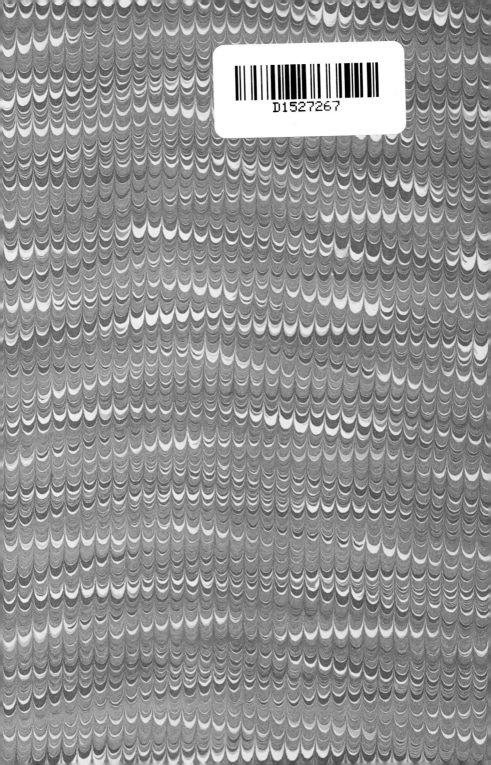

Reprinted 1985 from the 1904 edition.
Cover design © 1981 Time-Life Books Inc.
Library of Congress CIP data following page 308.

This volume is bound in leather.

WAR FROM THE INSIDE

COLONEL FREDERICK L. HITCHCOCK

MONUMENT OF 132D REGIMENT, P. V.
ERECTED BY THE STATE OF PENNSYLVANIA ON BATTLE-FIELD OF ANTIETAM, MD.
DEDICATED SEPT. 17, 1904

It stands about two hundred yards directly in front of the battle line upon which this regiment fought, on the side of the famous "Sunken Road" occupied by the Confederates.

This road has since been widened and macadamized as a government road leading from "Bloody Lane" towards Sharpsburg.

WAR
FROM THE INSIDE

THE STORY OF THE 132ND REGIMENT
PENNSYLVANIA VOLUNTEER INFAN-
TRY IN THE WAR FOR THE SUP-
PRESSION OF THE REBELLION

1862-1863

BY

FREDERICK L. HITCHCOCK

LATE ADJUTANT AND MAJOR
132ND PENNSYLVANIA
VOLUNTEERS.

Published by authority of the 132nd Regiment Pennsylvania
Volunteer Infantry Association.

PRESS OF J. B. LIPPINCOTT COMPANY
PHILADELPHIA
1904

PREFACE

THIS narrative was originally written without the least idea of publication, but to gratify the oft-repeated requests of my children. During the work, the ubiquitous newspaper reporter learned of it, and persuaded me to permit its publication in a local paper, where it appeared in weekly instalments. Since then the demand that I should put it in more permanent form has been so persistent and wide-spread, that I have been constrained to comply, and have carefully revised and in part rewritten it. I have endeavored to confine myself to my own observations, experiences, and impressions, giving the inner life of the soldier as we experienced it. It was my good fortune to be associated with one of the best bodies of men who took part in the great Civil War; to share in their hardships and their achievements. For this I am profoundly grateful. Their story is my own. If these splendid gray-headed " boys"—those who have not yet passed the mortal firing-line—shall find some pleasure in again tramping over that glorious route, and recalling the historic scenes, and if the younger generation shall gather inspiration for a like patriotic dedication to country

Preface

and to liberty, I shall be more than paid for my imperfect work. In conclusion, I desire to acknowledge my indebtedness to Major James W. Oakford, son of our intrepid colonel, who was the first of the regiment to fall, and to Mr. Lewis B. Stillwell, son of that brave and splendid officer, Captain Richard Stillwell, Company K, who was wounded and disabled at Fredericksburg, for constant encouragement in the preparation of the work and for assistance in its publication.

Scranton, Pa., April 5, 1904.

CONTENTS

LIST OF ILLUSTRATIONS

After the lapse of more than forty years, I hardly hoped to be able to publish pictures of all our officers, and have been more than pleased to secure so many. The others, I regret to say, could not be obtained. The youthful appearance of these officers will be remarked. All, I believe, with the exception of Colonel Oakford were below thirty years, and most between twenty and twenty-five.

WAR FROM THE INSIDE

CHAPTER I

FIRST LESSONS; OR, DOING THE IMPOSSIBLE

I WAS appointed adjutant of the One Hundred and Thirty-second Regiment, Pennsylvania Volunteers, by our great war Governor, Andrew G. Curtin, at the solicitation of Colonel Richard A. Oakford, commanding the regiment, my commission dating the 22d day of August, 1862. I reported for duty to Colonel Oakford at Camp Whipple, where the regiment was then encamped, on the 3d day of September, 1862. This was immediately following the disasters of " Chantilly" and " Second Bull Run," and as I passed through Washington to Camp Whipple, I found the greatest excitement prevailing because of these reverses, and a general apprehension for the safety of the capital in consequence. The wildest rumors were abroad concerning the approach of the victorious rebel troops, and an alarm amounting almost to a panic existed. Being without a horse or other means of transportation, I was obliged to make my way, valise in hand, on foot from Washington over the " long bridge" across the Potomac, to Camp Whipple, some two miles up the river nearly opposite Georgetown. From the wild rumors floating about Washington, I did not know but I should be captured bag and baggage before reaching camp. Undertaking this trip under those circumstances, I think, required almost as much nerve as " real work" did later on.

Getting beyond the long bridge there were abundant evidences of the reported disasters. Straggling troops, army wagons, etc., were pouring in from the " front" in great disorder. I reached camp about three o'clock P.M. and found Colonel Oakford out with the regiment on battalion drill. An hour later I reported to his office (tent) as ready for duty. The colonel had been a lifelong personal friend, and I was received, as I expected, most cordially. I was assigned quarters, and a copy of the daily routine orders of camp was placed in my hands, and my attention specially called to the fact that the next " order of business" was " dress parade" at six o'clock. I inquired the cause of this special notice to me, and was informed that I was expected to officiate as adjutant of the regiment at that ceremony. I pleaded with the colonel to be allowed a day or so in camp to see how things were done before undertaking such difficult and important duties; that I knew absolutely nothing about any part of military service; had never served a day in any kind of military work, except in a country fire company; had never seen a dress parade of a full regiment in my life, and knew nothing whatever about the duties of an adjutant.

My pleadings were all in vain. The only reply I received was a copy of the " Army Regulations," with the remark that I had two hours in which to study up and master the details of dress parade, and that I could not

First Lessons; or, Doing the Impossible

learn my duties any easier nor better than by actual practice; that my condition was no different from that of my fellow officers; that we were all there in a camp of instruction learning our duties, and there was not a moment to lose. I then began to realize something of the magnitude of the task which lay before me. To do difficult things, without knowing how; that is, to learn how in the doing, was the universal task of the Union volunteer officer. I took up my " Army Regulations" and attacked the ceremony of dress parade as a life and death matter. Before my two hours were ended, I could repeat every sentence of the ceremony verbatim, and felt that I had mastered the thing, and was not going to my execution in undertaking my duties as adjutant. Alas for the frailty of memory; it failed me at the crucial moment, and I made a miserable spectacle of myself before a thousand officers and men, many of them old friends and acquaintances, all of whom, it seemed to me, were specially assembled on that occasion to witness my début, and see me get " balled up." They were not disappointed. Things tactically impossible were freely done during that ceremony. Looking back now upon that scene, from the long distance of forty years, I see a green country boy undertaking to handle one thousand men in the always difficult ceremony of a dress parade. (I once heard Governor Hartranft, who attained the rank of a major-general during the war, remark, as he witnessed this ceremony, that he had seen thousands of such parades, and among them all, only one that he considered absolutely faultless.) I wonder now that we got through it at all. Think of standing to give your first command at the right of a line of men five hundred abreast, that is, nearly one thousand feet in length, and trying to make the men farthest away hear your small, unused, and untrained voice. I now can fully forgive my failure. The officers and men were considerate of me, however, and, knowing what was to be done, went through with it after a fashion in spite of my blunders.

The regiment was one of the " nine months' " quota; it had been in the service barely two weeks at this time. It was made up of two companies, I and K, from Scranton (Captains James Archbald, Company I, and Richard Stillwell, Company K), Company A, Danville, Pa.; B, Factoryville; C, Wellsboro and vicinity; E, Bloomsburg; F and G, Mauch Chunk, and H, Catawissa. It numbered, officers and men, about one thousand. Its field officers were Colonel Richard A. Oakford, Scranton; Lieutenant-Colonel Vincent M. Wilcox, Scranton; Major Charles Albright, Mauch Chunk; staff, Frederick L. Hitchcock, first lieutenant and adjutant, Scranton; Clinton W. Neal, first lieutenant and quartermaster, Bloomsburg; Rev. Schoonmaker, first lieutenant and chaplain, Scranton.

The transition from home life to that of an army in the field can only be appreciated from a stand-point of actual experience. From a well-ordered, well-cooked meal, served at a comfortable table with the accessories of home, howsoever humble, to a " catch as catch can" way of getting " grub," eating what, and when and where, you are fortunate enough to get to eat; and from a good, comfortable bed, comfortably housed in a comfortable home, to a blanket " shake down" under the beautiful sky, mark some of the features of this transition.

CAPT. MARTIN M. BROBST
CO. H

CAPT. WARNER H. CARNOCHAN
CO. D

CAPT. GEO. W. WILHELM
CO. F

CAPT. SMITH W. INGHAM
CO. B

CAPT. CHAS. M'DOUGAL
CO. C

CAPT. RICHARD STILLWELL
CO. K

CAPT. JAMES ARCHBALD, JR.
CO. I

CAPT. CHARLES C. NORRIS
CO. A

CAPT. JACOB D. LACIAR
CO. F

CAPT. JACOB B. FLOYD
CO. K

CAPT. ROBERT A. ABBOTT
CO. G

First Lessons; or, Doing the Impossible

Another feature is the utter change in one's individual liberty. To be no longer the arbiter of your own time and movements, but to have it rubbed into you at every turn that you are a very small part of an immense machine, whose business is to march and fight; that your every movement is under the control of your superior officers; that, in fact, you have no will of your own that can be exercised; that your individuality is for the time sunk, is a trial to an American freeman which patriotism alone can overcome. Not the least feature of this transition is the practical obliteration of the Lord's day. This is a great shock to a Christian who has learned to love the Lord's day and its hallowed associations. Routine duty, the march, the fighting, all go right on, nothing stops for Sunday.

On the morning after reaching camp I had the pleasure of seeing Major-General John Pope, who commanded the Union forces in the recent battles of Chantilly and Second Bull Run, and his staff, riding past camp into Washington. He hailed us with a cheery "Good-morning" in reply to our salute. He did not look like a badly defeated general, though he undoubtedly was—so badly, indeed, that he was never given any command of importance afterwards.

On Saturday, September 6, we received orders to join the Army of the Potomac—again under the command of " Little Mac"—at Rockville, Md., distant about eighteen miles. This was our first march. The day was excessively hot, and Colonel Oakford received permission to march in the evening. We broke camp about six o'clock P.M. It was a lovely moonlight night, the road was excellent, and for the first six miles the march was a delight. We marched quite leisurely, not making over two miles an hour, including rests, nevertheless the last half of the distance was very tiresome, owing to the raw and unseasoned condition of our men, and the heavy load they were carrying. We reached the bivouac of the grand Army of the Potomac, of which we were henceforth to be a part, at about three o'clock the next morning. Three miles out from the main camp we encountered the outpost of the picket line and were duly halted. The picket officer had been informed of our coming, and so detained us only long enough to satisfy himself that we were all right.

Here we encountered actual conditions of war with all its paraphernalia for the first time. Up to this time we had been playing at war, so to speak, in a camp of instruction. Now we were entering upon the thing itself, with all its gruesome accessories. Everything here was business, and awful business, too. Here were parks of artillery quiet enough just now, but their throats will speak soon enough, and when they do it will not be the harmless booming of Fourth of July celebrations. Here we pass a bivouac of cavalry, and yonder on either side the road, in long lines of masses, spread out like wide swaths of grain, lie the infantry behind long rows of stacked guns. Here were upward of seventy-five thousand men, all, except the cordon of pickets, sound asleep. In the midst of this mighty host the stillness was that of a graveyard; it seemed almost oppressive.

Halting the regiment, Colonel Oakford and I made our way to the head-quarters of Major-General Sumner, commanding the Second Army Corps, to whom the colonel was ordered to report. We finally found him asleep in his head-quarters wagon. A tap on the canvas top of the wagon quickly brought the response, " Hello! Who's there? What's wanted?"

Colonel Oakford replied, giving his name and rank, and that his regiment was here to report to him, according to orders.

" Oh, yes, colonel, that is right," replied the general. " How many men have you?"

Receiving the colonel's answer, General Sumner said:

" I wish you had ten times as many, for we need you badly. Glad you are here, colonel. Make yourselves as comfortable as you can for the rest of the night, and I will assign you to your brigade in the morning."

Here was a cordial reception and hospitality galore. " Make yourselves comfortable"—in Hotel " Dame Nature!" Well, we were all weary enough to accept the hospitality. We turned into the adjacent field, " stacked arms," and in a jiffy were rolled up in our blankets and sound asleep. The mattresses supplied by Madame Nature were rather hard, but her rooms were fresh and airy, and the ceilings studded with the stars of glory. My last waking vision that night was a knowing wink from Jupiter and Mars, as much as to say, " sleep sweetly, we are here."

The morning sun was well up before we got ourselves together the next morning. The " reveille" had no terrors for us greenhorns then. We found ourselves in the midst of a division of the bronzed old Army of the Potomac veterans. They were swarming all over us, and how unmercifully they did guy us! A regiment of tenderfeet was just taffy for those fellows. Did our " Ma's know we were out?" " Get off those purty duds." " Oh, you blue cherub!" etc., etc., at the same time accepting (?) without a murmur all the tobacco and other camp rarities they could reach.

We were soon visited by Brigadier-General Nathan Kimball, a swarthy, grizzly-bearded old gentleman, with lots of fire and energy in his eyes. He told the colonel our regiment had been assigned to his brigade. He directed the colonel to get the regiment in line, as he had something to say to the men, after which he would direct us where to join his troops. General Kimball commanded a brigade which had achieved a great reputation under McClellan in his West Virginia campaign, and it had been named by him the " Gibraltar brigade." It had also been through the Peninsular and Second Bull Run campaigns. It had comprised the Fourth and Eighth Ohio, Fourteenth Indiana and Seventh West Virginia regiments, all of which had been reduced by hard service to mere skeleton regiments. The Fourth Ohio had become so small as to require its withdrawal from the army for recuperation, and our regiment was to take its place.

To step into the shoes of one of these old regiments was business, indeed, for us. Could we do it and keep up our end? It was certainly asking a great deal of a two weeks' old regiment. But it was the making of us. We were now a part of the old Gibraltar brigade. Our full address now was " One Hundred and Thirty-second Pennsylvania Volunteers, First Brigade, Third Division, Second Army Corps, Army of the Potomac." Our own reputation we were now to make. We were on probation in the brigade,

First Lessons; or, Doing the Impossible

so to speak. These veterans were proud, and justly so, of their reputation. What our relation to that reputation was to be, we could see was a mooted question with them. They guyed us without measure until the crucial test, the "baptism of fire," had been passed. This occurred just ten days later, at the battle of Antietam, the greatest battle of the war thus far, where for four bloody hours we held our section of the brigade line as stanch as a rock. Here we earned our footing. Henceforth we belonged to them. There was never another syllable of guying, but in its place the fullest meed of such praise and comradeship as is born only of brave and chivalrous men.

CHAPTER II

THE ORGANIZATION AND MAKE-UP OF THE FIGHTING MACHINE CALLED "THE ARMY."

WE remained a day in bivouac after joining the Gibraltar brigade at Rockville, during which rations of fresh beef, salt pork, and "hardtack" (the boys' nickname for hard bread) were issued to the army, also ammunition.

The method of issuing rations was as follows: Colonels of regiments were directed to send in requisitions for so many days' rations, depending on the movements on hand, of hard bread and pork, and usually one day's rations of fresh beef. At brigade head-quarters these requisitions were consolidated, making the brigade requisition, and forwarded to division head-quarters. Here they were again consolidated into a division requisition, and so on until the army head-quarters was reached. Then the corps commissary received in bulk enough for his corps, and distributed it to the divisions in bulk, thence to brigades in bulk, thence to regiments, and finally from the regiment to the companies, and to the men. A long string of red tape, surely; and it might have been considerably shortened to the advantage of all, as it was later on.

An interesting feature of the issue of rations was the method of supplying the fresh beef. Live cattle were driven to the army and issued alive to the several corps,

REV. A. H. SCHOONMAKER
CHAPLAIN

J. W. ANAWALT
MAJOR AND SURGEON

G. K. THOMPSON
FIRST LIEUT. AND ASS'T SURGEON

Make-up of the Fighting Machine

from which details were made of men who had been butchers, who killed and dressed the beef. The animals were driven into an enclosure and expert marksmen shot them down as wanted. This seemed cruel work, but it was well done; the animal being hit usually at the base of its horns, death was instantaneous. This fresh meat, which we got but seldom after the march began, was cooked and eaten the day it was issued. Enough for one day was all that was issued at a time, and this, after the non-eatable portions had been eliminated, did not overburden the men.

The hard bread was a square cracker about the size of an ordinary soda cracker, only thicker, and very hard and dry. It was supposed to be of the same quality as sea biscuit or pilot bread, but I never saw any equal to that article. The salt pork was usually good for pork, but it was a great trial to us all to come down to camp fare, " hardtack and pork." Sometimes the " hardtack" was very old and poor. I have seen many a one placed in the palm of the hand, a smart blow, a puff of breath, and mirabile! a handful of " squirmers"—the boys' illustration of a " full hand." It came to be the rule to eat in daylight for protection against the unknown quantity in the hardtack. If we had to eat in the dark, after a prolonged march, our protection then lay in breaking our cracker into a cup of boiling coffee, stir it well and then flow enough of the coffee over to carry off most of the strangers and take the balance on faith.

On the march each man carried his own rations in haversacks. These were made of canvas and contained pockets for salt, sugar and coffee, besides room for about two days' rations of hard bread and pork. Sometimes five, six, and seven days' rations were issued, then the balance had to be stowed away in knapsacks and pockets of the clothing. When, as was usual in the latter cases, there was also issued sixty to one hundred rounds of ammunition, the man became a veritable pack-mule.

For the first month many of our men went hungry. Having enormous appetites consequent upon this new and most strenuous mode of life, they would eat their five days' supply in two or three, and then have to " skirmish" or go hungry until the next supply was issued. Most, however, soon learned the necessity as well as the benefit of restricting their appetites to the supply. But there were always some improvident ones, who never had a supply ahead, but were always in straights for grub. They were ready to black boots, clean guns, in fact, do any sort of menial work for their comrades for a snack to eat. Their improvidence made them the drudges of the company.

Whatever may be said about other portions of the rations, the coffee was always good. I never saw any poor coffee, and it was a blessing it was so, for it became the soldiers' solace and stay, in camp, on picket and on the march. Tired, footsore, and dusty from the march, or wet and cold on picket, or homesick and shivering in camp, there were rest and comfort and new life in a cup of hot coffee. We could not always have it on picket nor on the march. To make a cup of coffee two things were necessary besides the coffee, namely, water and fire, both frequently very difficult to obtain. On picket water was generally plentiful, but in the immediate presence of the enemy, fire was forbidden, for obvious reasons. On the march both were usually scarce, as I shall show later on. How was our coffee made? Each man was provided with a pint tin cup. As much coffee as could comfortably be lifted from the haversack by the thumb and two fingers—depending somewhat on the supply—was placed in the cup, which was filled about three-fourths full of water, to leave room for boiling. It was then placed upon some live coals and brought to a boil, being well stirred in the meantime to get the strength of the coffee. A little cold water was then added to settle it. Eggs, gelatin, or other notions of civilization, for settling, were studiously (?) omitted. Sometimes sugar was added, but most of the men, especially the old vets, took it straight. It was astonishing how many of the " wrinkles of grim visaged war" were temporarily smoothed out by a cup of coffee. This was the mainstay of our meals on the march, a cup of coffee and a thin slice of raw pork between two hardtacks frequently constituting a meal. Extras fell in the way once in a while. Chickens have been known to stray into camp, the result of a night's foraging.

Among the early experiences of our boys was an incident related to me by the " boy" who was " it." He said he had a mighty narrow escape last night.

I asked, " How was that?"

" Out hunting for chickens, struck a farmhouse, got a nice string, and was sneaking my way out. Dark as tar. Ran up against man, who grabbed me by the collar, and demanded ' what are you doing here?' I was mum as an owl. He marched me out where there was a flickering light, and sure as blazes it was old General Kimball. I didn't know that house was brigade head-quarters.

" ' What regiment do you belong to?'

War from the Inside

"'Dunno.'

"'You've heard about the orders against marauding, eh?'

"'Dunno.'

"'Hand up those chickens, you rascal.'

"I handed them out from behind my shaking legs.

"'How many have you got?'

"'Dunno'—I had two pair of nice ones. The old man took out his knife and slowly cut out one pair, looking savagely at me all the time.

"'There! You get back to camp as quick as your legs will carry you, and if I ever get my hands on you again you'll remember it.'" He said he thought he'd try and forage away from head-quarters next time. General Kimball was a rigid disciplinarian, but withal a very kind-hearted man. He no doubt paid for those chickens rather than have one of his boys suffer for his foraging escapade. Perhaps I ought to say a word about these foraging expeditions to eke out the boys' larder. These men were not thieves in any sense and very few attempted this dubious method, but the temptation was almost beyond the power of resistance. The best way to test this temptation is to diet yourself on "hardtack" and pork for just about one week. Then the devil's argument—always present—was practically true there, "the chickens will be taken (not stolen) by some of the army, and you might as well have one as anybody."

The following story of a neighboring regiment will show that even officers high in rank sometimes found that "circumstances alter cases." The troops were nearing bivouac at the close of the day, and, as usual, the

Make-up of the Fighting Machine

colonel ordered the music to start up and the men to fall into step and approach camp in order (the march is usually in route step,—*i.e.*, every man marches and carries his gun as he pleases). The fifes and the snare-drums promptly obeyed, but the big bass drum was silent. The men fell into cadence step in fine shape, including the bass drummer, but his big shell gave forth no sound. The colonel called out, " What's the matter with the bass drum?" Still no response. A second ejaculation from head-quarters, a little more emphatic, fared no better. Patience now exhausted, the colonel yelled, " What in h—l's the matter, I say, with——" when a sotto voice reached his ear, with " Colonel, colonel, he's got a pair of chickens in his drum, and one is for you." " Well, if the poor fellow is sick, let him fall out."

A little explanation now about how the army is organized will probably make my story clearer. That an army is made of three principal arms, viz., artillery, cavalry, and infantry, is familiar to all; that the cavalry is mounted is also well known, but that in actual fighting they were often dismounted and fought as infantry may not be familiar to all. The cavalry and infantry—or foot troops—are organized practically alike, viz., first into companies of 101 men and officers; second, into regiments of ten companies, or less, of infantry and twelve companies, more or less, of cavalry, two or more companies of cavalry constituting a " squadron," and a like number of companies of infantry a " battalion;" third, into brigades of two or more—usually four—regiments; fourth, divisions of two or more—usually three—brigades; fifth, army corps, any number of divisions—usually not more than three. Logically, the rank of officers commanding these several subdivisions would be colonel, commanding a regiment; brigadier-general, his rank being indicated by one star, a brigade; a major-general, two stars, a division; a lieutenant-general, three stars, an army corps; and the whole army a general, his rank being indicated by four stars. This was carried out by the Confederates in the organization of their armies. But not so with ours. With few exceptions—ours being one—the brigades were commanded by the senior colonels, and towards the end of the war this was sometimes temporarily true of divisions; the divisions by brigadiers, whilst we had no higher rank than that of major-general until General Grant was made, first, lieutenant-general, and finally general.

The artillery was organized into companies commonly called batteries. There were two branches, heavy and light artillery. The former were organized more like infantry, marched on foot and were armed with muskets in addition to the heavy guns they were trained to use. The latter were used against fortifications and were rarely brought into field work. The light artillery were mounted either on the horses or on the gun-carriages, and, though organized into a separate corps under the direction of the chief of artillery, were usually distributed among the divisions, one or two batteries accompanying each division.

In addition to these chief branches of the service, there was the signal corps, the "eyes" of the army, made up mostly of young lieutenants and non-commissioned officers detailed from the several regiments. There were two such officers from Scranton, namely, Lieutenant Fred. J. Amsden, One Hundred and Thirty-sixth Pennsylvania Volun-

Make-up of the Fighting Machine

teers, and Lieutenant Frederick Fuller, Fifty-second Pennsylvania Volunteers, besides a number of enlisted men.

Another important branch of the service was the telegraph corps. It was remarkable the celerity with which wires would be run along the ground and on brush, day by day, keeping the several corps constantly in touch with the commanding general. There were comparatively few telegraph operators that could be detailed, and many had to be hired,—some boys who were too young to enlist. Dr. J. Emmet O'Brien, of this city, was one of the most efficient of the latter class.

It was Dr. O'Brien, then operating below Petersburg, who caught the telegraphic cipher of the rebels and by tapping their wires caught many messages which were of material assistance to General Grant in the closing movements of the war. It was he also who in like manner caught the movements of Jeff Davis and his cabinet in their efforts to escape, and put General Wilson on his track, resulting in his final capture. Mr. Richard O'Brien, the doctor's older brother, for many years superintendent of the Western Union Telegraph lines in this end of the State, was at that time Government Superintendent of Telegraphs, in charge of all its telegraphic operations in Virginia and North Carolina. He could tell many a hair-raising experience. He related to me the following incident, which occurred during Grant's operations around Petersburg, to illustrate the enterprise of the enemy in trying to get our telegrams, and the necessity of sending all messages in cipher. They never succeeded in translating the Union cipher. But one day an operator at

War from the Inside

Washington, either too lazy or too careless to put his message in cipher, telegraphed to the chief commissary at a place below City Point that fifteen hundred head of beef cattle would be landed at that point on a certain day. The message was caught by the rebels. The beef cattle were landed on time, but in the meantime Wade Hampton had swept in with a division of rebel cavalry and was waiting to receive the cattle. With them were captured a handsome lot of rations and a number of prisoners, including all of Mr. O'Brien's telegraph operators at that post. Mr. O'Brien said he cared a good deal more about the loss of his operators than he did for the loss of the cattle and rations, for it was very hard to get competent operators at that time. There was at least one vacancy at Washington following this incident.

Still another arm of the service was the pontoniers, whose duty it was to bridge non-fordable rivers. They were armed and drilled as infantry, but only for their own protection. Their specialty was laying and removing pontoon bridges. A pontoon train consisted of forty to fifty wagons, each carrying pontoon boats, with plank and stringers for flooring and oars and anchors for placing. In laying a bridge these boats were anchored side by side across the stream, stringers made fast across them, and plank then placed on the stringers. Every piece was securely keyed into place so that the bridge was wide enough and strong enough for a battery of artillery and a column of infantry to go over at the same time. The rapidity with which they would either lay or take up a bridge was amazing. If undisturbed they would bridge a stream two hundred yards wide in thirty minutes. They

Make-up of the Fighting Machine

bridged the Rappahannock at Fredericksburg under fire on the 12th of December, 1863, in a little over an hour, losing heavily in the act.

Having now given some account of the organization of this great human fighting machine, it will be proper to show how it was handled. For this purpose there were four staff departments, namely, the adjutant-general's, the quartermaster-general's, the commissary-general's, and the ordnance departments. The first named was the mouthpiece of the army. All orders were issued by and through that officer. It was the book-keeper of the army. Each subdivision of the army had its adjutant-general down to the office of adjutant in the regiment, who was charged with issuing all orders, and with attending to their execution. He was secretary, so to speak, of the commanding officer, and his chief executive officer as well. Extraordinary executive talent and tireless energy were required in these positions. The adjutant must be able at all times to inform his chief of the condition of every detail of the command whether an army corps or regiment, exactly how many men were fit for duty, how many sick or disabled, and just where they all are. In fact, he must be a walking encyclopædia of the whole command; added to this he was usually chief of staff, and must be in the saddle superintending every movement of the troops. Always first on duty, his work was never finished.

Two of the best adjutants-general the world has produced literally wore themselves out in the service—Seth Williams and John B. Rawlins. The first named was McClellan's adjutant-general, the latter was Grant's. Mc-Clellan is credited with having organized the grand old

Army of the Potomac, the main fighting force by which the rebellion was finally crushed. This was doubtless true, he being its first commanding officer. But the executive ability by which that magnificent machine was perfected was largely the work of Seth Williams, a very quiet, modest man, but a master of the minutest details of every department and an indefatigable worker. It was said his chief could wake him in the middle of the night and get from his memory a correct answer as to the number of men fit for duty in any one of the hundreds of regiments in the army, and just where it was, and what duty it was doing. When one remembers that this knowledge was acquired only by a daily perusal of the consolidated reports of the various regiments, brigades, divisions, and corps of the army, and that he could have found time for one reading only, it will be seen how marvellous his memory was.

Rawlins was said to possess much the same quality. It may truthfully be said that the Army of the Potomac was organized and began its remarkable career in the life blood of Seth Williams, and it completed its work in a blaze of glory, in the life blood of John B. Rawlins. Seth Williams died in the service. Rawlins came home with the victorious army only to die. A beautiful bronze equestrian statue was erected at Washington under the influence of his beloved chief, Grant, to commemorate the services of Rawlins. So far as I know, Seth Williams shares the fate of most of his humbler comrades,—an unmarked grave.

I have said all orders were sent out through the adjutant-general's office. This, of course, applies to all regular routine work only, for during the movements of troops on campaigns and in battle orders had in the nature of the case to be delivered verbally. For this purpose each general had a number of aides-de-camp. In sending such orders, the utmost courtesy was always observed. The formula was usually thus, " General Kimball presents his compliments to Colonel Oakford and directs that he move his regiment to such and such a point." To which Colonel Oakford responds returning his compliments to General Kimball and says " his order directing so and so has been received and shall be immediately obeyed."

The quartermaster's department was charged with all matters connected with transportation; with the supplying of clothing, canvas, and equipage of all sorts. Both the commissary and the ordnance departments were dependent upon the quartermaster for the transportation of their respective stores. The wagon trains required by the Army of the Potomac for all this service were prodigious. They were made up of four and six mule teams with heavy " prairie schooners" or canvas-covered wagons. I have seen two thousand of them halted for the night in a single park, and such trains on the march six to ten miles long were not unusual. It will readily be seen that to have them within easy reach, and prevent their falling into the hands of an alert enemy, was a tremendous problem in all movements of the army.

The army mule has been much caricatured, satirized, and abused, but the soldier had no more faithful or indispensable servant than this same patient, plodding, hard-pulling, long-eared fellow of the roomy voice and nimble heels. The " boys" told a story which may illustrate the mule's education. A " tenderfoot" driver had gotten his team stalled in a mud hole, and by no amount of persuasion could he get them to budge an inch. Helpers at the wheels and new hands on the lines were all to no purpose. A typical army bummer had been eying the scene with contemptuous silence. Finally he cut loose:

" Say! You 'uns dunno the mule language. Ye dunno the dilec. Let a perfesser in there."

He was promptly given the job. He doffed cap and blouse, marched up to those mules as if he weighed a ton and commanded the army. Clearing away the crowd, he seized the leader's line, and distending his lungs, he shot out in a voice that could have been heard a mile a series of whoops, oaths, adjectives, and billingsgate that would have silenced the proverbial London fish vender. The mules recognized the " dilec" at once, pricked up their ears and took the load out in a jiffy.

" Ye see, gents, them ar mules is used to workin' with a perfesser."

The commissary department supplied the rations, and the ordnance department the arms and ammunition, etc. Still another branch of the service was the provost-marshal's department. This was the police force of the army. It had the care and custody of all prisoners, whether those arrested for crime, or prisoners of war—those captured from the enemy. In the case of prisoners sentenced to death by court-martial, the provost guard were their executioners.

CHAPTER III

WE are bound northward through Maryland, the vets tell us, on a chase after the rebs. The army marches in three and four parallel columns, usually each corps in a column by itself, and distant from the other columns equal to about its length in line of battle, say a half to three-fourths of a mile. Roads were utilized as far as practicable, but generally were left to the artillery and the wagon trains, whilst the infantry made roads for themselves directly through the fields.

The whole army marches surrounded by " advance and rear guards," and " flankers," to prevent surprise. Each column is headed by a corps of pioneers who, in addition to their arms, are provided with axes, picks and shovels, with the latter stone walls and fences are levelled sufficiently to permit the troops to pass, and ditches and other obstructions covered and removed. It is interesting to see how quickly this corps will dispose of an ordinary stone wall or rail fence. They go down so quickly that they hardly seem to pause in their march.

We learn that the Johnnies are only a couple of days ahead of us. That they marched rapidly and were on their good behavior, all maurading being forbidden, and they were singing a new song, entitled " My Maryland," thus trying to woo this loyal border State over to the Confederacy. We were told that Lee hung two soldiers for stealing chickens and fruit just before they entered Frederick City.

Much could be written about the discomforts of these marches, the chief of which was the dust more than the heat and the fatigue. No rain had fallen for some time, and the roads and the fields through which we passed were powdered into fine dust, which arose in almost suffocating clouds, so that mouth, lungs, eyes, and ears were filled with it. Sometimes it became so dense that men could not be seen a dozen yards away. The different regiments took turns in heading the columns. There was comparative comfort at the head, but there were so many regiments that during the whole campaign our regiment enjoyed this privilege but once.

Another feature of the march was inability to satisfy thirst. The dust and heat no doubt produced an abnormal thirst which water did not seem to satisfy. The water we could get was always warm, and generally muddy and filthy. The latter was caused by the multitude of men using the little streams, springs, or wells. Either of these, ordinarily abundant for many more than ever used them, were hardly a cup full apiece for a great army. Hence many a scrimmage took place for the first dash at a cool well or spring. On our second or third day's march, such a scrap took place between the advanced columns for a well, and in the mêlée one man was accidentally pushed down into it, head first, and killed. He belonged to one of the Connecticut regiments, I was told. We passed by the well, and were unable to get water, because a dead soldier

On the March

lay at the bottom of it. His regiment probably got his body out, but we had to march on without stopping to learn whether they did or not. The problem of water for our army we found to be a troublesome one. Immediately we halted, much of our rest would be taken up in efforts to get water. We lost no opportunity to fill our canteens. Arriving in bivouac for the night, the first thing was a detail to fill canteens and camp kettles for supper coffee. We always bivouacked near a stream, if possible. But, then, so many men wanting it soon roiled it for miles, so that our details often had to follow the stream up three and four miles before they could get clean water. This may seem a strong statement, but if one will stop a moment and think of the effect upon even a good-sized stream, of a hundred thousand men, besides horses and mules, all wanting it for drinking, cooking, washing, and bathing (both the latter as peremptory needs as the former), he will see that the statement is no exaggeration.

An interesting feature of our first two days' march was the clearing out of knapsacks to reduce the load. Naturally each man was loaded with extras of various sorts, knicknacks of all varieties, but mostly supposed necessaries of camp life, put in by loving hands at home, a salve for this, a medicine for that, a keepsake from one and another, some the dearest of earth's treasures, each insignificant in itself, yet all taking room and adding weight to over-burdened shoulders. At the midday halt, on the first day knapsacks being off for rest, they came open and the sorting began. It was sad, yet comical withal, to notice the things that went out. The most bulky and least treasured went first. At the second halting, an hour later, still an-

War from the Inside

other sorting was made. The sun was hot and the knapsack was heavy. After the second day's march, those knapsacks contained little but what the soldier was compelled to carry, his rations, extra ammunition, and clothing. Were these home treasures lost? Oh, no! Not one. Our friends, the vets, gathered them all in as a rich harvest. They had been there themselves, and knowing what was coming, were on hand to gather the plums as they fell. The only difference was, that another mother's or sweetheart's "boy" got the treasures.

On September 11 we were approaching Frederick City. Our cavalry had a skirmish with the rebel cavalry, showing that we were nearing their army. And right here I ought to say that what an individual officer or soldier—unless perhaps a general officer—knows of events transpiring around him in the army is very little. Even the movements he sees, he is seldom able to understand, his vision is so limited. He knows what his own regiment and possibly his own brigade does, but seldom more than that. He is as often the victim of false rumor as to movements of other portions of the army, as those who are outside of it. On this date we encamped near Clarksville. It was rumored that the rebels were in force at Frederick City. How far away that is we do not know. The only certainty about army life and army movements to the soldier is a constant condition of uncertainty. Uncertainty as to where or when he will eat, sleep, or fight, where or when the end will come. One would almost doubt the certainty of his own existence, except for the hard knocks which make this impossible.

The celebrated Irish brigade, commanded by Brigadier-

On the March

General Thomas Francis Meagher, was in Richardson's division. They were a "free and easy" going crowd. General Richardson impressed me as a man of great determination and courage. He was a large, heavy man, dressed roughly and spoke and acted very brusquely. French (who commanded our division) was also thick-set, probably upwards of sixty years old, quite gray and with a very red face. He had an affection of the eyes which kept him winking or blinking constantly, from which he earned the sobriquet, " Old Blink Eye." I saw General Burnside about this time. He was dressed so as to be almost unrecognizable as a general officer; wore a rough blouse, on the collar of which a close look revealed two much-battered and faded stars, indicating his rank of major-general. He wore a black "slouch" hat, the brim well down over his face, and rode along with a single orderly, without the least ostentation. The men of the other regiments knew him and broke out into a cheer, at which he promptly doffed his hat and swung it at the boys. His hat off, we recognized the handsome author of the " Burnside" whiskers. He was not only very popular with his own corps—the Ninth—but with the whole army, and chiefly, I think, because of his modest, quiet way of going about. This was so different from General McClellan.

On our third day's march we were halted for rest, when an orderly rode through the lines saying to the different colonels, " General McClellan will pass this way in ten minutes." This meant that we were to be ready to cheer " Little Mac" when he came along, which, of course, we all did. He came, preceded by a squadron of cavalry and accompanied by a very large and brilliantly caparisoned staff, followed by more cavalry. He was dressed in the full uniform of a major-general and rode a superb horse, upon which he sat faultlessly. He was certainly a fine-looking officer and a very striking figure. But whether all this " fuss and feathers" was designed to impress the men, or was a freak of personal vanity, it did not favorably impress our men. Many of the old vets, who had been with him on the Peninsula, and now greeted him again after his reinstatement, were very enthusiastic. But notwithstanding their demonstrations, they rather negatived their praises by the remark, " No fight to-day; Little Mac has gone to the front." " Look out for a fight when he goes to the rear." On the other hand, they said when " Old Man Sumner"—our corps commander—" goes to the front, look out for a fight."

General Sumner was an old man—must have been nearly seventy—gray, and his color indicated advanced age, though he seemed quite vigorous. He went about very quietly and without display. He had a singular habit of dropping his under jaw, so that his mouth was partially open much of the time.

We bivouacked on the 12th of September in front of Frederick City, Md., in a field occupied the night before by the rebels, so the people told us, and there was abundant evidence of their presence in the filth they left uncovered, for they had slaughtered beef for their troops and the putrid offal therefrom was polluting the air. Still there we had to sleep. We marched the latter part of the day in the rain, and were soon well covered with mud. We managed to keep some of the water out with our gum blankets, and when we came to fix for the night, the men going in

On the March

pairs made themselves fairly comfortable under their shelter tents. I should have explained that the only " canvas" supplied to the men on the march was shelter tents, which consisted of a square of stout muslin with buttonholes on one side and buttons on the other. Two of these buttoned together and stretched taut over a ridge-pole and made fast on the ground, would keep out the heaviest shower, provided the occupants were careful not to touch the muslin. A hand or elbow accidentally thrust against the tent brought the water through in streams. There is a knack in doing this, which the experience of the vets with whom we were brigaded soon taught us. Choosing ground a little slanting, so the water would run away from them, they would sleep fairly dry and comfortable, even in a hard storm. As for us officers who were without shelter tents, we had to shift for ourselves as best we might. A favorite plan, when fences were available, was to place three or four rails endwise against the fence and make a shelter by fastening a gum blanket on top.

This worked fairly well against a stone wall for a backing, but against an ordinary fence one side was unprotected, yet with another gum blanket, two of us could so roll ourselves up as to be comparatively water-proof. My diary states that in a driving rainstorm here I never slept better in my life. I remember awakening with my head thoroughly drenched, but otherwise comparatively dry.

This night I succeeded in getting a " bang up" supper— a cooked meal—at a reb farm-house. It consisted of pork-steak, potatoes, and hot coffee with bread and butter. It was a great treat. I had now been without a square meal for nearly ten days. The old gentleman, a small farmer,

War from the Inside

talked freely about the war, not concealing his rebel sympathies. He extolled Stonewall Jackson and his men, who, he said, had passed through there only a day ahead of us. He firmly believed we would be whipped. He evidently had an eye for the " main chance," for he was quite willing to cook for us at twenty-five cents a meal, as long as he had stuff to cook and his good wife had strength to do the work. She seemed to be a nice old lady, and, hungry as I was, I felt almost unwilling to eat her supper, she looked so tired. I told her it was too bad. She smiled and said she was tired, but she couldn't bear to turn away these hungry boys. She said she had a son in the rebel army, and she knew we must be hungry and wet, for it was still raining hard.

The officers at this time experienced difficulty in getting food to eat. The men were supplied with rations and forced to carry them, but rations were not issued to officers —though they might purchase of the commissary such as the men had, when there was a supply. The latter were supposed to provide their own mess, for which purpose their mess-kits were transported in a wagon supplied to each regiment. The field and staff usually made one mess, and the line or company officers another. Sometimes the latter messed with their own men, carrying their rations along on the march the same as the men. This was discouraged by the government, but it proved the only way to be sure of food when needed, and was later on generally adopted. We had plenty of food with our mess-kit and cook, but on the march, and especially in the presence of the enemy, our wagons could never get within reach of us. Indeed, when we bivouacked, they were generally from eight to ten miles away. The result was we often went hungry, unless we were able to pick up a meal at a farm-house—which seldom occurred, for the reason that most of these farmers were rebel sympathizers and would not feed us " Yanks," or they would be either sold out, or stolen out, of food. The tale generally told was, " You 'uns has stolen all we 'uns had." This accounts for the entry in my diary that the next morning I marched without breakfast, but got a good bath in the Monocacy—near which we encamped—in place of it. I got a " hardtack" and bit of raw pork about 10 A.M.

On the 13th of September, we passed through the city of Frederick, Md. It is a quaint old town, having then probably three thousand or more inhabitants and a decided business air. The rebels, they claimed, had cleaned them out of eatables and clothing, paying for them in Confederate scrip, and one man told me they would not take the same scrip in change, but required Union money; that this was demanded everywhere. General McClellan passed through the streets while we were halted, as did General Burnside shortly after. A funny incident occurred with the latter. General Burnside, as usual, was accompanied by a single orderly, and had stopped a moment to speak to some officers, when a handsome, middle-aged lady stepped out of her house and approached. She put out her hand and, as the general clasped it, she raised herself up on her toes in an unmistakable motion to greet him with a kiss.

The general so understood her, and, doffing his hat, bent down to meet her pouting lips, but, alas, he was too high up; bend as low as he might and stretch up as high as she

War from the Inside

could, their lips did not meet, and the kiss hung in mid-air. The boys caught the situation in a moment, and began to laugh and clap their hands, but the general solved the problem by dismounting and taking his kiss in the most gallant fashion, on which he was roundly cheered by the men. The lady was evidently of one of the best families. She said she was a stanch Union woman, and was so glad to see our troops that she felt she must greet our general. There was " method in her madness," however, for she confined her favors to a general, and picked out the handsomest one of the lot. It is worthy of note, that during this incident, which excited uproarious laughter, not a disrespectful remark was made by any of the hundreds of our " boys" who witnessed it. General Burnside chatted with her for a few moments, then remounted and rode away.

Approaching Frederick City, the country is exceptionally beautiful and the land seemed to be under a good state of cultivation. In front of us loomed up almost against the sky the long ridge called the South Mountain. It was evidently a spur of the Blue Ridge. Another incident occurred soon after reaching bivouack, just beyond the city. We had arranged for our night's "lodging" and were preparing supper, when one of the native farmers came into camp and asked to see the colonel. Colonel Oakford and Lieutenant-Colonel Wilcox were temporarily absent, and he was turned over to Major Albright, to whom he complained that " you 'uns" had stolen his last pig and he wanted pay for it. The major, who was a lawyer, began to cross-question him as to how he knew it was our men who had stolen it; there were at least fifty other regiments besides ours on the ground. But he would not be denied.

44

COLONEL CHARLES ALBRIGHT

On the March

He said they told him they was " a hundred and thirty-two uns," and he also saw those figures on their caps. The major asked how long ago they took it. He replied that they got it only a little while ago, and offered to go and find it if the major would allow him. But the latter was confident he was mistaken in his men—that some of the old " vets" had got his pig. His chief argument was that our men were greenhorns and knew nothing about marauding; that some of the " vets" had doubtless made away with his pig and had laid it on our men. So persuasive was the major that the man finally went off satisfied that he had made a mistake in his men. The man was only well out of camp when one of our men appeared at the major's quarters with a piece of fresh pork for his supper, with the compliments of Company ——. Now, the orders against marauding were very severe, and to have been caught would have involved heavy punishment. But the chief point of the incident, and which made it a huge joke on the major, lay in the fact that the latter who was a thoroughly conscientious man, had successfully fought off a charge against his men, whom he really believed to be innocent, only to find that during the very time he was persuading his man of their innocence, the scamps were almost within sound of his voice, actually butchering and dressing the pig. How they managed to capture and kill that pig, without a single squeal escaping, is one of the marvels of the service. Certainly vets could have done no better. The man was gone, the mischief was done, the meat was spoiling, and we were very hungry. With rather cheerful sadness, it must be confessed, we became *particeps criminis*, and made a supper on the pork.

45

CHAPTER IV

DRAWING NEAR THE ENEMY—BATTLE OF SOUTH MOUN-
TAIN—PRELIMINARY SKIRMISHES

SUNDAY, September 15, we broke camp at daylight and marched out on the Hagerstown "pike." Our division had the field this day. We crossed the ridge in rear of Frederick City and thence down into and up a most beautiful valley. We made only about seven miles, though we actually marched over twelve. We were in the presence of the enemy and were manœuvred so as to keep concealed. We heard heavy cannonading all day, and part of the time could see our batteries, towards which we were marching.

Towards night we heard the first musketry firing. It proved to be the closing of the short but sanguinary battle of South Mountain. General Reno, commanding the Ninth Corps, whose glistening bayonets we had seen across the valley ahead of us, had overtaken the rebel rear guard in South Mountain pass and a severe action had ensued. General Reno himself was killed. His body was brought back next morning in an ambulance on its way to Washington. We reached the battle-ground about midnight, whither we had been hurried as supports. The batteries on both sides were still at work, but musketry firing had ceased. It had been a beautiful though very warm day, and the night was brilliantly moonlight, one of those exceptionally bright nights which almost equalled daylight. And this had been Sunday—the Lord's day! How dreadful the work for the Lord's day!

Here I saw the first dead soldier. Two of our artillerymen had been killed while serving their gun. Both were terribly mangled. They had been laid aside, while others stepped into their places. There they still lay, horrible evidence of the " hell of war." Subsequently I saw thousands of the killed on both sides, which made scarcely more impression on me than so many logs, but this first vision of the awful work of war still remains. Even at this writing, forty years later, memory reproduces that horrible scene as clearly as on that beautiful Sabbath evening.

It was past midnight when we bivouacked for the little rest we were to have before resuming the "chase." Being now in the immediate "presence of the enemy," we rested on "our arms," that is, every soldier lay down with his gun at his side, and knapsack and accoutrements ready to be "slung" immediately on the sounding of the "call." We officers did not unsaddle our horses, but dismounted and snatched an hour's sleep just as we were. Bright and early next morning we were on our way again. It was a most beautiful morning.

We soon passed the field where the musketry did its work the night before, and there were more than a hundred dead rebels scattered over the field, as the result of it. Two or three were sitting upright, or nearly so, against stumps. They had evidently been mortally wounded, and died while waiting for help. All were dressed in coarse butternut-colored stuffs, very ugly in appearance, but admirably well calculated to conceal them from our troops.

We rapidly passed over the mountain (South Mountain) and down into the village of Boonsborough. There was abundant evidence of the rebel skedaddle down the mountain ahead of our troops in the way of blankets, knapsacks, and other impedimenta, evidently dropped or thrown away in the flight. We passed several squads of rebel prisoners who had been captured by our cavalry and were being marched to the rear under guard. They were good-looking boys, apparently scarcely more than boys, and were poorly dressed and poorly supplied. Some freely expressed themselves as glad they had been captured, as they were sick of the fighting.

My own experiences this day were a taste of "the front," that is, the excitement attending a momentarily expected "brush" with the enemy. Part of the time my heart was in my mouth, and my hair seemed to stand straight up. One can have little idea of this feeling until it has been experienced. Any effort to describe it will be inadequate. Personal fear? Yes, that unquestionably is at the bottom of it, and I take no stock in the man who says he has no fear. We had been without food until late in the afternoon for reasons heretofore explained. Towards night one of my friends in Company K gave me a cup of coffee and a " hardtack."

Just before reaching Boonsborough, a pretty village nestling at the foot of the South Mountain, our cavalry had a sharp skirmish with the rebel rear-guard, in which Captain Kelley, of the Illinois cavalry, was killed, I was

Battle of South Mountain

told. At Boonsborough we found the field hospitals with the rebel wounded from the fight of the day previous. Their wounded men said their loss was over four hundred killed, among them two brigadiers-general, one colonel, and several officers of lesser rank. A rebel flag of truce came into our lines here to get the bodies of these dead officers and to arrange for burying their dead and caring for their wounded. The houses of Boonsborough had been mostly vacated by the people on the approach of the rebel army and the fighting, and the latter had promptly occupied as many of them as they needed for their wounded. Imagine these poor villagers returning from their flight to find their homes literally packed with wounded rebel soldiers and their attendants. Whatever humble food supplies they may have had, all had been appropriated, for war spares nothing. Some of the frightened people of the village were returning as we passed through, and were sadly lamenting the destruction of almost everything that could be destroyed on and about their homes by this besom of destruction,—war. Food, stock, fences, bed and bedding, etc., all gone or destroyed. Some of the houses had been perforated by the shells,—probably our own shells, aimed at the enemy. One man told me a shell had entered his house and landed on the bed in the front room, but had not exploded. Had it exploded, he would have had a bigger story to tell.

The rebels, we learned, had been gone but a few hours, and we were kept in pursuit. We marched out the Shepherdstown road a few miles, reaching and passing through another village—Keedysville. We were continuously approaching heavy cannonading. Indeed, we had been

4   49

War from the Inside

marching for the past three days within hearing of, and drawing closer to, the artillery barking of the two armies. Old vets said this meant a big fight within the next few hours. If so, I thought I shall better know how to diagnose similar symptoms in the future.

A mile beyond Keedysville we bivouacked for the night, after a hard, hot, and exciting day's chase. Lieutenant-Colonel Wilcox came into camp with a great trophy, nothing less than a good old-fashioned fat loaf of home-made bread. He was immediately voted a niche in the future hall of fame, for two acts of extraordinary merit, namely, first, finding and capturing the bread, and, second, bringing it into camp intact, the latter act being considered supremely self-sacrificing. It was magnanimously divided by him, and made a supper for three of us. Our mid-day meal had been made up of dust and excitement.

All sorts of rumors were afloat as to the movements of the enemy, as well as of our own army. It was said Jackson was across the Potomac with a large force; that Hooker was engaging him, and that we were likely to bag the balance of Lee's army soon. One thing I learned, namely, that I could be sure only of what I saw, and that was very little, indeed, of the doings of either army. The soldier who professes to know all about army movements because he "was there," may be set down either as a bummer, who spent most of his time up trees, safely ensconced where he could see, or as a fake.

My diary records a night of good rest September 16, 1862, in this camp on the Shepherdstown road. The morning was clear, beautiful, and cheery. This entry will look

COLONEL VINCENT M. WILCOX

Battle of South Mountain

somewhat remarkable in view of that which follows, namely, " No breakfast in sight or in prospect." Later one of our men gave me half his cup of coffee and a couple of small sweet potatoes, which I roasted and ate without seasoning,

The " ball" opened soon after daylight by a rebel battery, about three-quarters of a mile away, attempting to shell our lines. Our division was massed under the shelter of a hill. One of our batteries of 12-pounder brass guns promptly replied, and a beautiful artillery duel ensued, the first I had ever witnessed at close quarters. Many of us crept up to the brow of the hill to see the " fun," though we were warned that we were courting trouble in so doing. We could see columns of rebel infantry marching in ranks of four, just as we marched, en route, and as shell after shell from our guns would explode among them and scatter and kill we would cheer. We were enjoying ourselves hugely until presently some additional puffs of smoke appeared from their side, followed immediately by a series of very ugly hissing, whizzing sounds, and the dropping of shells amongst our troops which changed the whole aspect of things. Our merriment and cheering were replaced by a scurrying to cover, with blanched faces on some and an ominous, thoughtful quiet over all.

This was really our first baptism of fire, for though at South Mountain we had been in range and were credited with being in the fight as supports, none of the shells had actually visited us. Several of these came altogether too close for comfort. Colonel Oakford, Lieutenant-Colonel Wilcox, and I were sitting on our horses as close together

51

as horses ordinarily stand, when one of these ugly missiles dropped down between us. It came with a shrieking, screeching sound, like the pitch of an electric car with the added noise of a dozen sky-rockets. It did not explode. It created considerable consternation and no little stir with horses and men, but did no damage further than the scare and a good showering of gravel and dust. Another struck between the ranks of our brigade as they were resting under the hill with guns stacked,—only a few feet away from us. It also, happily, failed to explode, but we were sure some one must have been killed by it. It did not seem possible that such a missile could drop down upon a division of troops in mass without hitting somebody; but, strange as it may seem, it did no damage beyond knocking down a row of gun-stacks and tumbling topsy-turvy several men, who were badly bruised, but otherwise uninjured. The way the concussion tossed the men about was terrific. Had these shells exploded, some other body would probably have had to write up this narrative.

Another shell incident occurred during this artillery duel that looked very funny, though it was anything but funny to the poor fellow who suffered. He, with others, had been up near our battery, on the knoll just above us, witnessing the firing, when one of these rebel shells came ricochetting along the ground towards him as he evidently thought, for he started to run down the hill thinking to get away from it, but in fact running exactly in front of the shell, which carried away one heel. He continued down the hill at greatly accelerated speed, but now hopping on one foot. Had he remained where he was the mis-

Battle of South Mountain

sile would have passed him harmlessly. Except when nearly spent, shells are not seen until they have passed, but the screeching, whizzing, hissing noise is sufficient to make one believe they are hunting him personally. Veteran troops get to discount the terrors of these noises in a measure, and pay little attention to them, on the theory that if one is going to be hit by them he will be anyway, and no amount of dodging will save him, so they go right on and " take their chances." But with new troops the effect of a shell shrieking over or past them is often very ludicrous. An involuntary salaam follows the first sound, with a wild craning of the necks to see where it went. Upon marching troops, the effect is like that of a puff of wind chasing a wave across a field of grain.

Returning to our artillery duel, so far as we could judge, our battery had the best of the practice, but not without paying the price, for the second rebel shell killed the major (chief of artillery of our division), who sat on his horse directing the fire, and besides there were a number of casualties among the battery men. I had seen many a battery practice on parade occasions with blank cartridges. How utterly different was the thing in war. Infinitely more savage, the noise deafeningly multiplied, each gun, regardless of the others, doing its awful worst to spit out and hurl as from the mouth of a hell-born dragon these missiles of death at the enemy.

The duel continued for upwards of two hours, until the enemy's battery hauled off, having apparently had enough. Evidences of the conflict were sadly abundant. A number were killed, others wounded and several of the battery horses were killed. The work of the men in this hell of fire was magnificent. They never flagged for a moment, and at the conclusion were not in the least disabled, notwithstanding their losses. I think it was Nimm's battery from Pittsburg. This was the chief incident of the day. It was said the two armies were manœuvring for position, and that a great battle was imminent. This from my diary. It proved to be true, and that all the skirmishes and "affaires" for the preceding ten days had been only preliminary to the great battle of Antietam, fought on the next day, the 17th.

We remained in bivouac here the remainder of the day and night. Burnside's Ninth Corps passed to "the front" during the afternoon, a splendid body of veteran troops, whose handsome and popular general was heartily cheered. He was a large, heavily-built man, and sat his handsome horse like a prince.

CHAPTER V

NEVER did day open more beautiful. We were astir at the first streak of dawn. We had slept, and soundly too, just where nightfall found us under the shelter of the hill near Keedysville. No reveille call this morning. Too close to the enemy. Nor was this needed to arouse us. A simple call of a sergeant or corporal and every man was instantly awake and alert. All realized that there was ugly business and plenty of it just ahead. This was plainly visible in the faces as well as in the nervous, subdued demeanor of all. The absence of all joking and play and the almost painful sobriety of action, where jollity had been the rule, was particularly noticeable.

Before proceeding with the events of the battle, I should speak of the " night before the battle," of which so much has been said and written. My diary says that Lieutenant-Colonel Wilcox, Captain James Archbald, Co. I, and I slept together, sharing our blankets; that it rained during the night; this fact, with the other, that we were close friends at home, accounts for our sharing blankets. Three of us with our gum blankets could so arrange as to keep fairly dry, notwithstanding the rain.

The camp was ominously still this night. We were not allowed to sing or make any noise, nor have any fires—

except just enough to make coffee—for fear of attracting the fire of the enemies' batteries. But there was no need of such an inhibition as to singing or frolicking, for there was no disposition to indulge in either. Unquestionably, the problems of the morrow were occupying all breasts. Letters were written home—many of them "last words" —and quiet talks were had, and promises made between comrades. Promises providing against the dreaded possibilities of the morrow. "If the worst happens, Jack." "Yes, Ned, send word to mother and to ——, and these; she will prize them," and so directions were interchanged that meant so much.

I can never forget the quiet words of Colonel Oakford, as he inquired very particularly if my roster of the officers and men of the regiment was complete, for, said he, with a smile, "We shall not all be here to-morrow night."

Now to resume the story of the battle. We were on the march about six o'clock and moved, as I thought, rather leisurely for upwards of two miles, crossing Antietam creek, which our men waded nearly waist deep, emerging, of course, soaked through, our first experience of this kind. It was a hot morning and, therefore, the only ill effects of this wading was the discomfort to the men of marching with soaked feet. It was now quite evident that a great battle was in progress. A deafening pandemonium of cannonading, with shrieking and bursting shells, filled the air beyond us, towards which we were marching. An occasional shell whizzed by or over, reminding us that we were rapidly approaching the "debatable ground." Soon we began to hear a most ominous sound which we had never before heard, except in the far distance at South

The Battle of Antietam

Mountain, namely, the rattle of musketry. It had none of the deafening bluster of the cannonading so terrifying to new troops, but to those who had once experienced its effect, it was infinitely more to be dreaded. The fatalities by musketry at close quarters, as the two armies fought at Antietam and all through the Civil War, as compared with those by artillery, are at least as 100 to 1, probably much more than that.

These volleys of musketry we were approaching sounded in the distance like the rapid pouring of shot upon a tinpan, or the tearing of heavy canvas, with slight pauses interspersed with single shots, or desultory shooting. All this presaged fearful work in store for us, with what results to each personally the future, measured probably by moments, would reveal.

How does one feel under such conditions? To tell the truth, I realized the situation most keenly and felt very uncomfortable. Lest there might be some undue manifestation of this feeling in my conduct, I said to myself, this is the duty I undertook to perform for my country, and now I'll do it, and leave the results with God. My greater fear was not that I might be killed, but that I might be grievously wounded and left a victim of suffering on the field.

The nervous strain was plainly visible upon all of us. All moved doggedly forward in obedience to orders, in absolute silence so far as talking was concerned. The compressed lip and set teeth showed that nerve and resolution had been summoned to the discharge of duty. A few temporarily fell out, unable to endure the nervous strain, which was simply awful. There were a few others, it must be said, who skulked, took counsel of their cowardly legs, and, despite all efforts of " file closers" and officers, left the ranks. Of these two classes most of the first rejoined us later on, and their dropping out was no reflection on their bravery. The nervous strain produced by the excitement and danger gave them the malady called by the vets, the " cannon quickstep."

On our way into "position" we passed the " Meyer Spring,"—a magnificent fountain of sweet spring water. It was walled in, and must have been ten or twelve feet square and at least three feet deep, and a stream was flowing from it large enough to make a respectable brook. Many of us succeeded in filling our canteens from this glorious spring, now surrounded by hundreds of wounded soldiers. What a Godsend it was to those poor fellows.

About eight o'clock we were formed into line of battle and moved forward through a grove of trees,* but before actually coming under musketry fire of the enemy we were moved back again, and swung around nearly a mile to the left to the base of a circular knoll to the left of the Roulette farm-house and the road which leads up to the Sharpsburg pike, near the Dunkard church. The famous " sunken road"—a road which had been cut through the other side of this knoll—extended from the Roulette Lane directly in front of our line towards Sharpsburg. I had ridden by the side of Colonel Oakford, except when on duty, up and down the column, and as the line was formed by the colonel and ordered forward, we dismounted and sent our horses to the rear by a servant. I was immediately sent by the colonel to the left of the line to assist

* Now known as East Woods.

COLONEL RICHARD A. OAKFORD
Killed at battle of Antietam, September 17, 1862

The Battle of Antietam

in getting that into position. A rail fence separated us from the top of the knoll. Bullets were whizzing and singing by our ears, but so far hitting none where I was. Over the fence and up the knoll in an excellent line we went. In the centre of the knoll, perhaps a third of the way up, was a large tree, and under and around this tree lay a body of troops doing nothing. They were in our way, but our orders were forward, and through and over them we went.

Reaching the top of the knoll we were met by a terrific volley from the rebels in the sunken road down the other side, not more than one hundred yards away, and also from another rebel line in a corn-field just beyond. Some of our men were killed and wounded by this volley. We were ordered to lie down just under the top of the hill and crawl forward and fire over, each man crawling back, reloading his piece in this prone position and again crawling forward and firing. These tactics undoubtedly saved us many lives, for the fire of the two lines in front of us was terrific. The air was full of whizzing, singing, buzzing bullets. Once down on the ground under cover of the hill, it required very strong resolution to get up where these missiles of death were flying so thickly, yet that was the duty of us officers, especially us of the field and staff. My duty kept me constantly moving up and down that whole line.

On my way back to the right of the line, where I had left Colonel Oakford, I met Lieutenant-Colonel Wilcox, who told me the terrible news that Colonel Oakford was killed. Of the details of his death, I had no time then to inquire. We were then in the very maelstrom of the battle. Men were falling every moment. The horrible noise of the battle was incessant and almost deafening. Except that my mind was so absorbed in my duties, I do not know how I could have endured the strain. Yet out of this pandemonium memory brings several remarkable incidents. They came and went with the rapidity of a quickly revolving kaleidoscope. You caught stupendous incidents on the instant, and in an instant they had passed. One was the brave death of the major of this regiment that was lying idle under the tree. The commanding officer evidently was not doing his duty, and this major was endeavoring to rally his men and get them at work. He was swinging his hat and cheering his men forward, when a solid shot decapitated him. His poor body went down as though some giant had picked it up and furiously slammed it on the ground, and I was so near him that I could almost have touched him with my sword.

The inaction of this regiment lying behind us under that tree was very demoralizing to our men, setting them a bad example. General Kimball, who commanded our brigade, was seated on his horse just under the knoll in the rear of our regiment, evidently watching our work, and he signalled me to come to him, and then gave me orders to present his compliments to the commanding officer of that regiment and direct him to get his men up and at work. I communicated this order as directed. The colonel was hugging the ground, and merely turned his face towards me without replying or attempting to obey the order. General Kimball saw the whole thing, and again called me to him and, with an oath, commanded me to repeat the order to him at the muzzle of my revolver, and shoot

The Battle of Antietam

him if he did not immediately obey. Said General Kimball: " Get those cowards out of there or shoot them." My task was a most disagreeable one, but I must deliver my orders, and did so, but was saved the duty of shooting by the other officers of the regiment bravely rallying their men and pushing them forward to the firing-line, where they did good work. What became of that skulking colonel, I do not know.

The air was now thick with smoke from the muskets, which not only obscured our vision of the enemy, but made breathing difficult and most uncomfortable. The day was excessively hot, and no air stirring, we were forced to breathe this powder smoke, impregnated with saltpetre, which burned the coating of nose, throat, and eyes almost like fire.

Captain Abbott, commanding Company G, from Mauch Chunk, a brave and splendid officer, was early carried to the rear, a ball having nearly carried away his under jaw. He afterwards told me that his first sensation of this awful wound was his mouth full of blood, teeth, and splintered bones, which he spat out on the ground, and then found that unless he got immediate help he would bleed to death in a few minutes. Fortunately he found Assistant Surgeon Hoover, who had been assigned to us just from his college graduation, who, under the shelter of a hay-stack, with no anæsthetic, performed an operation which Dr. Gross, of Philadelphia, afterwards said had been but once before successfully performed in the history of surgery, and saved his life. Lieutenant Anson C. Cranmer, Company C, was killed, and the ground was soon strewn with the dead and wounded. Soon our men began to call for more ammunition, and we officers were kept busy taking from the dead and wounded and distributing to the living. Each man had eighty rounds when we began the fight. One man near me rose a moment, when a missile struck his gun about midway, and actually capsized him. He pulled himself together, and, finding he was only a little bruised, picked up another gun, with which the ground was now strewn, and went at it again.

Directly, a lull in the enemy's firing occurred, and we had an opportunity to look over the hill a little more carefully at their lines. Their first line in the sunken road seemed to be all dead or wounded, and several of our men ran down there, to find that literally true. They brought back the lieutenant-colonel, a fine-looking man, who was mortally wounded. I shook his hand, and he said, " God bless you, boys, you are very kind." He asked to be laid down in some sheltered place, for, said he, " I have but a few moments to live." I well remember his refined, gentlemanly appearance, and how profoundly sorry I felt for him. He was young, lithely built, of sandy complexion, and wore a comparatively new uniform of Confederate gray, on which was embroidered the insignia of the " 5th Ga.,* C. S. A." He said, " You have killed all my brave boys; they are there in the road." And they were, I saw them next day lying four deep in places as they fell, a most awful picture of battle carnage. This lull was of very short duration, and like the lull of a storm presaged

---

* This is from my diary, but investigations since the war make it evident that it must be a mistake; that the 5th Ga. was not in that road, but it was the 6th Ga., and this officer was probably Lieutenant-Colonel J. M. Newton of that regiment.

SILENCED CONFEDERATE BATTERY IN FRONT OF DUNKER CHURCH
SHARPSBURG ROAD, ANTIETAM

This little brick church lay between the opposing lines, and both
Union and Confederate wounded were gathered in it

The Battle of Antietam

a renewal of the firing with greater fury, for a fresh line of rebel troops had been brought up. This occurred three times before we were relieved.

During the fiercest of the firing, another remarkable incident occurred, which well illustrated the fortunes of war. I heard a man shouting, " Come over here men, you can see 'em better," and there, over the brow of the knoll, absolutely exposed, was Private George Coursen, of Company K, sitting on a boulder, loading and firing as calmly as though there wasn't a rebel in the country. I yelled to him to come back under the cover of the hill-top, but he said he could see the rebels better there, and refused to leave his vantage-ground. I think he remained there until we were ordered back and did not receive a scratch. His escape was nothing less than a miracle. He seemed to have no idea of fear.

A remarkable fact about our experience during this fight was that we took no note of time. When we were out of ammunition and about to move back I looked at my watch and found it was 12.30 P.M. We had been under fire since eight o'clock. I couldn't believe my eyes; was sure my watch had gone wrong. I would have sworn that we had not been there more than twenty minutes, when we had actually been in that very hell of fire for four and a half hours.

Just as we were moving back, the Irish brigade came up, under command of General Thomas Francis Meagher. They had been ordered to complete our work by a charge, and right gallantly they did it. Many of our men, not understanding the order, joined in that charge. General Meagher rode a beautiful white horse, but made a show of himself by tumbling off just as he reached our line. The boys said he was drunk, and he certainly looked and acted like a drunken man. He regained his feet and floundered about, swearing like a crazy man. The brigade, however, made a magnificent charge and swept everything before it.

Another incident occurred during the time we were under fire. My attention was arrested by a heavily built general officer passing to the rear on foot. He came close by me and as he passed he shouted: " You will have to get back. Don't you see yonder line of rebels is flanking you?" I looked in the direction he pointed, and, sure enough, on our right and now well to our rear was an extended line of rebel infantry with their colors flying, moving forward almost with the precision of a parade. They had thrown forward a beautiful skirmish line and seemed to be practicallly masters of the situation. My heart was in my mouth for a couple of moments, until suddenly the picture changed, and their beautiful line collapsed and went back as if the d—l was after them. They had run up against an obstruction in a line of the " boys in blue," and many of them never went back. This general officer who spoke to me, I learned, was Major-General Richardson, commanding the First Division, then badly wounded, and who died a few hours after.

Our regiment now moved back and to the right some three-quarters of a mile, where we were supplied with ammunition, and the men were allowed to make themselves a cup of coffee and eat a " hardtack." I was faint for want of food, for I had only a cup of coffee in the early morning, and was favored with a hardtack by one of the men, who were always ready and willing to share their rations with us. We now learned that our brigade had borne the brunt of a long and persistent effort by Lee to break our line at this point, and that we were actually the third line which had been thrown into this breach, the other two having been wiped out before we advanced; that as a matter of fact our brigade, being composed so largely of raw troops—our regiment being really more than half the brigade in actual number—was designed to be held in reserve. But the onslaught of the enemy had been so terrific, that by eight o'clock A.M. our reserve line was all there was left and we had to be sent in. The other three regiments were veterans, old and tried. They had an established reputation of having never once been forced back or whipped, but the One Hundred and Thirty-second was new and, except as to numbers, an unknown quantity. We had been unmercifully guyed during the two preceding weeks, as I have said before, as a lot of " greenhorns," " pretty boys" in " pretty new clothes," " mamma's darlings," etc., etc., to the end of the vets' slang calendar. Now that we had proved our metal under fire, the atmosphere was completely changed. Not the semblance of another jibe against the One Hundred and Thirty-second Pennsylvania Volunteers.

We did not know how well we had done, only that we had tried to do our duty under trying circumstances, until officers and men from other regiments came flocking over to congratulate and praise us. I didn't even know we had passed through the fire of a great battle until the colonel of the Fourteenth Indiana came over to condole with us on the loss of Colonel Oakford, and incidentally told us that this was undoubtedly the greatest battle of the war thus far, and that we probably would never have such another.

After getting into our new position, I at once began to look up our losses. I learned that Colonel Oakford was killed by one of the rebel sharp-shooters just as the regiment scaled the fence in its advance up the knoll, and before we had fired a shot. It must have occurred almost instantly after I left him with orders for the left of the line. I was probably the last to whom he spoke. He was hit by a minie-ball in the left shoulder, just below the collar-bone. The doctor said the ball had severed one of the large arteries, and he died in a very few minutes. He had been in command of the regiment a little more than a month, but during that brief time his work as a disciplinarian and drill-master had made it possible for us to acquit ourselves as creditably as they all said we had done. General Kimball was loud in our praise and greatly lamented Colonel Oakford's death, whom he admired very much. He was a brave, able, and accomplished officer and gentleman, and his loss to the regiment was irreparable.

Had Colonel Oakford lived his record must have been brilliant and his promotion rapid, for very few volunteer officers had so quickly mastered the details of military tactics and routine. He was a thorough disciplinarian, an able tactician, and the interests and welfare of his men were constantly upon his heart.

My diary records the fact that I saw Captain Willard, of the Fourteenth Connecticut, fall as we passed their line on our way to the rear; that he appeared to have

The Battle of Antietam

been hit by a grape-shot or piece of shell. I did not know him, only heard that he was a brother of E. N. Willard, of Scranton. The Fourteenth Connecticut men said he was a fine man and splendid officer.

Among the wounded—reported mortally—was Sergeant Martin Hower, of Company K, one of our very best non-commissioned officers. I saw him at the hospital, and it was very hard to be able to do nothing for him. It seemed our loss must reach upward of two hundred killed, wounded and missing. Out of seven hundred and ninety-eight who answered to roll-call in the morning, we had with us less than three hundred at the close of the fight. Our actual loss was: Killed—Officers, two (Colonel Oakford and Lieutenant Cranmer; men, twenty-eight; total, thirty. Wounded—Officers, four; men, one hundred and ten; total, one hundred and forty-four. To this should be added at least thirty of the men who died of their wounds within the next few days, which would make our death loss in this battle upward of sixty. Of the missing, many of them were of those who joined the Irish brigade in their charge, and who did not find us again for a day or so. It may seem strange that a man should not be able to find his regiment for so long a time, when really it is so close at hand. But when one remembers that our army of about seventy-five thousand men had upward of two hundred regiments massed within say two square miles, and that they were constantly changing position, it will be seen that looking for any one regiment is almost like looking for a needle in a hay-mow.

CHAPTER VI

THE BATTLE OF ANTIETAM—CONTINUED

DURING the afternoon of this day we were again moved further to the right and placed as supports of a battery. We were posted about two hundred yards directly in front of the guns on low ground. The battery was evidently engaged in another artillery duel. We were in a comparatively safe position, so long as the rebel guns directed their firing at our battery; but after a time they began "feeling for the supports," first dropping their shells beyond our guns, then in front of them, until they finally got a pretty good range on our line and filled the air with bursting shells over our heads. One and another was carried to the rear, wounded, and the line became very restive. We were required to lie perfectly quiet. We found this very much more trying than being at work, and the line began to show symptoms of wavering, when General Kimball, who with his staff had dismounted and was resting near us, immediately mounted his horse and, riding up and down the line, shouted: "Stand firm, trust in God, and do your duty."

It was an exceedingly brave act, and its effect was electric upon the men. There was no more wavering, and the rebel battery, evidently thinking they had not found the "supports," soon ceased firing upon us. It was now near night and the firing very perceptibly slackened in our vicinity, though a mile or more to the left it still continued very heavy. This, we afterwards learned, was the work at what has passed into history as " Burnside's" bridge—the effort of Burnside's corps to capture the stone bridge over Antietam creek, near the village of Sharpsburg, and the heights beyond. These were gallantly carried after a terrific fight quite late in the afternoon.

Our work, so far as this battle was concerned, was done. We rested " on our arms" where we were for the next forty-eight hours, expecting all the next day a renewal of the fighting; but nothing was done in our neighborhood beyond a few shots from the battery we were supporting. On the second day it became known that Lee had hauled off, and there was no immediate prospect of further fighting. Our companies were permitted to gather up their dead, and burying parties were organized.

We were allowed to go over the field freely. It was a gruesome sight. Our own dead had been cared for, but the rebel dead remained as they had fallen. In the hot sun the bodies had swollen and turned black. Nearly all lay with faces up and eyes wide open, presenting a spectacle to make one shudder. The distended nostrils and thickened lips made them look like negroes, except for their straight hair. Their limbs and bodies were so enlarged that their clothing seemed ready to burst. Some ghouls had been among them, whether from their own lines or from ours, could not be known, but every man's pockets had been ripped out and the contents taken.

In company with Captain Archbald I went over the position occupied by our regiment and brigade, the famous " sunken road,"—that is, the lane or road extending from near the " Roulette house" towards Sharpsburg. For some distance it had been cut through the opposite side of the knoll upon which we fought, and had the appearance of a sunken road. It was literally filled with rebel dead, which in some places lay three and four bodies deep. We afterwards saw pictures of this road in the illustrated papers, which partially portrayed the horrible scene. Those poor fellows were the Fifth * Georgia regiment. This terrible work was mostly that of our regiment, and bore testimony to the effectiveness of the fire of our men.

The position was an alluring one: the road was cut into the hill about waist high, and seemed to offer secure protection to a line of infantry, and so no doubt this line was posted there to hold the knoll and this Sharpsburg road. It proved, however, nothing but a death-trap, for once our line got into position on the top of this crescent-shaped ridge we could reach them by a direct fire on the centre and a double flanking fire at the right and left of the line, and only about one hundred yards away. With nothing but an open field behind them there was absolutely no escape, nothing but death or surrender, and they evidently chose the former, for we saw no white flag displayed. We could now understand the remark of their lieutenant-colonel, whom our boys brought in, as already mentioned: " You have killed all my poor boys. They lie there in the road." I learned later that the few survivors of this regiment were sent South to guard rebel prisoners.

---

* Probably the 6th Ga.

SECTION OF FAMOUS SUNKEN ROAD IN FRONT OF LINE OF 132D P. V., NEAR ROULETTE LANE
The dead are probably from the Sixth Georgia Confederate troops

The Battle of Antietam

The lines of battle of both armies were not only marked by the presence of the dead, but by a vast variety of army equipage, such as blankets, canteens, haversacks, guns, gun-slings, bayonets, ramrods, some whole, others broken, —verily, a besom of destruction had done its work faithfully here. Dead horses were everywhere, and the stench from them and the human dead was horrible. " Uncle" Billy Sherman has said, " War is hell!" yet this definition, with all that imagination can picture, fails to reveal all its bloody horrors.

The positions of some of the dead were very striking. One poor fellow lay face down on a partially fallen stone wall, with one arm and one foot extended, as if in the act of crawling over. His position attracted our attention, and we found his body literally riddled with bullets—there must have been hundreds—and most of them shot into him after he was dead, for they showed no marks of blood. Probably the poor fellow had been wounded in trying to reach shelter behind that wall, was spotted in the act by our men, and killed right there, and became thereafter a target for every new man that saw him. Another man lay, still clasping his musket, which he was evidently in the act of loading when a bullet pierced his heart, literally flooding his gun with his life's blood, a ghastly testimonial to his heroic sacrifice.

We witnessed the burying details gathering up and burying the dead. The work was rough and heartless, but only comporting with the character of war. The natural reverence for the dead was wholly absent. The poor bodies, all of them heroes in their death, even though in a mistaken cause, were " planted" with as little feeling as though they had been so many logs. A trench was dug, where the digging was easiest, about seven feet wide and long enough to accommodate all the bodies gathered within a certain radius; these were then placed side by side, cross-wise of the trench, and buried without anything to keep the earth from them. In the case of the Union dead the trenches were usually two or three feet deep, and the bodies were wrapped in blankets before being covered, but with the rebels no blankets were used, and the trenches were sometimes so shallow as to leave the toes exposed after a shower.

No ceremony whatever attended this gruesome service, but it was generally accompanied by ribald jokes, at the expense of the poor " Johnny" they were " planting." This was not the fruit of debased natures or degenerate hearts on the part of the boys, who well knew it might be their turn next, under the fortunes of war, to be buried in like manner, but it was recklessness and thoughtlessness, born of the hardening influences of war.

Having now given some account of the scenes in which I participated during the battle and the day after, let us look at another feature of the battle, and probably the most heart-breaking of all, the field hospital. There was one established for our division some three hundred yards in our rear, under the shelter of a hill. Here were gathered as rapidly as possible the wounded, and a corps of surgeons were busily engaged in amputating limbs and dressing wounds. It should be understood that the accommodations were of the rudest character. A hospital tent had been hurriedly erected and an old house and barn utilized. Of course, I saw nothing of it or its work until

The Battle of Antietam

the evening after the battle, when I went to see the body of our dead colonel and some of our Scranton boys who were wounded. Outside the hospital were piles of amputated arms, legs, and feet, thrown out with as little care as so many pieces of wood. There were also many dead soldiers—those who had died after reaching the hospital—lying outside, there being inside scant room only for the living. Here, on bunches of hay and straw, the poor fellows were lying so thickly that there was scarce room for the surgeon and attendants to move about among them. Others were not allowed inside, except officers and an occasional friend who might be helping. Our chaplain spent his time here and did yeoman service helping the wounded. Yet all that could be done with the limited means at hand seemed only to accentuate the appalling need. The pallid, appealing faces were patient with a heroism born only of the truest metal. I was told by the surgeons that such expressions as this were not infrequent as they approached a man in his " turn" : " Please, doctor, attend to this poor fellow next; he's worse than I," and this when his own life's blood was fast oozing away.

Most of the wounded had to wait hours before having their wounds dressed, owing to insufficient force and inadequate facilities. I was told that not a surgeon had his eyes closed for three days after this battle. The doctors of neighboring towns within reach came and voluntarily gave their services, yet it is doubtless true that hundreds of the wounded perished for want of prompt and proper care. This is one of the unavoidable incidents of a great battle—a part of the horrors of war. The rebel wounded necessarily were second to our own in receiving care from the surgeons, yet they, too, received all the attention that was possible under the circumstances. Some of their surgeons remained with their wounded, and I am told they and our own surgeons worked together most energetically and heroically in their efforts to relieve the sufferings of all, whether they wore the blue or the gray. Suffering, it has been said, makes all the world akin. So here, in our lines, the wounded rebel was lost sight of in the suffering brother.

We remained on the battle-field until September 21, four days after the fight.

My notes of this day say that I was feeling so miserable as to be scarcely able to crawl about, yet was obliged to remain on duty; that Lieutenant-Colonel Wilcox, now in command, and Major Shreve were in the same condition. This was due to the nervous strain through which we had passed, and to insufficient and unwholesome food. As stated before, we had been obliged to eat whatever we could get, which for the past four days had been mostly green field corn roasted as best we could. The wonder is that we were not utterly prostrated. Nevertheless, I not only performed all my duties, but went a mile down the Antietam creek, took a bath, and washed my underclothing, my first experience in the laundry business.

We had been now for two weeks and more steadily on the march, our baggage in wagons somewhere en route, without the possibility of a change of clothing or of having any washing done. Most of this time marching in a cloud of dust so thick that one could almost cut it,

and perspiring freely, one can imagine our condition.
Bathing as frequently as opportunity offered, yet our
condition was almost unendurable. For with the accu-
mulation of dirt upon our body, there was added the ever-
present scourge of the army, body lice. These vermin,
called by the boys " graybacks," were nearly the size of a
grain of wheat, and derived their name from their bluish-
gray color. They seemed to infest the ground wherever
there had been a bivouac of the rebels, and following
them as we had, during all of this campaign, sleeping
frequently on the ground just vacated by them, no one
was exempt from this plague. They secreted themselves
in the seams of the clothing and in the armpits chiefly. A
good bath, with a change of underclothing, would usually
rid one of them, but only to acquire a new crop in the
first camp. The clothing could be freed of them by boiling in salt water or by going carefully over the seams
and picking them off. The latter operation was a frequent occupation with the men on any day which was
warm enough to permit them to disrobe for the purpose.
One of the most laughable sights I ever beheld was the
whole brigade, halted for a couple of hours' rest one hot
day, with clothing off, " skirmishing," as the boys called
it, for " graybacks." This was one of the many unpoet-
ical features of army life which accentuated the sacrifices
one made to serve his country.

How did we ordinarily get our laundrying done? The
enlisted men as a rule always did it themselves. Occasionally in camp a number of them would club together
and hire some " camp follower" or some other soldier to
do it. Officers of sufficient rank to have a servant, of

War from the Inside

course, readily solved the question. Those of us of lesser rank could generally hire it done, except on the march. Then we had to be our own laundrymen. Having, as in the above instance, no change of clothing at hand, the washing followed a bath, and consisted in standing in the running water and rubbing as much of the dirt out of the underwear as could be done without soap, for that could not be had for love or money; then hanging them on the limb of a tree and sitting in the sun, as comfortable as possible, whilst wind and sun did the drying. A "snap-shot" of such a scene would no doubt be interesting. But "snap-shots" unfortunately were not then in vogue, and so a picture of high art must perish. We could not be over particular about having our clothes dry. The finishing touches were added as we wore them back to camp.

My diary notes that there were nine hundred and ninety-eight rebel dead gathered and buried from in front of the lines of our division. This line was about a quarter of a mile long, and this was mostly our work (our division), although Richardson's division had occupied part of this ground before us, but had been so quickly broken that they had not made much impression upon the enemy. Our division had engaged them continuously and under a terrific fire from eight o'clock A.M. until 12.30 P.M. It may be asked why during that length of time and under such a fire all were not annihilated. The answer is, that inaccuracy and unsteadiness in firing on both sides greatly reduce its effectiveness, and taking all possible advantage of shelter by lying prone upon the ground also prevents losses; but the above number of rebel dead, it

FIELD HOSPITAL

The Battle of Antietam

should be remembered, represents, probably, not more than twenty to twenty-five per cent. of their casualties in that area of their lines; the balance were wounded and were removed. So that with nine hundred and ninety-eight dead it can be safely estimated that their losses exceeded four thousand killed and wounded in that area. This would indicate what was undoubtedly true, that we were in the very heart of that great battle.

Here I wish to say that some chroniclers of battles have undertaken to measure the effectiveness and bravery of the different regiments, batteries, etc., by the numbers they have lost in certain battles; for example, one historian has made a book grading the regiments by the number of men they lost in action, assuming that the more men killed and wounded, the more brilliant and brave had been its work. This assumption is absolutely fallacious. Heavy losses may be the result of great bravery with splendid work. On the other hand, they may be the result of cowardice or inefficiency. Suppose, under trying circumstances, officers lose their heads and fail to properly handle their men, or if the latter prove cowardly and incapable of being moved with promptness to meet the exigency, great loss usually ensues, and this would be chargeable to cowardice or inefficiency. According to the loss way of estimating fighting regiments, the least deserving are liable to be credited with the best work. The rule is, the better drilled, disciplined, and the better officered, the less the losses in any position on the firing-line.

One regiment I have in mind, with which we were afterwards brigaded, illustrates this principle. It was the First Delaware Volunteer infantry. It was a three years' regiment and had been in the field more than a year when we joined them. All things considered, it was the best drilled and disciplined regiment I saw in the service. It was as steady under fire as on parade. Every movement in the tactics it could execute on the jump, and its fire was something to keep away from. The result was that, pushed everywhere to the front because of its splendid work, it lost comparatively few men. Every man was a marksman and understood how to take all possible advantage of the situation to make his work most effective and at the same time take care of himself. This regiment, whose record was one unbroken succession of splendid achievements during its whole period of service, might never have gotten on a roll of fame founded on numbers of men lost. How much more glorious is a record founded on effective work and men saved!

CHAPTER VII

NEITHER side seemed anxious to resume the fighting on
the 18th, though there was picket firing and some cannonading. We remained the next day where the darkness
found us after the battle, ready and momentarily expecting to resume the work. All sorts of rumors were afloat
as to the results of the battle, also as to future movements.
Whether we had won a great victory and were to press
immediately forward to reap the fullest benefit of it, or
whether it was practically a drawn battle, with the possibilities of an early retreat, we did not then know. We
had no idea of what the name of the battle would be. My
diary calls it the battle of " Meyer's Spring," from that
magnificent fountain, on our line of battle, described in
the last chapter. The Confederates named it the battle of
Sharpsburg, from the village of that name on the right
of their line. Two days later, after the rebels had hauled
off—which they did very leisurely the next day and night
—we received " Little Mac's" congratulatory order on the
great victory achieved at " Antietam."

So far as our part of the battle was concerned, we knew
we had the best of it. We had cleaned up everything in
our front, and the " chip was still serenely resting on our

shoulder." But what had been the outcome elsewhere on the line we did not know. That our army had been terrifically battered was certain. Our own losses indicated this. We were therefore both relieved and rejoiced on receiving the congratulatory order. I confess to have had some doubts about the extent of the victory, and whether, had Lee remained and shown fight, we would not have repeated the old story and " retired in good order." As it was, the tide had evidently turned, and the magnificent old Army of the Potomac, after so many drubbings, had been able to score its first decisive victory.

On the twenty-second day of September we were again on the march, our regiment reduced in numbers, from casualties in the battle and from sickness, by nearly three hundred men. Lieutenant-Colonel Wilcox was now in command. The body of our late colonel had been shipped to Scranton under guard of Privates S. P. Snyder and Charles A. Meylert, Company K, the " exigencies of the service" permitting of no larger detail nor any officer to accompany it.

We were told the army was bound for Harper's Ferry, distant some eight to ten miles. We passed through the village of Sharpsburg—what there was left of it. It had been occupied by the rebels as the extreme right of their line on the morning of the battle. It presented abundant evidence of having been well in the zone of the fight. Its buildings were riddled with shells, and confusion seemed to reign supreme. We learned that Burnside, with the left wing of the army, had a very hot argument with Lee's right during the afternoon for the possession of the stone bridge over Antietam creek at the foot of the hill entering the village; that after two repulses with heavy loss, Colonel Hartranft (afterwards Governor of Pennsylvania) led his regiment, the Fifty-first Pennsylvania Volunteers and the Fifty-first New York, in a magnificent charge and carried the bridge and the heights above, and Sharpsburg was ours. If any one would like to get an idea of what terrific work that charge was they should examine that bridge and the heights on the Sharpsburg side. The latter rise almost perpendicularly more than three hundred feet. One of the "boys" who went over that bridge and up those heights in that memorable charge was Private Edward L. Buck, Fifty-first Pennsylvania Volunteers, formerly Assistant Postmaster of Scranton, and ever since the war a prominent citizen of this city. That bridge is now known as "Burnside's Bridge." Forty-one years afterwards, I passed over it, and was shown a shell still sticking in the masonry of one of the arches. It was a conical shell probably ten inches long, about half of it left protruding.

Little of special interest occurred on this march until we reached the Potomac, a short distance above Harper's Ferry. Here we were shown the little round house where John Brown concealed his guns and "pikes" prior to his famous raid three years before. This was his rendezvous on the night before his ill-starred expedition descended upon the State of Virginia and the South, in an insane effort to free the slaves. Our division was headed by the Fourteenth Connecticut, and as we approached the river opposite Harper's Ferry its fine band struck up the then new and popular air, "John Brown's Body," and the whole division took up the song, and we forded the

6   81

river singing it. Slavery had destroyed the Kansas home of old John Brown, had murdered his sons, and undoubtedly driven him insane, because of his anti-slavery zeal. The great State of Virginia—the " Mother of Presidents"—had vindicated her loyalty to the " peculiar institution," and, let it be added, her own spotless chivalry, by hanging this poor, crazy fanatic for high treason! Was there poetic justice in our marching into the territory where these events transpired singing:

"John Brown's body lies a mouldering in the grave,
His soul goes marching on?"

This couplet,

" We'll hang Jeff Davis to a sour apple-tree,"

was sung with peculiar zest, though I never quite understood what the poet had against the sour apple-tree.

We marched through the quaint old town of Harper's Ferry, whose principal industry had been the government arsenal for the manufacture of muskets and other army ordnance. These buildings were now a mass of ruins, and the remainder of the town presented the appearance of a plucked goose, as both armies had successively captured and occupied it. We went into camp on a high plateau back of the village known as Bolivar Heights. The scenic situation at Harper's Ferry is remarkably grand. The town is situated on the tongue or fork of land at the junction of the Potomac and Shenandoah rivers. From the point where the rivers join, the land rises rapidly until the summit of Bolivar Heights is reached, several hundred feet above the town, from which a view is had of one of the most lovely valleys to be found anywhere in

Harper's Ferry

the world—the Shenandoah Valley. Across the Potomac to the east and facing Harper's Ferry rises Maryland Heights, a bluff probably a thousand feet high, while across the Shenandoah to the right towers another precipitous bluff of about equal height called Loudon Heights. Both of these bluffs commanded Bolivar Heights and Harper's Ferry.

It was the sudden and unexpected appearance of Stonewall Jackson's batteries upon both of these supposed inaccessible bluffs that ten days before had forced the surrender of the garrison of ten thousand Union troops which had been posted here to hold Harper's Ferry. It was said that the rain of shot and shell from those bluffs down upon our forces was simply merciless, and Jackson had cut off all avenues of escape before opening his batteries. The cavalry, I believe, cut their way out, but the infantry, after twenty-four hours of that storm of shot and shell, were forced to hoist the white flag. How they could have lived half that time in such a hell of fire is a marvel. Everything above ground bore evidence of this fire. There were unexploded shells lying about in great numbers.

An incident that might have been anything but funny occurred the day after we encamped here. A new regiment joined the army and marched past our division to a point farther up the heights and went into camp. They were a fine-looking regiment, full in numbers, and with new, clean uniforms. Their reception at the hands of the " vets" was very like our own three weeks before. Our boys, however, were " vets" now, and joined in the " reception" with a zest quite usual under such circumstances.

War from the Inside

However, the "tenderfeet" incident had passed, and we were preparing our evening meal, when bang! bang! bang! bang! rang out a half-dozen shots in quick succession. Every man jumped as though the whole rebel army was upon us. It was soon discovered that the explosions came from the camp of the "tenderfeet." Some of those greenhorns had gathered a number of those unexploded shells, set them up on end for a fireplace, and were quietly boiling their coffee over them when they, of course, exploded. Why none of them were seriously injured was a miracle. At the moment of explosion no one happened to be very near the fire. A moment before a dozen men had been standing over it. Does Providence graciously look out for the tenderfoot? Some of them, I fear, were made to feel that they would rather be dead than take the guying they got for this evidence of their verdancy.

Camp life at Bolivar Heights soon resolved itself into the usual routine of drill and picket duty. How many corps of the army were encamped here I did not know, but we were a vast city of soldiers, and there was no end of matters to occupy attention when off duty. These included bathing expeditions to the Shenandoah, a mile and a half away; the "doing" of the quaint old town of Harper's Ferry, and rambles up Maryland and Loudon Heights, both of which were now occupied by our troops. This was our first experience in a large encampment in the field. One feature of it was exceedingly beautiful, and that was its system of "calls." The cavalry and artillery were encamped on one side of us. Each battery of artillery and battalion of cavalry had its

Harper's Ferry

corps of "trumpeters" or "buglers," while the infantry regiments had their drum corps, whose duty it was to sound the various "camp calls." The principal calls were "reveille," the getting up or morning roll-call, at sunrise usually; the guard mount, the drill, the meal calls, the "retreat" (evening roll-call), and the "taps," the "turning in" or "lights out" call. The reveille, the retreat, and taps were required to be sounded by each battery, troop, and regiment in consecutive order, commencing at the extreme right. The firing of the morning gun was the signal for the first corps of cavalry buglers to begin the reveille, then in succession it was repeated first through the bugler corps and then by the drum corps back and forth through the lines until it had gone through the whole army. As a martial and musical feature it was exceedingly beautiful and inspiring. But as its purpose was to hustle out sleepy men to roll-call, it is doubtful if these features were fully appreciated; that its advent was an occasion for imprecation rather than appreciation the following story may illustrate.

A group of "vets" were discussing what they would do when they got home from the war. Several plans had been suggested—the taking into permanent camp of the soldier's sweetheart being the chief goal, of course. When Pat's turn came to tell what he was going to do, he said:

"I'll be takin' me girl and settling down wid her housekeepin', and thin i'll be hirin' of a dhrum corps to come an' play the ravalye iviry mornin' under me chamber windi."

"What will you do that for? Haven't you had enough of the reveille here?"

85

War from the Inside

" I'll just h'ist me windi, an' I'll yell, ' To h—l wid yer ravalye; I'll slape as long as I plase.' "

Many of these " calls" were parodied by the men. Here is the reveille:

> I can't get 'em up, I can't get 'em up,
> I can't get 'em up at all, sir;
> I can't get 'em up, I can't get 'em up,
> I can't get 'em up at all.
> I'll go and tell the captain,
> I'll go and tell the captain,
> I'll go and tell the captain,
> I can't get 'em up at all.

This is the sick call:

> Get your quinine, get your quinine,
> And a blue pill too, and a blue pill too.
> Get your quinine.

And so on down the list. The retreat call at sundown was really enjoyed and was made more of. The day's work was then over, and each corps elaborated its music, the bands frequently extending it into an evening concert.

The almost universal time-killer was cards. Of course various games were played, but " poker" was king. A game of the latter could be found in almost every company street, officers as well as men took a " twist at the tiger." At the battle of Chancellorsville I saw a game in full blast right under fire of the rebel shells. Every screeching shell was greeted with an imprecation, while the game went on just the same.

After our return home I was told of one man who made

enough money at cards to successfully start himself in business. It was said he performed picket duty by hired proxies during the following winter in camp at Falmouth, and gave his time wholly to the game. A New York City regiment lay adjoining our camp that winter, and a truer lot of sports, from colonel down, never entered the service. These men, officers and all, were his patrons. They came to "do the Pennsylvania novice," but were themselves done in the end.

On the 3d of October our brigade made what was termed a reconnoissance in force out through Loudon County, Virginia, to Leesburg. It was reported that Jeb. Stuart was there with a force of cavalry and infantry. General Kimball was sent with our brigade to capture him if possible. Our orders on the evening of October 2 were to report at brigade head-quarters at seven o'clock A.M., with three days' rations and sixty rounds of ammunition. This meant "business," and was a welcome change from the monotony of camp life. A regiment of cavalry and two batteries of artillery had been added to our brigade for this expedition. The morning dawned bright and beautiful, but the day proved a very hot one, and the first three or four miles of our march was around the base of Loudon Heights, close under the mountain over a very rocky road, and where there was not a breath of air stirring. We were delayed by the artillery in getting over this portion of the route, and then we were marched almost on the run to make up for the lost time. General Kimball had gone forward with the cavalry, leaving his adjutant-general to bring up the balance of the column as rapidly as possible. In his efforts to hurry the men forward the latter overdid the matter. The result was the men dropped in scores utterly exhausted, so that within three hours our number had been reduced more than half, and at the end of the march in the evening there were just twenty-five officers and men of our regiment present for duty, and of the whole infantry force, three thousand strong at the start, there were less than two hundred present at the finish. This was due to an utter lack of judgment in marching.

The distance covered had been twenty-three miles. The day had been hot, the road rough, and the men, in heavy marching order with three days' rations and sixty rounds of ammunition, had carried upwards of ninety pounds each. With such a load and under such conditions, to expect men to march any distance at the hurried pace required was criminal folly. It bore its natural fruit. Our men were scattered on the route from Harper's Ferry to Leesburg, a demoralized lot of stragglers. My diary mentions this experience with much indignation and attributes the folly to the effects of whiskey. Of course, this was only a surmise.

General Kimball was not directly responsible for it. In his anxiety to capture Jeb. Stuart he had pushed ahead with the cavalry, and knew nothing of our condition until the forlorn party came straggling into his bivouac in the evening. He was very indignant, and said some words that cannot be recorded here. He was chagrined to find Stuart gone, but now was greatly relieved that such was the fact. Otherwise, said he, we would have stood an excellent chance for a journey south under rebel escort.

On our way out we passed through several small villages, in none of which did we find evidence of decided Union sentiment, except in Waterford. This was a prosperous-looking town, and the people seemed hospitable, and manifested their Union sentiments by furnishing us fruit and water freely. Our cavalry caught four of Stuart's men in a picture-gallery and marched them to the rear. I had the good fortune to secure a loaf of nice bread and a canteen of sweet milk. If any one wishes to know how good bread and milk is, let him step into my shoes on that weary night.

Conditions compelled us to remain at Leesburg that night. We rested on our arms, fearing Stuart might get an inkling of our plight and pounce upon us. My diary says I was unable to sleep because of suffering from a sprained knee and ankle, caused by my horse stumbling and falling on me just at dusk.

The next morning we were off bright and early on the back track for camp, but by another route, so as to avoid being cut off by Stuart. We had started out bravely to capture this wily rebel. Now we were in mortal danger of being captured by him. A detail was made to go back over the route we came and gather up the stragglers. On our way back I was refused a canteen of water by the " Missus" of one of the plantation dwellings; but on riding around to the rear, where the slaves lived, old " Aunt Lucy" supplied us freely with both milk and water. This was a sample of the difference between the aristocrat in the mansion and the slave in the hovel. The latter were always very friendly and ready to help us in every possible way, while as a rule we met with rebuff at the hands of the former.

War from the Inside

Here we came in contact for the first time with plantation life under the institution of slavery. The main or plantation house was usually situated a quarter-mile or more back from the " pike." They were generally low, flat, one-story mansions, built of stone, while further to the rear, in the form of a square, were the wooden cabins of the slaves, each plantation a village by itself. We marched only about eight miles this day, and bivouacked near the village of Hillsboro. This evening we officers of the field and staff caught on to a great treat in the way of stewed chicken and corn cake for supper at a Union farmhouse, and thought ourselves very fortunate to be able to engage a breakfast at the same place for next morning. Alas for the uncertainties of war! We had barely rolled ourselves in our blankets for the night when a staff officer from General Kimball's head-quarters came and in a low tone of voice ordered us to arouse our men without the least noise and be off as quietly as possible; that scouts had reported that Stuart was after us in hot haste. We were off almost in a jiffy. The night was cool and foggy. The former favored our rapid march, and the latter hid us from the enemy, who succeeded in capturing only a couple of men who fell out.

We reached camp at Harper's Ferry shortly after sunrise, a thoroughly tired and battered crowd. The expedition proved absolutely fruitless, and had barely escaped being captured, owing to mismanagement. It was the most trying bit of service of our whole experience. Some of our men never recovered from the exhaustion of that first day's march, and had to be discharged as permanently disabled.

Harper's Ferry

Shortly after this another expedition relieved the monotony of camp life. General Hancock, commanding the Second Division of our corps, had been sent to make a reconnoissance in force towards Halltown, six to eight miles up the Shenandoah Valley. He had gone in the morning, and shortly after noon we had heard cannonading in that direction, showing that he had found "business." It was Hancock's reputation to make "business," if the "Johnnies" could be induced to tarry long enough for him to reach them. However, the firing shortly ceased, and the night set in with a terrific rain-storm. I remember, as I rolled myself in my blanket prepared for a good sleep in defiance of the rain, sympathizing with those poor fellows out on that reconnoissance in all this storm. My sympathy was premature. Just then I heard an ominous scratch on my tent, and the hand of an orderly was thrust through the flaps with an order. In much trepidation I struck a light. Sure I was of trouble, or an order would not have been sent out at such a time. My fears were realized. It directed our regiment to report at brigade head-quarters in heavy marching order with all possible despatch. Here was a "state of things." Was it ever so dark, and did it ever rain harder? Not in my recollection. But that order left no time for cogitations. Into boots, clothing, and gum blanket, out to the colonel's tent with the order, then with his orders to all the companies, the sounding of the long roll, the forming line, and away to brigade head-quarters in that inky blackness and drenching rain was the work of less than fifteen minutes. General Kimball complimented us as being the first regiment to report, and we were honored with the head of the column which was to support Hancock at Halltown. French's division had been ordered out as supports, and Kimball's brigade had the advance.

We marched rapidly up the valley of the Shenandoah, now as black as Erebus. But soon the rain ceased, the clouds broke away, and the stars appeared, completely transforming the scene, and except for the mud and our wet and uncomfortable condition it would have been an enjoyable march. After going about six miles we were directed into a woods to rest until morning. Inside the woods it was inky dark again, and we made headway with much difficulty. Men and horses stumbled and floundered over fallen logs and through brush at imminent peril of limbs, until a halt was made, and after details for picket had been sent out we were allowed to rest until daylight.

It was now about three o'clock. But to rest, soaking wet, almost covered with mud, in a woods that had been so drenched with rain that everything was like a soaked sponge, that was the problem. No fires were allowed, for no one knew how near the enemy might be. However, the men were tired enough to sleep, most of them, even under those conditions. I well remember the weary walking and stamping to keep warm until the sunshine came to our relief. But daylight revealed a condition of things relative to our position that, had the enemy known, we might again have been made an easy prey. Our details for water, after going out some distance, as they supposed in our rear, suddenly found themselves uncomfortably near the enemy's outposts, and hurried back to camp with the information. It was found that in the darkness our picket line had actually gotten turned around, so that our rear had been carefully guarded, whilst our front was left wholly exposed. The denseness of the woods and the darkness of the night had been our salvation. We shortly learned that Hancock had accomplished his purpose and was moving back to Harper's Ferry. We followed leisurely, reaching the camp about noon, thoroughly tired and bedraggled from the rain and mud.

CHAPTER VIII

WE remained on Bolivar Heights, at Harper's Ferry, without further special incident until the 31st of October, 1862. In the mean time Lieutenant-Colonel Wilcox had been promoted to colonel to fill the vacancy caused by the death of Colonel Oakford at Antietam. Major Albright had been promoted to lieutenant-colonel and the senior captain, Shreve, Company A, had been made major. Colonel Wilcox was on his back with a severe case of typhoid fever, and Lieutenant-Colonel Albright had been some ten days absent on sick leave, during which time Major Shreve had been in command. Lieutenant-Colonel Albright, hearing of the probable movement of the army, rejoined us in time to take command as we bade farewell to Harper's Ferry. To show how little a soldier can know of what is before him, I note the fact that we had just completed fixing up our quarters for cold weather at Camp Bolivar. This involved considerable labor and some expense. My diary records the fact that I had put up a " California stove" in my tent. This, if I remember rightly, was a cone-shaped sheet-iron affair, which had a small sliding door and sat on the ground, with a small pipe extending through the canvas roof just under the ridge-pole to the rear. It cost, I think,

94

about four dollars, and required some skill in " setting up," chiefly in fixing the pipe so that it would not tumble about one's ears with every blast of wind that shook the tent, and in windy weather would at least carry some of the smoke outside. A special course of engineering was almost needed to be able to properly handle those stoves. A little too much fire, and you had to adopt Pat's remedy when Biddy's temper got up—sit on the outside until it cooled down. Too little was worse than none, for your tent became a smoke-house. On the whole, they were much like the goose the aforesaid Pat captured and brought into camp, " a mighty unconvanient burr'd, a little too big for one and not big enough for two."

This fixing up of quarters had been done in contempla-tion of remaining here through the winter, and we had taken our cue from like actions of our brigade officers, who were supposed to know something about the move-ments of the army. When we got orders on the 29th of October to prepare for the march, I was assured by the adjutant-general of our brigade that it was nothing more than a day's reconnoissance, and that we were certainly not going to move our quarters. He knew as much about it as I did. Within an hour after this order another came directing us to move in heavy marching order, with three days' rations and sixty rounds of ammunition. And so we moved out of Harper's Ferry on the 31st of October, leaving our fixed-up quarters, with my four-dollar stove, to Geary's division, which succeeded to our camp.

We crossed the Shenandoah on a pontoon bridge and skirted the mountain under Loudon Heights over the same route south that we had taken on our way in from the

War from the Inside

Leesburg raid. We marched very leisurely, making during the first four days only about twenty-five miles, to a village bearing the serious (?) name of Snickersville. Here we had the first evidence of the presence of the enemy. We were hurried through this village and up through the gap in the mountain called " Snicker's Gap" to head off the rebels. We soon came on to their scouts and pickets, who fled precipitately without firing a gun. Part of our division halted on the top of the gap, while a couple of regiments skirmished through the woods both sides of the road down to the foot of the mountain on the other side. The enemy had taken " French leave," and so our men returned and our division bivouacked here for the night.

We now learned that these giant armies were moving south in parallel columns, the mountain separating them. At every gap or pass in the mountain a bristling head or a clinched fist, so to speak, of one would be thrust through and the other would try to hit it. This was our mission, as we double-quicked it through this gap. When we got there the "fist" had been withdrawn, and our work for the time was over. But our bivouac here—how beautiful it was! The fields were clean and green, with plenty of shade, for right in the gap were some good farms. Then the cavalry had not cleaned the country of everything eatable, as was usual, they being always in the advance. There was milk and bread to be had, and somehow—I never dared to inquire too closely about it—some good mutton came into camp that night, so that we had a splendid breakfast next morning. Some fine honey was added to the bill of fare. The man who brought in the latter claimed that a rebel hive of bees attacked him whilst on picket duty, and he confiscated the honey as a measure of retaliation.

But the special feature that makes that camp linger in my memory was the extraordinary beauty of the scene in the valley below us when the evening camp-fires were lighted. We were on a sort of table-land two or three hundred feet above the broad valley, which widened out at this point and made a most charming landscape. As the darkness drew on the camp-fires were lighted, and the scene became one of weird, bewitching beauty. Almost as far as the eye could reach, covering three and possibly four square miles, were spread out the blazing camp-fires of that mighty host of our " Boys in Blue." No drums were beaten and the usual retreat call was not sounded, but the thousands of camp-fires told of the presence of our men. A martial city was cooking its evening coffee and resting its weary limbs in the genial camp-fire glow, whilst weary hearts were refreshed with the accompanying chat about friends and dearer ones at home. The scouting " Johnny Rebs" (and there were no doubt plenty of them viewing the scene) could have gotten from it no comforting information to impart as to our numbers. Most of the Army of the Potomac, now largely augmented by new regiments, was there, probably not less than one hundred thousand men. It was a picture not of a lifetime, but of the centuries. It made my blood leap as I realized that I was looking down upon the grandest army, all things considered, of any age or time. Its mission was to save to liberty and freedom the life of the best government the world ever saw. In its ranks was the best blood of a free people. In intelligence it was far superior to any other army that ever existed. Scholars of all professions, tradesmen and farmers, were there, fighting side by side, animated by the same patriotic impulse. I said to myself, it is impossible that that army should be beaten. It is the strong right arm of the Union, and under God it shall assuredly deal the death-blow to the rebellion. This it certainly did, though at a fearful cost, for it was fighting the same blood. The inspiration of that scene made me glad from the bottom of my heart that I had the privilege of being just one in that glorious army. After forty years, what would I take for that association with all its dangers and hardships? What for these pictures and memories? They are simply priceless. I only wish I could so paint the pictures and reproduce the scenes that they might be an inspiration to the same patriotism that moved this mighty host.

One of our grizzly-headed "boys," after forty years, tells the following story of his experiences on a foraging expedition from the camp. Three of them started out after beef. Some young steers had been seen in the distance. They reached the field, a mile or more from camp. They found the game a mighty vigorous lot of young steers, and their troubles began when they tried to corral any one of them. Both ends seemed to be in business at the same time, whilst a tail-hold proved to have more transportation possibilities than they had ever dreamed of. Coaxing and persuasion proved utter failures, for the bovines seemed to have the same prejudices against our blue uniforms their owners had, and it would not do to fire a gun. However, after two hours of the hardest exercise they ever had, they succeeded in "pinching" their steer with nose, horn, and tail-holds. Neither of them had ever undertaken to butcher a beef before, and a good-sized jackknife was all they had to work with. But beef they came for and must have, and one was selected to do the trick. Here again they counted without their quarry. The latter evidently objected to being practised on by novices, for as the knife entered his neck he gave a jump which somehow nearly severed the would-be butcher's thumb. Nevertheless, he completed his work without a word, and the animal was skinned and divided. Just as they had him down a field officer rode almost on to them. They felt sure that their " fat was in the fire," for the officer—probably the field officer of the day— certainly saw them and saw what they were doing. But he turned and rode away without saying a word. It was evidently one of those things he did not want to see. Well, the fun was not yet over. They backed their beef to camp, and this was about as uncomfortable a job as they ever had. No more tired trio ever rolled themselves in blankets than they were that night. But there was compensation. They had an abundant supply of " fresh" on hand and their sleep was sweet. Alas for the uncertainties of camp life. Notwithstanding they took the extra precaution to roll their several portions in their coats and placed them under their heads for pillows, some " sons of Belial" from an adjacent regiment who had discovered them bringing their " game" into camp actually stole every ounce of the beef out from under their too soundly sleeping heads during the night and made off with it. After all their labor and trouble neither of them had a taste of that beef. Their nostrils were regaled with the savory fumes of the cooking meat. They had no difficulty in discovering where it was. Indeed, the whelps who stole it rather paraded their steal, knowing that the mouths of our men were sealed. They simply could not say a word, for marauding was punishable with death. The worst of the escapade was that the poor fellow whose thumb had been so nearly severed was made a cripple for life. He was never able to do another day's duty, and to shield him the other two—be it said to their everlasting honor—performed his picket duty in addition to their own until he was discharged.

My diary notes the fact that Fitz-John Porter's corps passed us just before night, and I saw its commander for the first time. He was a small, slender, young-looking man, with full black whiskers and keen black eyes. He was dressed very modestly and wore the usual high black slouch hat, with a much battered gold-tassel band. A pair of silver stars on his shoulder, much obscured by wear and dust, indicated his rank of major-general.

The next day, November 3, was cold and chilly and we were early on the march, still southward. We had now exhausted our supply of rations, and at a temporary halt wagon-loads of hardtack and pork were driven along our company lines and boxes of the bread and barrels of pork dumped out, and the men told to fill their haversacks. Barrel heads and boxes were soon smashed with the butts of guns and contents appropriated, each man taking all he would. Many a fine piece of the pork marched away on a bayonet, ready for the noon-day meal. I filled my own saddle-bags, as did the rest of us officers, preferring to take no further chances on the grub question.

We bivouacked about four o'clock, after a thirteen-mile march in a raw and very chilly air. Just going into bivouac I saw Major-General John F. Reynolds, who met such a tragic death at Gettysburg the next July. His corps—the First—was in the advance of ours. Our regiment was marching at the head of our brigade column. Lieutenant-Colonel Albright was temporarily absent and I was directing the column. General Reynolds's corps had passed into the field to the left and were already in bivouac; the other troops of our division were not visible at this point, and I was hesitating what direction to give the column. General Reynolds was sitting on his horse looking at us, evidently with much interest, and noticing my dilemma, rode up to my assistance at once. Addressing me as adjutant, he said: " Part of your corps has moved in yonder," pointing out the place. " If I were you I would go in here and occupy this field to the right in column of divisions, and you may say General Reynolds advised this, if you please." His manner and way of doing this little service were so pleasant that he captured me at once. Had he chosen to do so, he could have given me orders, as the senior officer present, but with a gentle courtesy he accomplished his purpose without that, and to reassure me gave his name and rank in this delicate way. I shall never forget his pleasant smile as he returned my salute after thanking him for his suggestion. He was a superb-looking man, dark complexioned, wearing full black whiskers, and sat his fine horse like a Centaur, tall, straight, and graceful, the ideal soldier. I do not remember to have ever seen this remarkable officer again. He was one of the few great commanders developed by the war. A quiet, modest man, he yet possessed a very decisive element of character, as illustrated by the following incident related to me by my friend Colonel W. L. Wilson, assistant adjutant-general of one of the divisions of Reynolds's corps, and shows his unwearied vigilance and his indefatigable capacity for work. The corps was in the presence of the enemy, an attack was deemed highly probable. Night had brought on a storm of rain and intense darkness. General Reynolds had given the proper officers very explicit instructions about locating his picket lines, and Colonel Wilson, knowing the critical nature of the work and his division chief's anxiety over it, about midnight went out over their part of the line to make doubly sure that everything was right. Among the first persons he encountered after reaching the outposts was General Reynolds, all alone, making his way over the line in that drenching rain, to be assured that the pickets were properly posted and doing their duty. Here is Colonel Wilson's account of the colloquy that ensued: " Who are you, sir? Where do you belong? What are you doing here?" he volleyed at me savagely. Being apparently reassured by my reply, he continued in a less peremptory tone, " Who ordered that line? How far out is it?" Receiving my reply, he exclaimed, " Push it out, push it out farther!" " How far, General?" I ventured to ask. " Push it out until you feel something!" This was Reynolds.

We continued our march down what I was told was

the valley of the Catochin. November 5 found us near Upperville, where we bivouacked alongside an old grave-yard, our head-quarters being established inside the enclosure, to get the protection of its stone wall from the cold wind that was blowing. The temperature had fallen during the past twenty-four hours, so that it was now decidedly chilly—good for marching, but cold in bivouac. My notes say that I was chilled through until my teeth chattered; that I slept in the hollow made by a sunken grave to get warm; that my dreams were not disturbed by any unsubstantial hobgoblins of the defunct member of an F. F. V. whose remains might have been resting below me. The letters F. F. V. meant much in those war days. They stood for " First Family of Virginia," an expression much in use by her slave-proud aristocracy, and, of course, much satirized by us of the North. On this day we passed several very handsome mansions with their slave contingents. One old " daddy" volunteered the information that his " Mars was a pow'ful secesh;" that he had three sons in the rebel army. My diary notes with indignation that these rich plantations were carefully guarded by our cavalry to prevent our soldiers entering to get water as they passed. They would doubtless have helped themselves to other things as well, especially things eatable, but the owners were rebels and deserved to have their property taken, we all felt.

The orders against marauding were punctuated by a striking example this day. The cavalry orderly of the general commanding our division, riding back to head-quarters after delivering a batch of orders, among them another on this hated subject, carried a pair of handsome turkeys strapped to his saddle. It is safe to say that entire flock came into our camp that night, and turkey was served at breakfast to some of the rank and file as well as to the general. Verily, " consistency thou art a jewel."

From Upperville we moved by easy marching down to Warrenton. The weather had grown much colder. On the 8th of November there was a fall of rain, succeeded by snow, and we marched in a very disagreeable slush. The bivouac in this snow was most trying. The result for myself was a severe attack of fever and ague. I had been much reduced in flesh from the fatigue and nervous strain of the strenuous life of the past two months. This attack prostrated me at once. I was placed in an ambulance, being unable to ride my horse. The shaking and jolting of that ambulance ride were something fearful. I can now sympathize with the wounded who were compelled to ride in those horrible vehicles. They were covered wagons, with seats on each side, and made with heavy, stiff springs, so as to stand the rough roads, which were frequently cut through the fields. This night General Kimball had me brought to his head-quarters, a brick farm-house, for shelter. It was a kindness I greatly appreciated. The next night our chaplain succeeded in getting me into a farm-house some little distance from the regiment. He secured this accommodation on the strength of Freemasonry. The owner's name I have preserved in my diary as Mr. D. L. F. Lake. He was one of Mosby's " cavalry," as they called themselves. We in our army called them " guerillas." They were the terror of our army stragglers. They were " good Union men" when our army was passing, but just as soon as the army had passed they were in their saddles, picking up every straggler and any who may have had to fall behind from sickness. In that way they got quite a few prisoners. This man did not hesitate to tell us the mode of their operations. He said his farm had been literally stripped of hay, grain, and cattle by our cavalry under General Stoneman. All he had left was one chicken. This his wife cooked for the chaplain and me. He brought out Richmond papers during the evening and freely discussed the issues of the war with the chaplain. I was too ill to pay much attention to what was said, only to gather that his idea of us Northern people was that we were a miserable horde of invading barbarians, destined to be very speedily beaten and driven out. He admitted, however, that in financial transactions he preferred " greenbacks" to the Confederate scrip, which I thought rather negatived his boasted faith in the success of the Confederacy. His wife, who had, not many years gone, been young and pretty, occasionally chimed in with expressions of great hate and bitterness. Perhaps the latter was not to be wondered at from their stand-point, and they had just now ample grounds for their bitter feelings in the fact that they had just been relieved of all their portable property by the Union forces. He had receipts for what Stoneman had taken, which would be good for their market value on his taking the oath of allegiance. But he said he would die rather than take that oath, so he considered his property gone. He no doubt thought better of this later on, and probably got pay for his stuff. His kindness to me on the score of our fraternal relations was generous to the full extent of his ability, and showed him to be a true man, notwithstanding his "secesh" proclivities. It was a great favor, for had I been compelled to remain out in that rough weather sick as I was, the consequences must have been most serious. On leaving I tried to pay him in gold coin for his hospitality, but he firmly declined my money, saying: "You know you could not have gotten into my house for money. Pay in like manner as you have received when opportunity affords." For this fraternal hospitality I shall always remember my "secesh" Masonic brother with gratitude, for I feel that it saved my life.

Another terrific day in that awful ambulance brought me to Warrenton, where I got a room at a so-called hotel. Here, upon the advice of our surgeon, I made application for leave of absence on account of sickness. The red tape that had to be "unwound" in getting this approved and returned almost proved my ruin. Captain Archbald was taken sick at this time, and his application for a like leave accompanied mine. The corps surgeon, Dr. Dougherty, called with our surgeon to examine us at the hotel, and said he would approve both applications; that it would be but a day or so before our leaves would be ready and returned to us. The next day orders for the army to move were issued, and we saw our men marching away. It made my heart ache not to be in my place with them. I was, however, barely able to sit up, so that was out of the question. Now another possibility confronted us, namely, being picked up and carried off as prisoners by my late host's comrades, Mosby's guerillas. The army was evidently evacuating Warrenton and vicinity, and unless our leaves of absence reached us within a very few hours we would be outside of the "Union lines" and transportation to Washington unobtainable, for the railroad trains did not pretend to run beyond the Union lines. The next day came, the last of our troops were moving out, and our leaves had not come. Captain Archbald and I resolved that we must cut that "red tape" rather than take the chances of going to Richmond. This we did by securing suits of citizens' clothes and making our way as citizens through the lines to Washington. From there we had no difficulty in reaching home in uniform. At Washington I wrote Colonel Albright of our dilemma and the way we had solved it, and asked that our leaves of absence be forwarded to us at Scranton. They came some two weeks later. Had we remained at Warrenton, they would never have reached us, unless in a rebel prison. Yet I suppose we had committed an offence for which we could have been court-martialled.

I should have mentioned that just at the time I was taken sick, on the 9th of November, whilst the army was approaching Warrenton, the order relieving General McClellan from the command of the Army of the Potomac was issued. He was ordered to report to his home in Trenton, N. J., on waiting orders. Great was the consternation among the veterans of that army on his retirement, for they really had a strong attachment for "Little Mac," as they fondly called him. He took his leave in an affectionate order, recounting the heroic deeds of this noble army. This was followed by a grand review, accompanied by battery salutes, and the military career of General George B. McClellan passed into history.

CHAPTER IX

I MUST pause long enough to speak of the days of that sick leave. Just before reaching Scranton I met on the train my old friend and employer, Joseph C. Platt, of the Lackawanna Iron & Coal Company, who insisted on taking me home with him. As I had no home of my own and no relations here, I accepted his kind hospitality. Had I been their own son I could not have been cared for more tenderly. Under the circumstances I am sure I was not a very prepossessing object to entertain. I well remember the warm bath and the glorious luxury of once more being actually clean, dressed in a civilized nightrobe, and in a comfortable bed. It must be remembered that a soldier must habitually sleep in his clothes. I had not had my clothes off, except for a wash, since I entered the army. I had evidently been living beyond my strength, and now the latter gave way and I found myself unable to leave my bed for the next two weeks. Dr. William Frothingham gave me most excellent medical treatment, and with the motherly nursing of Mrs. Platt I was soon on the mend.

On the 8th of December I started back for my regiment. I was by no means well, and the doctor was loath to let me go, as were all my kind friends; but a grand forward movement of the army was reported as in prog-

The Fredericksburg Campaign

ress, and I felt that I must be at my post. I reached Washington on the 9th, and it took the next two days to secure a pass and transportation to the front. The latter was somewhat difficult to obtain, owing to the fact that a movement of the army was in progress. What the character of the movement was no one seemed to know, not even the provost-marshal, who issued all passes.

I took a boat leaving at six o'clock A.M. on the 12th for Aquia Creek and thence went by rail in a cattle-car to its terminus in the open field opposite Fredericksburg. (The rebels were mean enough to refuse us depot privileges at the regular station in Fredericksburg.) I arrived there about one o'clock P.M. A brisk cannonade was in progress between the Union batteries posted on the heights back of Falmouth and the Confederate guns on Marye's Heights, back of Fredericksburg. The problem now was to find my regiment. A stranger standing near said, in answer to my inquiry, that the Union army had been encamped about a mile and a half back yonder, pointing to the hills in our rear, but that he was quite sure they had all gone across the river last night; that a big fight had taken place about laying the pontoon bridge over the river (the Rappahannock), and the Union forces had beaten the rebels back, laid the bridge and had crossed over and occupied the city. Fredericksburg was a city of probably five or six thousand people, lying on the west bank of the Rappahannock, which runs at this point nearly southeast. The river is probably one hundred and fifty to two hundred yards wide here, quite deep, with a rather swift current and high banks, so that one does not see the water until quite close to it. The railroad formerly ran from Aquia Creek to Richmond *via* Fredericksburg, the connection to Washington being by boat from Aquia Creek. The war stopped its operation, but so much of it as was in the Union lines had been seized by the government, and was being operated by the quartermaster's department for war purposes. The stations of the latter were wherever the troops were, and these were now operating against Fredericksburg, hence I was dumped down in an open field opposite that city as stated above. I was fortunate enough to find a man who was going to Hancock's old camp, and I concluded to go with him, believing that once there I could find our division camp belonging to the same corps.

I chartered a burly " contraban" to carry my luggage, and we started. The ground was very soft from recent rains, and the mud was something terrible. If one has never encountered Virginia mud, he can have no adequate idea of the meaning of the word. It gets a grip on your feet and just won't let go. Every rise of your pedal extremities requires a mighty tug, as if you were lifting the earth, as indeed you are—a much larger share of it than is comfortable.

A tramp of a mile and a half brought us to Hancock's old camp. In my weak condition I was thoroughly exhausted, and so my " contraban" claimed to be, for he positively refused to go another step. I got my quartermaster friend to take care of my baggage, whilst I continued my search for our division camp. I was not successful in finding it that night, and was obliged to accept the invitation of a sick officer of the Eighty-first Penn-

The Fredericksburg Campaign

sylvania Volunteers to share his quarters for the night. I had eaten breakfast at five o'clock that morning in Washington and had eaten nothing since, and it was now dusk. I was not only tired, but faint for want of food. This officer, whose name I regret I have forgotten, was a brother Mason, and kindly divided his meagre rations with me, which consisted of boiled rice and hardtack. He had a little molasses, with which the former was lubricated, and a good strong cup of coffee was added. It was not Waldorf-Astoria fare, to be sure, and the explanation was that the boys had taken almost everything eatable with them.

The next morning I picked up an old "crow-bait" of a horse, the only four-footed transportation possibly obtainable, and started for Fredericksburg to find my regiment. The only directions I had about disposing of this frame of a horse was to "turn the bones loose when you get through with him." He could go only at a snail's pace, and when I reached Fredericksburg it must have been nine o'clock. I crossed the pontoon bridge, which had been laid the morning before under circumstances of the greatest gallantry by Howard's division of our corps.

The "ball" was now well opened. Marye's Heights (pronounced Marie, with the accent on the last letter, as if spelled Maree), circling the city from the river above to a point below the city, was literally crowded with batteries of rebel artillery. These guns were firing at our batteries on the heights on the other side of the river, and also upon our troops occupying the city. The air was filled with screeching, bursting shells, and a deafening pandemonium was in progress. It was not a very inviting place to enter under these circumstances, but it was as safe for me as for my regiment, and my duty was to be with them. The trouble was to find it in that multitude of troops filling all the streets of the city. Our corps alone numbered probably twelve thousand men at that time, and the Ninth Corps was there besides. However, I soon found Kimball's brigade to my great delight, supposing our regiment was in it, as it was when I went away. General Kimball greeted me with great cordiality; but when I asked where my regiment was, he said he was sorry he could not inform me; that they had that morning been transferred, much against his will, to General Max Weber's brigade, and where that was he did not know. It was probably somewhere in the city. Said he:

" You cannot possibly find it now, and it is a waste of time to try. I can give you plenty of work to-day. Stay with me and serve as an aide on my staff."

The officers of his staff, all of whom were personal friends, urgently joined in the general's invitation. But I felt that I must be with the regiment if it were possible to find it, and so declined what would have been a distinguishing service. Some distance down the main street I ran on to the regiment just when I had abandoned all hope of finding it. My reception was exceedingly cordial, accompanied with the remark: " Just in time, adjutant, just in time." I found Lieutenant-Colonel Albright in command and with no help from our field and staff. Colonel Wilcox was still on sick leave. Major Shreve had returned to camp during the heavy cannonading of

The Fredericksburg Campaign

the day before, and Colonel Albright had lost his voice
from a severe cold, so that I had to supply voice for
him in the issuing of orders, in addition to my other
duties.

The situation was most portentous. We lay in the
main street under the shelter of the houses, which were
being bombarded by the rebel batteries in their efforts
to reach our troops. The houses were all vacant; the
people had fled on the approach of our army. Not a
soul did we see of the inhabitants of the city during the
two days we occupied it. They had evidently left in
great haste, taking but few things with them. I was told
that in some houses the boys found and ate meals that
had been prepared and left in their flight, and in all
there was more or less food, which was appropriated.
Flour was plentiful, and the night after the battle there
were army flapjacks galore. In some cases it might have
been said these were fearfully and wonderfully made,
but they went just the same.

An incident connected with this occupation of Fredericksburg comes to light after forty years. If General
Howard should see it the mystery of the sudden dis-
appearance of his breakfast on that morning might be
cleared up. Our regiment happened to be quartered
in the morning near his head-quarters. Rations were
scarce. General Howard's servant had prepared him a
most tempting breakfast from supplies found and confiscated from one of the houses. The sight of this repast and its savory fumes were too much for the empty
stomachs of two of our men, who shall be nameless
here. The trick was a neat one. One of them got the

8   113

attention of the cook and held it until the other reached into the tent and dumped the contents of the main dish, hot and steaming, into his haversack and quietly sauntered away. When the cook discovered his loss the other fellow was gone. These rascals said it was the best dish of ham and eggs they ever ate. Many houses had fine pianos and other musical instruments, and in some instances impromptu dances were on whilst Confederate shells whanged through the house above their heads. It is safe to say that there was little left of valuable bric-à-brac to greet the fugitive people on their return. And it is highly probable that pianos and handsome furniture needed considerable repairing after the exodus of the " Yank." This was not due to pure vandalism, although war creates the latter, but to the feeling of hatred for the miserable rebels who had brought on the war and were the cause of our being there. And it must be admitted there were some who pocketed all they could for the commercialism there might be in it, the argument again being, " somebody will take it, and I might as well have it as the other fellow." The first part of the argument was doubtless as true as the latter part was false. Many trinkets were hawked about among the men after the fight as souvenirs. Among them was a silver-plated communion flagon. Some scamp had filched it from one of the churches and was trying to sell it. Fortunately, he did not belong to our regiment. Our chaplain took it from him and had it strapped to his saddle-bag. His purpose was to preserve it for its owner if the time should come that it could be returned. But in the meantime its presence attached to his saddle made him the

The Fredericksburg Campaign

butt of any amount of raillery from both officers and men.

When I joined the regiment it was lying in front of the Court-House, from the steeple of which some sixty or seventy feet high, the flags of our signal-corps were most actively wagging. It occurred to me that those signal-men were mighty nervy fellows. They were a beautiful mark for the rebel batteries, which were evidently doing their best to knock them out. The steeple was a plain, old-fashioned affair, having an open belfry, which seemed to be supported by four upright posts or timbers. I saw one of those uprights knocked out by a rebel shell. A couple more equally good shots and our signal-fellows would come ignominiously—no, gloriously—down, for there could be no ignominy with such pluck. But the wig-wagging went on, I fancied, with a little more snap and audacity than before, and they maintained their station there in the very teeth of the rebel batteries until the army was withdrawn. So much for "Yankee nerve." I afterwards learned that the signal-officer there was none other than Lieutenant Frederick Fuller, of Scranton, one of my most intimate personal friends. Lieutenant Fuller told me that he was on duty at Burnside's head-quarters on that morning; that a station was ordered opened in the belfry of that Court-House, and another officer was despatched thither for that duty; that after waiting some time for the flags to appear he was ordered over to see what the trouble was. He found the other officer sitting under shelter, afraid to mount the belfry, nor could any persuasion induce him to face that storm of shell. Lieutenant Fuller thereupon climbed up into the belfry, opened the station himself, and ran it during the whole battle.

About ten o'clock the command " Forward" was sounded, and our brigade moved out towards Marye's Heights. Some idea of the topography of Fredericksburg and its rear I find is necessary to an understanding of what follows. Marye's Heights, which encircle the city back some five hundred yards, are the termination of a plateau which rises from one hundred and fifty to two hundred feet in an abrupt terrace from the plain upon which the city stands. These heights form a half-circle from the river above to a point below the city some little distance from the river, and are from a mile to a mile and a half long and are most admirably adapted for defensive purposes. The rebel batteries, numbering at least one hundred guns, were massed on these heights, and covered not only every street leading out from the city, but every square foot of ground of the plain below. A third of the way down the terrace was an earthwork filled with infantry, whilst at its foot ran the famous stone wall extending southward from the cemetery above the city, and was continued by an earthwork around the whole circle. Behind this stone wall was massed a double line of Confederate infantry. To enter either street leading out to those heights was to face the concentrated fire of that mass of artillery and the deadly work of those three lines of infantry. Yet that was just what we had before us.

Our division (French's) led the assault. Our regiment brought up the rear of our brigade column. As each regiment turned into the street leading out, it took up the run to cover this exposed ground as quickly as possible. Lieutenant-Colonel Albright was leading our regiment and I was by his side. We passed rapidly up the street, already covered with the dead and wounded which had fallen from the regiments that had preceded us, until we reached the embankment of a railroad, which was nearly parallel with the enemy's works. A temporary halt was made here preparatory to moving forward in line of battle.

Turning to see that our men were in position, I was amazed to find that we had but one company with us. It was my duty as adjutant to go back and find and bring up the balance of the regiment. The distance was about four hundred yards. I can truthfully say that in that moment I gave my life up. I do not expect ever again to face death more certainly than I thought I did then. It did not seem possible that I could go through that fire again and return alive. The grass did not grow under my feet going back. My sprinting record was probably made then. It may be possible to see the humorous side at this distance, but it was verily a life and death matter then. One may ask how such dangers can be faced. The answer is, there are many things more to be feared than death. Cowardice and failure of duty with me were some of them. I can fully appreciate the story of the soldier's soliloquy as he saw a rabbit sprinting back from the line of fire:

" Go it, cotton tail; if I hadn't a reputation at stake, I'd go to."

Reputation and duty were the holding forces. I said to myself, " This is duty. I'll trust in God and do it. If I fall, I cannot die better." Without the help and stimulus of that trust I could not have done it, for I doubt if any man was ever more keenly susceptible to danger than I, and the experience of Antietam had taught me the full force of this danger. The nervous strain was simply awful. It can be appreciated only by those who have experienced it. The atmosphere seemed surcharged with the most startling and frightful things. Deaths, wounds, and appalling destruction everywhere. As fast as I was running back over that street, my eyes caught an incident that I can see now, which excited my pity, though I had no time to offer help. A fine-looking fellow had been struck by a shot, which had severed one leg and left it hanging by one of the tendons, the bone protruding, and he was bleeding profusely. Some men were apparently trying to get him off the street. They had hold of his arms and the other leg, but were jumping and dodging at every shell that exploded, jerking and twisting this dangling leg to his horrible torture. I remember hearing him beseeching them to lay him down and let him die. They were probably a trio of cowards trying to get back from the front, and were using this wounded man to get away with, a not infrequent occurrence with that class of bummers.

I found the balance of the regiment had passed our street and were in confusion further down the main street. As the second company was about turning to follow the column a shell had exploded in their faces, killing and wounding some ten men and throwing it into disorder. Before it could be rallied the advancing column was out of sight. It was the work of but a few moments to straighten out the tangle and head them again for the front. No body of men could have more quickly and bravely responded, though they told me afterwards that they read in my pallid face the character of the work before them. Back we went up that street on the run, having to pick our way to avoid stepping on the dead and wounded, for the ground was now blue with our fallen heroes.

CHAPTER X

REACHING the place in the rear of that railroad embankment, where I had left the brigade, I found it had just gone forward in line of battle, and a staff officer directed me to bring the rest of the regiment forward under fire, which I did, fortunately getting them into their proper position. The line was lying prone upon the ground in that open field and trying to maintain a fire against the rebel infantry not more than one hundred and fifty yards in our front behind that stone wall. We were now exposed to the fire of their three lines of infantry, having no shelter whatever. It was like standing upon a raised platform to be shot down by those sheltered behind it. Had we been ordered to fix bayonets and charge those heights we could have understood the movement, though that would have been an impossible undertaking, defended as they were. But to be sent close up to those lines to maintain a firing-line without any intrenchments or other shelter, if that was its purpose, was simply to invite wholesale slaughter without the least compensation. It was to attempt the impossible, and invite certain destruction in the effort. On this interesting subject I have very decided convictions, which I will give later on.

Proceeding now with my narrative, we were evi-

FIRST LIEUT. JAMES A. ROGERS
CO. C

FIRST LIEUT. NOAH H. JAY
CO. K

FIRST LIEUT. A. C. MENSCH
CO. E

FIRST LIEUT. CHARLES E. GLADDING
CO. D

FIRST LIEUT. ISAIAH W. WILLITTS
CO. H

SECOND LIEUT. D. R. MELLICK
CO. E

The Battle of Fredericksburg

dently in a fearful slaughter-pen. Our men were being
swept away as by a terrific whirlwind. The ground was
soft and spongy from recent rains, and our faces and
clothes were bespattered with mud from bullets and fragments of shells striking the ground about us, whilst men
were every moment being hit by the storm of projectiles
that filled the air. In the midst of that frightful carnage
a man rushing by grasped my hand and spoke. I turned
and looked into the face of a friend from a distant city.
There was a glance of recognition and he was swept away.
What his fate was I do not know.

That same moment I received what was supposed to
be my death wound. Whilst the men were lying down,
my duties kept me on my feet. Lieutenant Charles Mc-
Dougal,* commanding the color company, called to me
that the color-guard were all either killed or wounded.
We had two stands of colors, the national and State flags.
These colors were carried by two color-sergeants, protected by six color-corporals, which made up the color-
guard. If either sergeant became disabled the nearest corporal took the colors, and so on until the color-guard were
down. This was the condition when this officer called to
me to replace these disabled men, so that the colors should
be kept flying. He had one flag in his hand as I approached him, and he was in the act of handing it to me
when a bullet crashed through his arm and wrist, spatter-
ing my face with his warm blood. I seized the staff as it

---

* Lieutenant, afterwards Captain, Charles McDougal was a Metho-
dist minister before he entered the army. If he could preach as well
as he could fight, he was worthy of a commission in the church mili-
tant.

fell from his shattered arm. The next instant a bullet cut the staff away just below my hand. An instant later I was struck on the head by the fragment of a shell and fell unconscious with the colors in my hand. How long I remained unconscious I do not know, possibly twenty minutes or more. What were my sensations when hit? I felt a terrific blow, but without pain, and the thought flashed through my mind, "This is the end," and then everything was black. I do not remember falling. It takes time to write this, but events moved then with startling rapidity. From the time we went forward from the embankment until the line was swept back could have been but a few minutes, otherwise all must have been killed.

When I revived I was alone with the dead and wounded. The line of battle had been swept away. The field about me was literally covered with the blue uniforms of our dead and wounded men. The firing had very perceptibly decreased. I had worn into the battle my overcoat, with my sword buckled on the outside. I had been hit on the left side of my head, and that side of my body was covered with blood down to my feet, which was still flowing. My first thought was as to my condition, whether mortally wounded or not. I was perceptibly weakened from loss of blood, but lying there I could not tell how much strength I had left. I did not dare move, for that would make me a target for the guns that covered that terrible wall, the muzzles of which I could plainly see. Many of them were still spitting out their fire with a venom that made my position exceedingly uncomfortable. What should I do? What could I do?

The Battle of Fredericksburg

To remain there was either to bleed to death or be taken prisoner and sent to Libby, which I felt would mean for me a sure lingering death. To make a move to get off the field would draw the fire of those guns, which would surely finish me. These were the alternatives.

I carefully stretched my legs to test my strength, and I made up my mind I had enough left to carry me off the field, and I resolved to take my chances in the effort. I determined that I would zigzag my course to the rear so as not to give them a line shot at me. So getting myself together I made a supreme effort and sprang up and off in jumps, first to the right, then to the left. As I expected, they opened on me, and the bullets flew thick and fast about me. The first turn I got a bullet through my right leg just above the ankle. It felt like the stinging cut of a whip and rather accelerated my speed. About fifty yards back was an old slab fence to my right, and I plunged headlong behind that, hoping to find shelter from those bullets. I fell directly behind several other wounded men, two of whom rolled over dead from bullets that came through the slabs and which were probably aimed at me. This flushed me again, and by the same zigzag tactics I succeeded in getting back to the railroad embankment, where, to my great joy, I found Colonel Albright with what remained of the regiment. Colonel Albright grasped me in his arms as I came over, with the exclamation, " We thought you were killed." Sergeant-Major Clapp told me that he had rolled me over and satisfied himself that I was dead before they went back.

As I reached cover under this embankment I remember noticing a field-officer rallying his men very near us on our right, and that instant his head was literally carried away by a shell. So intense was the situation that even this tragic death received only a passing thought. Then came the Irish brigade, charging over our line as they did at Antietam. They came up and went forward in fine form, but they got but a few yards beyond the embankment, when they broke and came back, what was left of them, in great confusion. No troops could stand that fire. Our division and the whole Second Corps, in fact, were now completely disorganized, and the men were making their way back to the city and the cover of the river-bank as best they could, whilst the splendid old Ninth Corps was advancing to take its place. Profiting by our experience, they did not advance by those streets through which we came, but made their way through houses and yards and so escaped that concentrated fire on the streets. Their advancing lines, covering the whole city front, looked magnificent, and it was dreadful to think that such a splendid body of men must march into such a slaughter-pen. Their movement was a repetition of ours. With bayonets unfixed they moved forward and attempted to maintain a firing-line under Marye's Heights on the ground from which we had been driven, only to be hurled mercilessly back as we had been. Our line had been the first to make this effort, and for some reason we had approached to within about one hundred yards of their main line of infantry, much closer than any of the troops that followed. The others had barely got beyond the embankment, when they were swept away. We, having approached nearer their line, were, of course, longer exposed to their fire and lost more heavily.

The Battle of Fredericksburg

I was always curious to know why we of the first line of that fateful movement succeeded in getting so much nearer their works than the equally brave and determined men who followed us. Some years afterwards on revisiting this location I met an ex-Confederate who commanded one of the rebel batteries on those heights that day. In answer to my questions, he said the first "Yankee" line was permitted to approach much nearer than those that followed, for, said he, "we knew they were our meat, and when we finally opened on them with our full force, the slaughter was so awful it made me heart sick. But you kept coming with such persistency that we did not dare repeat those tactics." This may have been partially true so far as concerned their infantry fire, but a more potent reason, in my judgment, was that we had developed the utter hopelessness of the attempt, and men could not put heart into the effort.

Recurring to myself again, Colonel Albright stanched the flowing of blood from my wound in the head by making a strong compress of my large bandana handkerchief. The other wound in my leg did not give me much trouble then. In that condition, accompanied by another wounded man, I made my way back into the city. We found it one vast hospital. Every house was literally crowded with wounded men. We were fortunate enough to run against our brigade surgeon, who had taken possession of a brick building on the main street for hospital purposes. The only thing he could give me to lie down upon was a wooden bench. We had dismounted and left our horses with a servant when we went forward, and our blankets, etc., were with them, and where they were now there was no means of knowing. I was therefore without those comforts. Everything of that nature left by the rebels had long before been appropriated. The doctor hastily examined my wounds, pronounced them not dangerous, ordered the hospital steward to dress them, and was away. He, however, appropriated my red handkerchief. I had been presented by a friend on leaving Scranton with two large old-fashioned red silk bandana handkerchiefs, and they were exceedingly useful. The doctor, seeing them, said, " I must have these to nail up over the outside door to show that this is a hospital," and, without so much as saying by your leave, carried them off. The effort was to secure as much protection as possible from the fire of the enemy, and to do this the red flag of the hospital must be displayed. It is against the rules of civilized warfare to fire upon a hospital. The doctor said my red silk handkerchiefs were the first red stuff of any kind he had been able to get hold of. Of course I was glad to part with them for that purpose, though they were worth at that time $2 each in gold. The wound in my head was fortunately a glancing blow from a fragment of a shell. It tore the scalp from the bone about three inches in length in the form of a V. It has never given me serious trouble, more than to be a barometer of changing weather. The wound in my leg nearly severed the big tendon. They both quickly healed, and I was off duty with them but the one day I took to get back to camp.

After my wounds had been dressed I tried to sleep, being not only very weak from loss of blood, but almost in a condition of nervous exhaustion. I laid down on my bench, but shells were continually crashing through the building, and sleep was impossible. I went out on the street. It was crowded with wounded and straggling soldiers. The stragglers were hunting for their regiments, the wounded for hospital room. It seemed as if the army must have disintegrated. This was practically true of the Second and Ninth Corps, which had made the assault. Towards night General French rode down the street, accompanied by his staff. Seeing me, he stopped his horse and exclaimed, "Adjutant, where is my division? Tell me where my men are. My God, I am without a command!" and the tears were flowing down his red, weather-beaten face. He was beside himself over the awful losses of his division. Well he might be, for a great number of them were lying on yonder field in front of Marye's Heights, and the balance were scattered through the houses and on the river-bank practically disorganized.

I was greatly alarmed for our safety that night. It seemed to me highly probable that General Lee would come down upon us and capture all that were in the city, as he could easily have done. Possibly he was satisfied with the damage already inflicted, and did not care to assume the care of our wounded, which that would have involved. I remained on my bench in that hospital through that long night without food or covering. I had eaten nothing since early morning. With the constant whanging of shells through ours and adjacent buildings and the moaning of the wounded lying all about me, sleep or rest was impossible. It was a night too dreadful to think of, and makes me shudder again as I write. We remained in the city the next day, Sunday, and I rejoined our regiment, which, with other troops, was lying under the shelter of the river-bank. Officers were getting their men together as far as possible and bringing order out of chaos. We had Sunday about two hundred for duty out of three hundred and fifty taken into the battle. On Monday, the 15th, we who were wounded were told to make our way across the river back to our old camps as best we could. I was now very weak, and my head and leg were very sore. The latter gave me much trouble in walking, nevertheless there was a three-mile tramp before us. Lieutenant Musselman, also wounded, went with me on this weary tramp. We did not reach camp that night, and so had to find shelter at a farm-house, already full of straggling and wounded soldiers. The owner was a widow, living with a grown-up daughter, and was a bitter rebel, although professing Union sentiments whilst our army was there. She was, of course, greatly annoyed by the presence of these soldiers, most of whom were eating up her provisions without paying for them. Some of them were "bummers," who had run away from the battle and had persuaded her to feed and shelter them for the protection they professed to afford her. She was in great wrath when we reached there and peremptorily forbade us entering. But I told her firmly that we were wounded men and must have shelter; that I would willingly pay for accommodations, but, permission or not, the latter we must have. This argument seemed to be convincing, and the daughter led us up to the garret, which, she said, was the only unoccupied room in the house. Here she spread a blanket on the floor for us to sleep on.

The Battle of Fredericksburg

I suppose this was the best she could do. Then, at our solicitation, she got us some supper, an exceedingly frugal meal, but we were glad to get that. The daughter did not seem to share her mother's bitterness, but as often as she could would interject a word in our favor, and really did all she could for us. I sincerely hope she was ultimately made a permanent prisoner by some good " boy in blue." Here would have been an excellent opportunity to have woven into this narrative the golden thread of romance. This pretty secesh girl, with flashing blue eyes and golden hair, rebel to the core, yet befriending a wounded Union soldier, etc. How readily it lends itself, but the truth must be told. The little arrow god had already driven home his shaft, and so the romance could not mature.

During the evening General Franz Sigel and staff came to the house and demanded supper. Our lady was very polite, assured him that it was impossible. " Very well," said General Sigel, " I think I shall want this place to-morrow for a hospital. Madam, your kindness will be reciprocated." He spoke very emphatically, whereat the pretty daughter began to cry, and the mother to stammer apologies, and said she would do the best she could for them, but she really had nothing to cook. The general retired very indignant. Whether or not his threat was carried out I do not know, for the next morning we were off without trying to get breakfast. On asking for her bill we were surprised to find her charges were evidently based on the highest war-time hotel rates. We had so poor a supper that we had no desire for breakfast there, and had slept on the garret floor. For this she demanded one dollar. We paid her fifty cents, which was more than double its worth, and left amidst a great volley of her choicest anathemas.

We reached camp towards noon, and found we had tramped about five miles out of our way. The regiment was there ahead of us, the troops having evacuated Fredericksburg on Monday, two days after the battle, without opposition. We were actually under fire in this battle, that is, from the time the assault began until we were swept back, probably not more than thirty minutes as against four and one-half hours at Antietam. Yet our losses were proportionately much heavier. During my absence on sick leave, our regiment, after leaving Warrenton, had been detailed on heavy " fatigue" duty, loading and unloading vessels and various kinds of laborer's work at Belle-plain, and in consequence many were on the sick list, others were on various details, so that when we went into this battle we had only three hundred and fifty men for duty, against seven hundred and fifty at Antietam. Of this number my diary, written the 15th, says we lost: Killed, 7; wounded, 80; missing, 20; total, 107. Lieutenant Hoagland, Company H, was killed. Of the wounded, four were officers,—Captain Richard Stillwell and First Lieutenant John B. Floyd, Company K; First Lieutenant Musselman, Company E, and First Lieutenant McDougal, commanding Company C. Lieutenant McDougal's arm was shattered by a minie-ball whilst handing me the colors, detailed above. Captain Stillwell received a very singular wound. A bullet struck the side of his neck near the big artery and appeared to have gouged out a bit of flesh and glanced off. It bled more than this circumstance would have seemed to war-

The Battle of Fredericksburg

rant, but the captain was sure he was not hurt and made light of it. Swelling and pain speedily developed in his shoulder, and it was found that the missile, instead of glancing off, had taken a downward course and finally lodged near his shoulder-joint, a distance of ten or twelve inches from where it entered. He was given leave of absence on account of wounds, and the ball was cut out after his return home, and ultimately the whole channel made by the ball had to be opened, when it was found lined with whiskers which the ball had carried in with it.

Most of those computed above as missing were undoubtedly killed, but had not been so reported at that time. Our loss in that half-hour was nearly one-third. One stand of our colors, the one whose staff was shot away in my hand, was missing, and the other was badly torn by shells and bullets.

CHAPTER XI

I PROMISED to give my convictions relative to the responsibility for the disaster of Fredericksburg, and I might as well do it here.

Recalling the fact heretofore stated that we seemed to have been thrown against Marye's Heights to be sacrificed; that we were not ordered to charge their works, but to advance and maintain a line of battle-fire where such a thing was absolutely impossible, I come to the inquiry, what was the character and purpose of the movement and why did it fail? So thoroughly impressed was I that there was something radically wrong about it, that I determined to solve that question if possible, and so made a study of the subject at that time and later after my return home. I had personal friends in the First and Sixth Corps, which had operated on the extreme left, and I discussed with them the movements that day. Finally, after my return home, I got access to Covode's congressional reports on the conduct of the war covering that campaign, and from all these sources learned what I then and now believe to be substantially the facts about that campaign. The army was divided into three grand divisions, composed of two army corps each, namely, the Second and Ninth, the right grand division, commanded by Sumner; the First and Sixth, the left grand division, commanded by Franklin, and the Third and Fifth, the centre, commanded by Hooker. The plan of battle was to hold Lee's army at Fredericksburg by a " feint in force" (which means an attack sufficiently strong to deceive the enemy into the belief that it is the real or main attack) at that point, whilst the left grand division was to throw a pontoon bridge across the river three miles below and turn his flank (*i.e.,* get behind them) in the rear of Marye's Heights. For this purpose the left grand division was to advance and attack vigorously. If successful, Lee would then have been between Franklin's forces on the left and our own on the right, with every possibility of being crushed. Hooker was to hold his division in readiness to support either wing. Had this plan been carried out, our work at the right would, at its conception, have been as it appeared to be, a mad sacrifice of men, but with an opportunity later on of pushing forward and reaping a victory. In that event, our position would have made us a tremendous factor in the result.

Now how was the plan carried out? The student will be puzzled on finding such a paucity of records concerning this disastrous movement. The official documents are remarkable for what they do not contain. A study of Covode's reports on the conduct of the war will, I think, justify my conclusions, viz., that the disaster of Fredericksburg was due not to accident, nor to a faulty plan of battle, but to a failure of the left grand division to perform the vital part assigned to it. My information gained at the time was that Franklin was to remain concealed until the signal for our attack came; then he was to cross over and attack vigorously, a military expression, meaning to put all possible vigor and power into the movement. The signal was given as our attack began. Whatever force may have crossed the river at that time, my information was that the division known as the Pennsylvania Reserve, now numbering probably not more than six thousand men, under General Meade, was the only body of troops which made a determined attack on Lee's right, in support of our work in front of Marye's Heights. Realizing the opportunity, General Meade pushed forward with his usual vigor and, though meeting strenuous opposition, soon found himself well in Lee's rear, but without support. He sent back aide after aide to hurry forward the supporting lines, but without avail, finally galloping back himself. He found General Birney resting near the bridge with his division. An eye-witness * to Meade's interview with Birney says the language of General Meade as he upbraided Birney for not coming to his support was enough to " almost make the stones creep;" that Meade was almost wild with rage as he saw the golden opportunity slipping away and the slaughter of his men going for naught. He said Birney responded that he agreed with General Meade fully, and was ready and most anxious to come to his support, but that his orders

---

* This eye-witness was Captain Haviland, Company G, One Hundred and Forty-second Pennsylvania Volunteers, whose regiment was attached to the Pennsylvania Reserves, and which lost in that charge two hundred and forty-three men killed and wounded. Captain Haviland had been wounded, and was making his way with Major John Bradley, also wounded, to the hospital. They happened to be passing Birney's head-quarters when Meade rode up, and heard the whole interview.

were peremptory to await further orders in his present position: that he had been for an hour trying to find General Franklin to obtain permission to move forward. This loss of time and want of support to Meade's charge changed a possible victory into a fearful disaster. This was substantially the testimony of Major-General Reynolds, commanding the First Corps, before the Committee on the Conduct of the War. Burnside rode down to the left and vigorously expostulated with Franklin for his failure to carry out his orders, and peremptorily ordered him to make the attack as originally directed, whilst he repeated the movement at the right. It was now considerably after noon, and this order was undoubtedly a mistake. The plan of battle had been revealed, and there was practically no hope of success. Had the left grand division vigorously performed its part in the earlier movement, can any one doubt the result? I cannot think so. Had Meade, Reynolds, or Hancock been in command on the left that day, I feel confident that Fredericksburg would have been recorded a glorious victory instead of a horrible slaughter.

Now, why did the left grand division fail to make the attack as ordered? Halleck, in his report on the operations at Fredericksburg, says " alleged misunderstanding of orders." Here is his language:

" It was intended that Franklin's grand division, consisting of the corps of Reynolds (First) and Smith (Sixth), should attack the enemy's right and turn his position on the heights in the rear of Fredericksburg, while Sumner and Hooker attacked him in front. But by some alleged misunderstanding of orders Franklin's operations were limited to a mere reconnoissance, and the direct attacks of Sumner and Hooker were unsupported." "Rebellion Records," vol. xxi., page 47.

Is the theory of a misunderstanding of orders tenable? The records show that on the 11th of December, two days before the battle, Burnside ordered his division commanders to so dispose their troops as to bring them within easy reach of Fredericksburg, and that on that day at twelve o'clock noon these officers were ordered to meet him personally at his head-quarters for final instructions. There are no records of what those instructions were, but is it credible that either general retired from that conference with a misunderstanding as to the plan of battle or of his own part in it? Certain it is that neither Sumner nor Hooker misunderstood.

And the excuse said to have been made by Franklin, that he did not deem the attack on the left practicable, is not consistent with the idea of misunderstanding. Otherwise, why did he attack at all? General Halleck's guarded language clearly indicates where he placed the responsibility for that disaster, and that he did not credit the "misunderstanding of orders" theory. It is plainly evident Burnside did not accept that excuse, as appears from his celebrated Order No. 8, issued a month later, relieving Franklin, Smith, Newton, Cochran, and Ferrero, and stating as his reason that "it being evident that these officers can be of no further service to this army,"—the first named being the commander of the left grand division, the second the commander of the Sixth Corps, and the others subordinate commanders in that wing of the army. General Burnside explained to the Committee

Why Fredericksburg was Lost

on the Conduct of the War * that in asking the President to approve this order, and making that a condition upon which he would consent to remain at the head of the army, he had explicitly stated, "that was the only condition on which he could command the Army of the Potomac." In other words, he could not command that army with those officers as his subordinates. The inference that there had been insubordination is inevitable. It was the current belief amongst us officers of the army that the battle of Fredericksburg had been lost through a want of hearty co-operation, if not direct disobedience of orders, on the part of the officer commanding on the left that day, and some of his subordinates, and that this was due to a spirit of jealousy. McClellan had but recently been removed from the command of the army, and the officers relieved were strong personal friends and partisans of the latter. Again, Burnside, his successor, was alleged to be junior in actual rank to Franklin. Whether either of these facts supplied the motives for the jealousy which lost that battle, if such was true, the judgment day alone will reveal. It is devoutly to be hoped that the light of

---

* This order was dated January 23, 1863, and can be found in the Annual American Cyclopædia, 1863, page 79, with a copious extract from the report of the Committee of Congress on the Conduct of the War. It is there stated that this order was issued subject to the President's approval, and was sent to Washington for that purpose, General Burnside soon following and interviewing the President. It is also stated that it was not approved and was not published. How, then, did I come in possession of its main features, so as to note them in my diary at the time? And how should my recollection of them be so clear, as they certainly are, unless it had been made public. Possibly the press may have published it. It was certainly published in some form.

that day will relieve the terrible disaster of Fredericksburg of this awful shadow, and that nothing worse than a " misunderstanding of orders" was responsible for it.

That Order No. 8 was disapproved at Washington, and General Burnside promptly tendered his resignation of the command of the Army of the Potomac. He felt that he had not received and was not likely to receive the cordial and hearty support of all his subordinate officers, and under those circumstances he did not want the responsibility of command. He expressed himself as anxious to serve his country and willing to work anywhere it might please the President to place him. He was not relieved, however, until a month or so later. In writing the foregoing I know that many brave men will take exception. I would say, however, that I have made a somewhat careful study of the subject from an absolutely unprejudiced stand-point, and such are the conclusions I reached, and they were shared by many of my fellow-officers who were in that campaign. The losses in this battle amount to nearly one-third the troops actually engaged, a most remarkable fact, and which stamps this engagement as one of the bloodiest in all history. Burnside reports his loss as twelve hundred and eighty-four killed and nine thousand six hundred wounded, making a total loss, including the missing, of twelve thousand six hundred and fifty-three. Of this loss the right grand division (the Second and Ninth Corps) lost five thousand three hundred and eleven. The left grand division, Franklin's (First and Sixth Corps, which numbered considerably more than the right grand division), lost three thousand four hundred and sixty-two, and most of this was sustained in the

Why Fredericksburg was Lost

second attack in the afternoon. These facts sustain the belief above referred to in the army, that the main attack in the morning on the left was not what it should have been, and was the cause of the disaster.

A remarkable fact connected with this loss is the great number of wounded as compared with the killed. Usually the former exceeds the latter in the proportion of three and four to one, but at Fredericksburg it was nearly nine to one. How this is to be explained I never understood, unless it be that most of the casualties were from exploding shells. The minute fragments of a shell scatter very widely and wound, whilst there are fewer of the large pieces which kill. For example, the shell that exploded in the front of our second company, as it was turning to enter the street leading out towards Marye's Heights, previously described, knocked out ten men, only one of whom was instantly killed. It is safe to estimate that of the nine thousand six hundred reported as wounded, one-third died or were permanently disabled therefrom.

To show how quickly troops can recover from such a shock as the disaster of Fredericksburg, the Second Corps had a grand review back of Falmouth the second week after the battle. Major-General Edwin V. Sumner, commanding the right grand division, was the reviewing officer. I have spoken before of this distinguished officer. This was his farewell to the Second Corps, which he had long commanded and to which he was greatly attached, a sentiment which was most cordially reciprocated by the men. He was now probably the oldest in years of all the officers in the amy, yet still vigorous, intrepid, and efficient. He was relieved from active command in the field and assigned to the command of the Department of the Ohio, but a few months later died peacefully at his home in New York. Is it not singular that this old hero should have escaped the numberless missiles of death in all the battles through which he had passed, so soon to succumb in the quietude of retirement?

Our regiment had present at this review but few over two hundred men, and the other regiments were proportionally small, so that the corps was scarcely larger than a good-sized division, yet it appeared in splendid condition. Its depleted numbers and battle-scarred flags alone told the story of its recent experiences. The following week our regiment was detailed for a ten-days' tour of picket duty, and was encamped some distance above Falmouth in a pretty grove. This change of service was a welcome one to the men in many respects, for there was better foraging opportunities, and there was also considerable excitement attending this service in the presence of the enemy. The Rappahannock River was the dividing line of the two armies, and their respective pickets lined its banks. At this time the two lines were kept as far as possible concealed from each other, though there was practically no picket firing. Later on the two lines were posted in full view of each other, and by agreement under a " flag of truce" all picket firing was strictly forbidden. Thereafter, although forbidden, there was more or less conversation carried on between the two lines.

CHAPTER XII

In addition to our heavy loss of men at Fredericksburg was the loss of our colors, the stand whose staff had been shot away in my hand as described in a former chapter.

It can be well understood that we felt very keenly the loss of our flag, although we knew that it had been most honorably lost. It was known to have been brought off the field in the night by Corporal William I. D. Parks, Company H, one of the color-guard, who was mortally wounded, and left by him in a church used as a temporary hospital. Corporal Parks was removed to a hospital at Washington, where he died shortly afterwards, and the colors mysteriously disappeared. The act of this color-bearer in crawling off the field with his colors, wounded as he was to the death, was a deed of heroism that has few parallels. We made every effort to find the flag, but without success, and had concluded that it must have been left in Fredericksburg, and so fallen into the hands of the enemy, when a couple of weeks after the battle, on returning from a ride down to Falmouth, I noticed a regiment of our troops having dress parade. I rode near them, and my attention was at once attracted to the fact that they paraded three stands of colors, a most unusual circumstance. My suspicion was at once aroused that here were our lost colors. Riding closer, my joy was great on recognizing our number and letters on their bullet- and shell-tattered folds, " 132 P. V." Anger immediately succeeded my joy as I saw that our precious colors were being paraded as a sort of trophy. This flag, under whose folds so many of our brave men had fallen, and which had been so heroically rescued from the field, exhibited to the army and the world as a trophy of the battle by another regiment! It was, in effect, a public proclamation of our cowardice and dishonor and of their prowess in possessing what we had failed to hold and guard, our sacred colors. It stung me to the quick. I do not remember ever to have been more beside myself with anger. It was with difficulty that I contained myself until their ceremony was over, when I rode up to the colonel, in the presence of all his officers, and in a voice which must have betrayed my emotion, demanded to know why he was parading our colors. His reply was, "Those are the colors of a d——d runaway regiment which my men picked up on the battle-field of Fredericksburg." My hair and whiskers were somewhat hot in color those days, and I have not kept a record of my language to that colonel for the next few minutes. I sincerely hope the recording angel has not. Still, I am sure it was the explosion of a righteous indignation.

Full of wrath I galloped at topmost speed to camp and made known my discovery to Colonel Albright. If I was "hot," what shall be said of him? Of a fiery, mercurial disposition, his temper flew in a moment. He mounted his horse and bade me lead him to this regiment. The brave heralds who carried "the good news

142

Lost Colors Recovered

from Ghent to Aix," did not gallop faster than did we two, and the wicked fellow who was hired to say two dollars' worth of " words" for the Quaker did not do his work a bit more effectively than did my brave colonel in denouncing the man who had made that charge of cowardice against our regiment. Well, he began to hedge immediately. He evidently saw that there was trouble ahead, and offered to give us the colors at once, but Colonel Albright peremptorily refused to accept them that way, and said he would demand a court of inquiry and would require full and complete vindication, cost what it might. A court of inquiry was at once asked for and granted. It was made up of officers outside of our division, and was directed to investigate the loss of our flag, and how it came into the possession of this other regiment. Colonel Albright was a good lawyer and conducted his own case before the court. It came out in the investigation that in making his report of the part his regiment took in the battle of Fredericksburg this colonel had used substantially the same language he had to me concerning how he came into possession of the flag. Here is the paragraph referring to our colors, taken from his report printed in the " Rebellion Records," vol. xxi., page 275 :

" I would also state that some cowardly members of a regiment unknown (?) abandoned their colors, which were recovered by Captain Northrup, of my regiment, and saved the disgrace of falling into the hands of the enemy." My diary notes that I interviewed this Captain Northrup, and he promptly stated that he took the colors from the hospital and brought them with him when their regiment left Fredericksburg. He said he did not know how they got into the hospital, but supposed a wounded sergeant had left them there. He disclaimed any idea of their having been abandoned in a cowardly manner, and could not understand why his colonel had made such a declaration. The statement that his men rescued them from an unknown regiment was false upon its face, for our name was inscribed on its folds in plain letters, " 132d P. V." Why he made such a statement, and why he treated the colors as he did, I could never understand, for had the statement been true it was outrageously unmilitary to proclaim to the world the cowardice of one of our own regiments. It was his duty to promptly send the colors to head-quarters, with a statement of the facts, so that the alleged runaways could be properly disciplined. As it was, it seemed a most contemptible effort to secure a little cheap, unearned glory. It was heartlessly cruel and unworthy of a brave soldier.

The result of the court of inquiry was a full and complete vindication of our regiment, as shown by the following paragraph from an order issued by Major-General O. O. Howard, commanding the Second Corps: " The last color-bearer, badly wounded, left his regiment after dark, and in the town entered a church used as a hospital, taking his colors with him. He was carried away from this place and the colors left behind. The very fidelity of the color-bearer holding to his colors as long as he was conscious was the occasion of their loss to the regiment. Not only no fault should be found with this regiment, but it should receive unqualified commendation."

General French, commanding our division, published this order to the division, adding the following: " As the

commander of the division, and knowing the character
of the One Hundred and Thirty-second Pennsylvania
Volunteers, which has fought under my eye in two of the
bloodiest engagements of the war, and which has the
highest encomiums from its brigade commander, General
Kimball, who knows what brave men are, I have deemed
it my duty to make this record to go with whatever may
have transpired in reference to this subject during my
short absence." The above paragraphs were taken from
Bates's "History of Pennsylvania Volunteers." The
colors were ordered returned to us with proper military
honors. They were brought to General French's head-
quarters by a military escort from that regiment, and I
had the satisfaction of officially receiving them with a like
escort from our regiment, commanded by First Lieutenant
J. D. Laciar, of Company G. The ceremony was to us a
joyous and impressive occasion. It took place in the
presence of General Alfred Sully, temporarily commanding the division, and staff, and our brigade officers. The
two escorts were drawn up, facing each other. The order
of Major-General Howard, above referred to, was read.
This was followed by a little speech from General Sully,
in which we came in for some more praise; then both
escorts presented arms, whilst their color-bearer transferred the colors to ours, and the ceremony was over. A
happier escort never marched than was ours bearing home
those restored colors.

The weather was now getting very cold, and we set
about making ourselves as comfortable as possible in
camp. The men were allowed to fix up their tents as best
they could without much regard for architectural beauty

or regularity. Some of them dug cellars four to five feet deep, made puncheon floors,—that is, floors made of split logs smoothed off and laid the flat side up,—whilst the sides were made of logs plastered up with mud. Mud fireplaces were made with old barrels for chimneys. The roofs were canvas, of course, but fairly waterproof. A favorite bit of horse-play of the men at this time was to watch when the occupants of some tent were having a good time, and smoke them out by throwing a wet blanket over the top of their barrel chimney. In about a second the smoke would be almost dense enough to suffocate, and every fellow would pile out and hunt for the culprit. Woe be unto him if they found him. A favorite ruse on the part of the culprit was to plunge into his tent and be placidly snoring when the victims began their hunt. Sometimes the simulation would be too sonorous, and give him away, and then he had trouble on hand for the next hour. The ingenuity of these sons of Belial in their pranks was beyond description. I have laughed until absolutely exhausted many a time. How did I know so much about them? Well, I had two of the liveliest of these boys in my office as clerks, and, as they were generally in the fun, I was kept posted, and to tell the truth, as long as it did not seriously transgress, and there was fun in it, I knew nothing about it " officially." Often have I seen these boys put up a job on some fellow quietly sleeping, by smoking out his next-door neighbors and then directing their attention to him as the culprit. To see him hauled out of a sound sleep and mauled for something he was entirely innocent of, vehemently protesting his innocence, yet the more he protested getting the more punishment, the rascals who put up the job doing most of the punishing, I have nearly split my sides. Of course, no one was seriously hurt. The victim knew enough to keep his temper, and in the end enjoyed the lark as well as the rest. I speak of these things, for they were the oases in army life and drudgery. Except for them it would have been unendurable. Seldom were things so bad but that some bit of raillery would relieve the strain and get up a laugh, and everybody would feel better.

We had a young fellow in one of the companies who was certainly the most comical genius I ever saw. He was known by a nickname only. No length of march and no severity of service could curb his spirits. When all were down in the dumps this fellow would perform some monkey-shine that would make even a horse laugh, and all would be in good spirits again. Colonel Albright used to say he was worth his weight in gold. He was with us until after Fredericksburg, where he was either killed or wounded, and I do not remember to have seen him afterwards.

I have spoken of the men's winter-quarters. We officers had our wall tents, and had them fixed up with puncheon floors also, and sheet-iron stoves, so that as long as we kept a fire burning all were fairly comfortable. But wood fires would last but an hour or so without replenishing, and so during the night we had great difficulty in keeping warm. Some of the coldest nights my clerks and myself took turns in keeping up our fire. I rather prided myself on the construction of my bed. It was made of two springy poles held in place by crotched sticks driven into the ground. On the poles nailed crosswise was a bottom made of barrel-staves, the hollow side down, and on these was laid a bed of hay, kept in place by some old canvas sacking. On cold nights the only article of clothing we took off was our shoes or boots. Then rolling ourselves in our blankets, with gum blanket outside tucked well around our feet and the whole surmounted with our overcoats, we managed to sleep pretty well. These puncheon floors were all the proceeds of foraging. No lumber of any kind was furnished by the government. The men cut the trees and split the logs wherever they could find them. Most of them were " backed" into camp anywhere from one to four miles.

After this little of note occurred in camp until Christmas. We had made ourselves as comfortable as we could with the materials at hand, which were not in superabundance. The weather was what we were told was characteristic of Virginia winters,—rather mild, slush and mud, with its raw, disagreeable dampness, being the prevailing conditions. It was exceedingly trying to our men, and many, in consequence, were on the sick list. My diary notes that on Christmas day we actually had a little sunshine, and that by way of adding good cheer to the occasion a ration of whiskey was issued to the men. The ration consisted of a gill for each man. Each company was marched to the commissary tent, and every man received his gill in his cup or drank it from the measure, as he preferred. Some of the men, who evidently were familiar with the intricacies of repeating in ward elections, managed in various ways to repeat their rations of this vile stuff until we had a good deal more than a gill of whiskey's worth of hilarity in camp. However, the noise was winked at, believing it would soon subside and pass off. All drills were suspended and the men were allowed passes freely out of camp, being required to be in quarters promptly at taps. The officers passed the day visiting and exchanging the compliments of the season. The wish for a "Merry Christmas" was about all there was to make it such. I remember our bill of fare for Christmas dinner consisted of boiled rice and molasses, "Lobskous" and stewed dried apples. The etymology of the euphonious word "Lobskous" I am unable to give. The dish consisted of hardtack broken up and thoroughly soaked in water, then fried in pork fat. I trust my readers will preserve the recipe for a side dish next Christmas. One of the boys, to show his appreciation of this extra fare for Christmas dinner, improvised the following blessing:

> "Good Lord of love
> Look down from above
> And see how a soldier's grub has mended,—
> Slushed rice, Lobskous, and shoat,
> Where only hardtack and hog were intended."

The day was not without its fun, however. Among other things, an impromptu foot-race was gotten up between the Fourth New York and our regiment. The former regiment, with which we were now brigaded, was from New York City, and in its general make-up was decidedly "sporty." They had in their ranks specimens of almost all kinds of sports, such as professional boxers, wrestlers, fencers, and runners. One of the latter had been practising in the morning, and some of our boys had remarked that "he wasn't much of a runner," whereupon they were promptly challenged to produce a man who could beat him, for a cash prize of twenty dollars in gold. Win or lose, our fellows were not to be bluffed, and so promptly accepted the challenge. Back they came to camp with their " bluff," to look up a man to meet this professional. So far as our men were concerned, it was another case of the Philistine defying the armies of Israel. Where was our David? All hands entered into the fun, from the colonel down. The race was to be a one-hundred-yard dash from a standing mark. We found our man in Corporal Riley Tanner, of Company I. He was a lithe, wiry fellow, a great favorite in his company, and in some trial sprints easily showed himself superior to all of the others. He, however, had never run a race, except in boys' play, and was not up on the professional tactics of such a contest. It was decided that the affair should take place at five o'clock P.M., on our regimental front, and should decide the championship of the two regiments in this particular. The course was duly measured and staked off, and was lined on both sides by a solid wall of the men, nearly our whole division being present, including most of the officers. If the championship of the world had been at stake, there could hardly have been more excitement, so much zest did every one put into it. On the minute the Goliath of the bloody Fourth appeared, clad in the most approved racing garb. He was a stockily built young Irishman, and looked decidedly formidable, especially when our poor little David appeared a moment later, with no other preparation than his coat and cap off and pants rolled up. Nevertheless, our boys thoroughly believed in him, and we all gave him a rousing cheer. The signal was given and away leaped our little champion

Lost Colors Recovered

like a frightened deer, literally running away from the professional from the start and beating him leisurely in the end by more than a dozen feet. Great was the furore which followed. The victor was carried on the shoulders of his comrades of Company I triumphantly back to his quarters, and afterwards through all the company streets, the victim of an immense popularity. Corporal Tanner, scarcely beyond his teens, was a good, brave, and true young man, popular with his comrades and faithful in all his duties. Was this little race, so short and gloriously won, prophetic of his life's brief course? He came home to survive but a few years, and then die of injuries received in the service. He was as much a sacrifice upon the altar of his country as if he had been killed in battle. He was long ago laid to rest in a soldier's grave. But he still lives in the hearts of his comrades.

Here let me say a few words of our " friends, the enemy," we had just beaten, the Fourth New York. Its colonel was a Scotchman named McGregor, and he was a true McGregor, a splendid officer. He was in command of the brigade after Colonel Andrews was wounded at Fredericksburg, until himself disabled by a wound. His lieutenant-colonel was a captain in the New York police force when he entered the service, and after the war as Inspector Jameson he achieved a national reputation. He was a splendid fellow personally, and physically a king among men. He stood six feet two inches, beautifully proportioned, square, and straight as an Indian, with heavy jet black hair and whiskers, and an eye that I imagine could almost burn a hole in a culprit. He could be both majestic and impressive when occasion required, and was

more gifted in all these things than any man I ever knew.
The following incident will illustrate his use of them. I
met him in Washington whilst returning to my regiment
the day before the battle of Fredericksburg. I joined him
just before reaching the wharf where we were to take the
boat. He had been up to Washington on a day's pass, all
any one could then get, and had for some reason overstayed his leave. I think he had missed his boat the day
before. In consequence he could not get a pass through
the lines to go back. I asked how he expected to get
through the provost guard. " Oh, that's easy," he said.
" Just watch me go through," and I did. There was a
double guard at the entrance to the boat and a sergeant
and lieutenant examining all passes. Jameson threw his
cape over his shoulders to conceal his shoulder-straps, put
on one of his majestic airs, looked the officer through, as
much as to say, you do not presume to question my rights
here, and waved him and the guards aside, and deliberately stalked aboard, as though he commanded the army.
I came meekly along behind, pass in hand. The officer
had by that time recovered himself sufficiently to ejacu-
late, " Who the h—l is that—general?" I repeated the
ejaculation to the colonel afterwards to his great amusement. He was all right, and on his way to rejoin his
regiment, where he was wounded next day, splendidly
doing his duty. Because he had overstayed his leave
twenty-four hours, red tape would have required him to
remain in Washington, submit to a court-martial or court
of inquiry, and probably after three or four weeks be sent
back, duly excused, the country being deprived of his services in the mean time.

Lost Colors Recovered

Well, to get back to Christmas. After the foot-race the men were given free rein until ten o'clock P.M., and passes out of camp were not required. As the evening wore on, it became evident that John Barleycorn had been getting in some extra work, from the character of the noise emanating from the company streets, and I became somewhat nervous about it. Lieutenant-Colonel Albright's tent adjoined mine, and I could see that he was becoming a little exercised over this extra noise. The fear was that we might get a peremptory summons from division headquarters to " explain immediately the causes of the unusual noises emanating from our regiment, and why it is not suppressed." Just about ten o'clock there was an extra outburst, and I noticed Colonel Albright, with sword dangling, pass rapidly out of his tent and down towards the company streets from whence the noise came. I feared trouble, and slipped on my boots and followed as quickly as possible. But before I reached the scene, the colonel had drawn his sword and ordered all the men to their quarters, at the same time striking right and left with the flat of his sword, hitting two of the men. One proved to be a sergeant who was trying to quell the noise and get his men into quarters. The latter resented the blow and made a sharp retort to the colonel, who immediately repeated it, whereupon the sergeant struck him a terrible blow in the eye with his fist, knocking him down. I got there just in time to see the colonel fall, and immediately seized the sergeant and placed him in arrest. He was handed over to the division provost guard. The colonel was found to be seriously hurt. His eye swelled up and turned black and gave him great pain all night.   And it was several days before he recovered the use of it.

The most serious thing about this unfortunate culmination of our Christmas festivities was not only the breach of discipline, but the present status of this sergeant.   He was an exceptionally good non-commissioned officer, with a splendid record in both battles and in all service, yet he had now committed an offence the punishment for which, in time of war, was death,—viz., striking his superior commissioned officer.   The next day Colonel Albright reported the affair to General French, commanding the division, who promptly advised him to prefer charges against the culprit and make an example of him.   The matter was generally discussed by both officers and men in camp, and although it was felt that the sergeant had committed a grave offence, yet that the colonel was in a measure responsible for it.   The latter was justly popular with all as a brave officer and good man, yet he had been guilty himself of an offence which had brought upon him the blow he had received.   He had no right to strike a soldier as he did, even with the flat of his sword.   Nor was it the proper thing for him to take the place of his " officer of the guard" or " officer of the day" in enforcing his own orders regulating camp discipline.   He should have sent for the latter and required them to do their duty in the matter.   As a matter of fact, this was just what the officer of the day was doing when the colonel appeared. The colonel sent for me next morning, on his return from General French's head-quarters, and freely told me of the advice of the latter, and indicated his purpose to proceed.

This splendid man has long since entered into rest.   No

Lost Colors Recovered

truer man or braver officer entered the service than he, and it has been one of the greatest satisfactions of my life that I was able to possess his confidence to the fullest degree. He invited my views now and he afterwards thanked me for the service I then rendered him by opposing his contemplated action. He was still suffering very much from his injury and was in a poor mood to brook opposition. Nevertheless I felt that if he subjected this man to the possible results of a court-martial, later on he would never forgive himself, and I so told him. I reminded him of the mistake he had made in assuming the duties of his " officer of the day," and of his graver error, if not offence, in striking the men; that such action would be very likely to produce similar results with almost any of the men upon whom it might be committed; that he had failed to respect the rights of his men even in matters of discipline, and that all this being true, it would be a mistake he would always regret if he failed to treat this affair in as manly and generous a way as discipline would permit. It was an occasion of keen regret that I had to differ with Colonel Albright, for I really loved the man. He dismissed me rather cavalierly with his thanks for my drastic frankness. By his direction a meeting of all the officers of the regiment was summoned to meet at his head-quarters in the afternoon to give their views as to the course to be pursued. The question, as submitted by the colonel being one purely of discipline, seemed to admit of but one treatment,—viz., court-martial; and this was the unanimous sentiment as expressed in this meeting, although outside, I well knew nearly all had expressed themselves differently. Perhaps the way the colonel took to get their views was partly responsible for his failure to get their real feelings. He began with the youngest lieutenant and asked each officer up to the senior captain, what he thought the offence merited. The answer was, " I suppose court-martial." None seemed willing to accuse the colonel of his own error, and to have answered otherwise would have involved that, so they simply replied as above.

The colonel said, after all had given their answers, that the adjutant did not agree with him nor them, and called on me to state my position, saying I was to be excused, as he supposed the sergeant was a personal friend. Whilst it was true that I had known him at home, I disclaimed being influenced by that fact in this matter. The colonel, to my relief, adjourned the meeting without announcing his determination. I felt sure that a little more time would bring him to my way of thinking, and so it turned out. I saw the sergeant over at the provost-guard tent, and found him very anxious about his situation and thoroughly sorry for his hasty conduct towards the colonel, whom he sincerely respected. He said he felt terribly hurt at being so roughly treated. He was not to blame for the noise, but was actually doing his best to quiet the noisy ones and get them into quarters when the first intimation he had of the colonel's presence was the blow from his sword. He said this blow hurt him and roused his anger and he replied sharply, and on getting the second blow he struck without stopping to think of the consequences. I told the colonel of this conversation, and said if he would permit this man to express to him personally his sorrow for his conduct, and, under the circumstances, restore him to duty with no greater punishment than a

Lost Colors Recovered

loss of his rank as sergeant, I felt sure he would win the hearts of all the men and do an act he would always be glad of. Two days later, to my great joy, he ordered me to prepare an order practically embodying my recommendations, the order to be read at dress parade that day, and the prisoner to be publicly released at that time. I think I never performed a more willing or difficult task than reading that order on parade that afternoon. Just before the ceremony, the sergeant had been brought by the provost guard to the colonel's tent and had, in a manly way, expressed his sorrow for his act. The colonel had stated this fact to the regiment, and then directed me to read the order releasing the prisoner and restoring him to duty. The tears blinded my eyes and my emotions almost choked my voice as I tried to read, and I doubt if there was a dry eye in the ranks when I had finished. The outcome of the unfortunate affair was exceedingly satisfactory. The colonel, always popular, had now the hearts of all—officers and men.

CHAPTER XIII

OUR brigade was now commanded by Lieutenant-Colonel Marshall, Tenth New York Volunteers, who was the senior officer present for duty, Colonels Kruger, First Delaware, and McGregor, Fourth New York, being absent on account of wounds received at Fredericksburg, and Colonel Wilcox, of our regiment, absent, sick. I mention this to show how the exigencies of the service thrust upon junior officers the duties and responsibilities of much higher grades. Here a lieutenant-colonel was discharging the duties appertaining to a general; sergeants frequently commanded companies, whilst a captain in command of a regiment was not an infrequent thing. These junior officers performing the duties of higher grades got no more compensation than the pay of their actual rank. On the 24th of January, Colonel Wilcox sent in his resignation, and Lieutenant-Colonel Albright was commissioned colonel. Major Shreve was promoted to be lieutenant-colonel, and I had the honor to receive the rare and handsome compliment of an election to the office of major, although, being a staff-officer, I was not in the regular line of promotion. Sergeant-Major Clapp succeeded to my position as adjutant, and Private Frank J. Deemer, Company K, who had been a clerk in my office, was appointed sergeant-major. Just at this time I had a somewhat singular ex-

The Winter at Falmouth

perience. I had received a three-days' leave of absence with permission to visit Washington on business for the officers. This detail I mention because no leaves of absence other than for sickness or disability were obtainable at this time, except on urgent business for the officers of a regiment, and for but one officer to a regiment, and three days was the limit. To get to Washington—only about sixty miles away—I had to start from camp before daylight in the morning, ride three miles to the railroad in a heavy, springless army wagon, across fields and over rutted roadways that were barely passable, the jolting of which was almost enough to shake one's bones loose; then ride twenty miles in a freight car, perched on whatever truck one could get a seat on, thence by boat to Washington. The morning was exceptionally cold and I had to leave without breakfast; the result was I caught a severe cold, and when I reached my destination I was suffering terribly from an attack of dysentery. I was barely able to get to the Ebbitt House, the clerk of which seeing my plight summoned a physician, who had me sent to the Seminary Hospital for Officers at Georgetown. Here I received most excellent care.

This institution was for officers only. There must have been upward of two hundred sick and wounded officers there at that time. It was under strict military rules. The surgeon in charge was its commanding officer, as absolute as though a general commanding a division in the field. When I reached the hospital I was registered, put to bed, and all clothing and personal effects taken from me. A warm bath followed with the assistance of a stalwart nurse and medicines were administered, and

I soon found relief in a refreshing sleep. A couple of days later I had a remarkable visit. I was not allowed to sit up yet, but a fine-looking old gentleman, wearing the insignia of a major-general, appeared at my cot and extended his hand. His face was an exceedingly kind one and his voice, if possible, more so. His hair was white and he had the unmistakable appearance of advanced age, though he stood fully six feet high and was still square and unbent in form. He proceeded to say he had learned that a young officer bearing the name of Hitchcock had been taken suddenly very ill and sent to this hospital, and inasmuch as his name was Hitchcock, he was doubly interested to know, first how I was, and second who I was. My visitor was none other than Major-General Hitchcock, military attaché of President Lincoln's cabinet and the first general commissioner for the exchange of prisoners of war. I think he was a retired regular army officer called from his retirement to special service as military adviser of the president and now in charge of the bureau for the exchange of prisoners of war. His call was very pleasant, and I learned from him that all of our name in this country were distantly related. That two brothers came to this country with the Regicides and settled, one in New Hampshire, the other at New Haven. He was of the former stock, whilst I was from the latter. On retiring he bade me call on him when well. I greatly regret I never had the opportunity of returning his gracious visit. On the cot next mine lay an officer convalescing from a wound received at Fredericksburg. I have forgotten his name, but we soon became well acquainted, and he proved a valuable and companionable acquaintance. He was the best posted man in military tactics I ever met, and was thoroughly familiar with all its branches from the school of the soldier to the grand tactics of a division. It was very profitable pastime for me to go over the tactics under his instruction, he illustrating each battalion movement by the use of matches on the coverlets of our cots. In that way I learned the various tactical movements as I had never been able to do before, and it was of immense value to me, having now been promoted to the position of a field-officer. This hospital was no better and in no wise different from those for private soldiers, except that we were charged a per diem for board, whereas there was no charge for the privates. I thought I could return at the end of a week, and asked to be discharged, but was rather curtly informed by the surgeon in charge that when the time came for my discharge he would inform me.

The papers now contained rumors of another movement on foot, and, of course, I was very anxious to return. A few days later, after an examination, the doctor gave me my discharge. It was now ten days since I had left camp on a three-days' leave, but my discharge from the hospital operated as an extension, and I had no difficulty in getting transportation and passes through the lines to rejoin my regiment. I performed my errands for the officers of the regiment, which consisted in getting various articles for their comfort, and in several cases a bottle of something to " keep the cold out." As I write, I have before me, in perfect preservation, all the official papers covering that trip. Here are copies of the papers required to get back to the regiment. They will give an idea of the conditions, getting in and out of Washington at that time, as well as of the load I had to carry back:

HEAD-QUARTERS MILITARY DISTRICT OF WASHINGTON,
WASHINGTON, D. C., January 22, 1863.
Lieutenant F. L. Hitchcock, 132d P. V., with servant, has permission to proceed to Falmouth, Va., for the purpose of rejoining his regiment, and to take the following articles for officers and men: (1) one drum, (3) three express packages, carpet sack containing liquors, (1) one box of provisions, (1) one box of clothing. Quartermaster please furnish transportation.
By Command of Brigadier-General Martindale, Military Governor of Washington.

JOHN P. SHERBURNE,
Assistant Adjutant-General.

No. 247.
ASSISTANT-QUARTERMASTER'S OFFICE, SIXTH STREET WHARF,
WASHINGTON, D. C., January 23, 1863.
Pass on government boat to Aquia Creek, three boxes and one drum, liquors and sutlers' stores strictly excluded.
For Adjutant F. L. Hitchcock, 132 Pa. Vols.

J. M. ROBINSON,
Captain and A. Q. M.

The word liquors above is erased with a pen. It is difficult at this day to realize that Washington was surrounded with a cordon of sentries. All places of entrance and exit were under the strictest military surveillance. General Martindale, as its military governor, was supreme in authority. No one could come or go, and nothing be taken in or out, without his permission.

The servant included in the above pass was a " contraband," picked up in Washington for the trip. There were hundreds of them clamoring for an opportunity to get down to the army. They were glad to do all one's drudgery for the chance of going, for once there,

The Winter at Falmouth

plenty of jobs could be found, besides the excitement and attractions of "Uncle Sam's" army were to them irresistible. I reached camp early in the evening and delivered my supplies, the officers being promptly on hand to receive them. The return of an officer from "civilization" was an event of no ordinary moment, and I had many calls that evening. The following anecdote of Major-General Howard was told that evening, apropos of the delivery of the "commissions" I had brought. The general was well known to be uncompromising in his opposition to the presence of liquor of any kind in camp, or elsewhere, and especially among the members of his official family. Yet shortly after the battle of Fredericksburg, one of his staff had a present of a bottle of "old Rye." He put it away until some time during the general's absence he could safely bring it out and treat his fellow-members of the staff. The opportunity came one day when his chief announced his absence at army headquarters for a couple of hours, and mounted and rode away. The hidden treasure was brought out and due preparation made for the delectation of all hands, and he was in the act of pulling the cork in front of his tent, when, suddenly hearing the clatter of horse's hoofs, he looked up just in time to see the general returning for a forgotten paper. He had barely time to swing the bottle behind his heels as he closed them in the position of a soldier, and arose and respectfully saluted. The position and salute were strictly according to army regulations, but with a general's own staff such formality was not usual. The general evidently caught the situation, for he was tantalizingly deliberate in acknowledging the salute, and finally

163

War from the Inside

remarked, with a twinkle in his eye, looking him full in the face: " Mr. ——, your position is faultless and your punctiliousness in saluting truly admirable. Were you getting it ready to send to the hospital? Very commendable, indeed; it will do so much good." And to the hospital, of course, it had to go, much to the chagrin of all the staff.

The event of special interest at this time was the movement later known as the " mud march." Troops had for three days been moving up the river, destination, of course, unknown to us, but now they were returning, a most sorry, mud-bedraggled looking crowd. We were glad enough not to have been with them. Our corps had been for a week under marching orders, to move at a moment's notice, but the final order never came, and we were spared this experience. Whatever the movement was designed to be, it was defeated by plain, simple MUD. It should be spelled in the largest capitals, for it was all-powerful at this time. Almost immediately after the movement began, it commenced to rain heavily. The ground was already soggy from previous rains, and it soon became a vast sea of mud. I have already spoken of Virginia mud. It beggars description. Your feet sink into it frequently ankle deep, and you lift them out with a sough. In some places it seemed as bottomless as a pit of quicksand. The old-established roads were measurably passable, but, as I have heretofore explained, most of the troops had to march directly across the fields, and here it proved absolutely impossible to move the wagon-trains and artillery any distance. This was the main reason why the movement had to be abandoned. I saw many wagons

164

down over their hubs, stalled in the mire. And the guns and caissons of a battery of artillery were stalled near our camp, and had to be abandoned for the time. The horses were saved from miring with great difficulty. A few days later the guns and caissons were hauled out with ropes.

There were dead mules and mired and broken wagons all along the route of the marching troops. The number of animals that perished in this futile march must have run up into thousands, killed by exposure over pulling or miring. It should be understood that when the army moves, and the mule trains of ammunition and rations are ordered to move, they must go as long as it is physically possible, mule or no mule. The lives of a thousand mules, more or less, is nothing compared with the necessity of having ammunition and rations at the proper place at the required time. I saw one mule team stalled in one of these sloughs. The heavy wagon was down so that the box was in the mud and the four mules were wallowing in a death struggle to get out. Harness was cut and they were freed, all to no purpose. Their struggles had made the slough like a stiff pudding, which was apparently bottomless; the more they struggled the deeper they got. Finally a chain was hooked about the neck of one of the leaders and fastened to another wagon and the mule hauled out, but with a broken neck. The experiment was repeated in a modified way with the other leader, now over back in the mire, but with no better results. The others had ceased to struggle and were slowly sinking, and were mercifully killed and allowed to bury themselves in the mire, which they speedily did. It may be asked why more civilized methods were not employed to extricate these valuable animals. Why fence rails or timbers were not placed under them as is usual? The answer is, there was not a fence rail nor anything of that nature probably within ten miles. Everything of this kind had long ago been used for fire-wood for the soldiers' cooking. And as for timbers there probably was not a stick nearer than Aquia Creek, more than ten miles away. Again it may be wondered why the chain was not passed around the mule's body rather than his neck. Simply because the former was impossible without running the risk of miring the driver in the slough, and he was not disposed to run any risk of that kind. Had this been practicable, it is doubtful if the result would have been any better, for without padding the chains would have killed or mangled the mule, and there were no means at hand for that purpose. The destruction of this class of property, always very severe under favorable circumstances in the army, was during this mud movement simply appalling. The loss of one or more mules meant an abandonment of the wagon and its contents to the weather in many instances, and the same was true where a team was mired.

The rebels were evidently interested observers of this mud march, for their pickets taunted ours with such questions as " How d'ye like Virginia mud?" " Why don't you 'uns come over?" " How are you, mud?" etc., and they put up rude sign-boards on which were scrawled in large letters, " Burnside stuck in the mud!" " Burnside's name is Mud!" etc.

The " mud march" had evidently settled it that there would be no further attempt to move until better weather conditions prevailed, which could not reasonably be looked

MAJOR FREDERICK L. HITCHCOCK
132D P. V.
A year later Colonel 25th U. S. C. T.

The Winter at Falmouth

for before April, and so we settled down for a winter where we were, back of Falmouth. The several corps were spread out, occupying an area extending from within three miles of Fredericksburg, nearly down to the Potomac. Our corps, the Second, was located nearest to the latter city, and our picket lines covered its front to Falmouth and some miles up the river. Our division, the Third (French's), had the line from the railroad bridge at Fredericksburg to Falmouth, something over two miles. Being now a field-officer, my name was placed on the roster of picket field-officers of the day. My first detail on this duty came almost as soon as my commission. My duties had hitherto been confined almost exclusively to the staff or executive business of the regiment. Further than making the necessary details of officers and men for picket duty, I had never had anything to do with that branch of the service. I had, therefore, only a smattering knowledge of the theory of this duty. It may well be judged, therefore, that I felt very keenly this lack, when I received my order to report for duty as division field-officer of the day, the following morning. Here I was suddenly confronted with the responsibility of the command of the picket forces covering the dividing line between the two hostile armies. A demonstration of the enemy was to be looked for any moment, and it was most likely to occur on our front. I had hoped to have a few days to study up and by observing its practical work get some little idea of my new duties. But here was the detail, and it must be obeyed. It should be explained that the picket line consists of a cordon of sentinels surrounding the army, usually from two to three miles from its camp. Its purpose is to watch the enemy, and guard against being surprised by an attack. Except for this picket line, the main body of troops could never sleep with any degree of safety. To guard against attacks of the enemy would require it to remain perpetually under arms. Whereas with its picket lines properly posted it may with safety relax its vigilance, this duty being transferred to its picket forces. This picket service being a necessity of all armies is a recognized feature of civilized warfare. Hence, hostile armies remaining any length of time in position near each other usually make an agreement that pickets shall not fire upon each other. Such agreement remains in force until a movement of one or the other army commences. Notice of such a movement is, of course, never given. The other party finds out the fact as best it can. Frequently the withdrawal or concealment of the picket line will be its first intimation. Ordinarily, picket duty is not only of the very highest responsibility, but an exceedingly dangerous duty. Until agreements to cease picket-firing are made, every sentinel is a legitimate target for the sentinels or pickets of the enemy, hence extreme vigilance, care, and nerve are required in the performance of this duty.

The picket line in the presence of the enemy is generally posted in three lines,—viz., First, the line of sentries; second, the picket supports, about thirty yards in rear of the sentries, and third, the guard reserves, about three hundred yards farther in the rear, depending upon the topography of the country. Each body constitutes one-third of the entire force, *i.e.,* one-third is constantly on duty as sentinels, one-third as picket supports, and one-

The Winter at Falmouth

third as grand reserves. The changes are made every two hours, usually, so that each sentry serves two hours on "post" and four hours off. The latter four hours are spent half on grand reserve and half as picket supports. The supports are divided into companies, and posted in concealed positions, near enough to the sentry line to be able to give immediate support in case of attack, while the grand reserves, likewise concealed, are held in readiness to come to the assistance of any part of the line. Ordinarily this part of the picket force is able to sleep during its two hours of reserve service. The supports, however, while resting, must remain alert and vigilant. It being the duty of the picket-line to prevent a surprise, it must repel any sort of attack with all its power. In the first instance the sentinel must promptly challenge any party approaching. The usual formula is: "Halt! Who comes there?" The approaching party failing to obey the command to halt, it is his duty to fire at once, even though he be outnumbered a hundred to one, and it cost him his life. Many a faithful sentinel has lost his life in his fidelity to duty under such circumstances. For although the picket is there to prevent a surprise, the attacking party is equally bent on getting the advantage of a surprise, if possible, and many are the ruses adopted to capture sentinels before they can fire their guns. He must fire his gun, even though he be captured or run through with a bayonet the next instant. This gives the alarm, and the other sentries and picket supports open fire at once, and the reserves immediately join them, if necessary, to hold or impede the progress of the enemy. It is thus seen that in case of an attack the picket force finds

itself maintaining a fight possibly against the whole opposing army, or whatever the attacking force may be.
Fight it must, cost whatever it may, so that time may be
gained to sound the "long roll" and assemble the army.
Many of our picket fights were so saucy and stubborn that
the attacks were nipped in the bud, the enemy believing
the army was there opposing them. In the mean time,
mounted orderlies would be despatched to army head-
quarters with such information of the attack as the officer
of the day was able to give.

Having now given some idea of picket service, I return to my own first experiences as field-officer of the
day. I was fated to have several rather singular experiences on that first day. The first occurred in connection
with my horse. I mounted and started for division head-
quarters, about a half-mile away, in ample time to reach
there a little before the appointed time—eight o'clock,
but reaching the outer edge of our camp my horse balked,
and in answer to my efforts to move him began to kick,
rear, and plunge. He tried to throw me, and did nearly
everything except roll over. Every time I headed him
forward, he would wheel around and start back for his
stable. I coaxed him, then tried the spur, all to no purpose. I was losing valuable time, besides having a very
uncomfortable kind of a fight on hand. I realized I must
make him obey me or I could never handle him again. An
orderly from General French came galloping over with
the expected peremptory message. One minute's delay
with him was almost a capital offence. I could only return
word that I was doing my best to get there. The general
and his staff then rode over to see my performance. He

DON AND I

And a glimpse of the camp of **Hancock's** Division, Second Army Corps, back of Falmouth, Va.,
winter of 1862–3. See page 171

reassured me with the remark, "Stick to him and make him obey you, or kill him." Well, it took just about one hour to conquer him, at the end of which time I had ploughed up several acres of ground, my horse was in a white lather, and I was in the same condition. When he quit, he did so at once, and went on as cleverly as though nothing had happened. The cause of this freak I never understood, he never having done so before, and never did again.

May I digress long enough to speak a little more of this remarkable horse. Dr. Holland says there is always hope for any man who has heart enough to love a good horse. Army life was well calculated to develop the sterling qualities of both man and beast. Hence, I suppose every man who had a good horse could safely regard him as "most remarkable." How many such have I heard cavalrymen talk about, descanting on the "remarkable" qualities of their half-human favorites, whilst the tears wet their cheeks. I had named this splendid animal "Don Fulano," after that superb horse in Winthrop's "John Brent," not because he was a magnificent black charger, etc.; on the contrary, in many respects he was the opposite of the original Don Fulano. Raised upon an unromantic farm near Scranton, an unattractive yellow bay, rather too heavy limbed and too stockily built to be called handsome, yet powerful, courageous, intelligent (he could almost talk), high spirited, with a heavy, shaggy mane and forelock, through which gleamed a pair of keen, fierce eyes, he had many of the qualities which distinguished his noble prototype. He had not the high honor to die carrying a slave to liberty, but when the final accounts come to be squared up in the horses' heaven, it is possible that the credit of having passed unflinchingly through the battles of Fredericksburg and Chancellorsville, and of having safely carried a wounded soldier off each field may prove to be a little something in favor of my splendid " Don." As a saddler, he came to me practically unbroken. He was sold from the farm because he would jump all fences, yet under the saddle, when I took him, he would not jump the smallest obstacle. This is really as much of an art on the part of the rider as with the horse. An unskilled rider is liable to seriously injure both the horse and himself in jumping. If he is unsteady, the motion of the horse as he rises to make his leap is liable to pitch him over his head. On the other hand, if he clings back, a dead weight in his saddle, he is liable to throw the horse backward. I have seen both done. The secret of successful jumping is to give the horse his head as he rises, feel your knees against his sides firmly, rising with him as he rises and be again in your seat before his feet reach the ground. This helps him and saves both a killing jounce. I finally trained him so that as a jumper he was without a peer in our part of the army. I have had the men hold a pole fully a foot higher than my head, as I stood on the ground, and have jumped him back and forth over it as readily as cats and dogs are taught to jump over one's arm. And the men insisted that he cleared the pole at least a foot each jump.

This jumping of horses was considered quite an accomplishment in the army, it being often a necessity on the march in getting over obstacles. One day I saw our general's son, a young West Pointer, attached to his

father's staff, trying to force his Kentucky thoroughbred
to jump a creek that ran past division head-quarters. The
creek was probably ten to twelve feet wide and, like all
Virginia creeks, its banks seemed cut vertically through
the soil and the water at the edges was about a foot deep.
After repeated trials the best the young man's horse could
do was to get his forefeet on the opposite bank. His
hindfeet always landed in the water. Mr. West Pointer
was way above noticing in any way a poor volunteer
plebeian like myself mounted on an old plug like Don.
But Don had taken in the situation as well as I, and when
I said, " Come, Don, let's us try it," he just gathered
himself and sailed over that creek like a bird, landing
easily a couple of feet on the other side, and swung around
for another try. The young fellow gathered up his thoroughbred and with an oath of disgust retired. Don and
I became great friends, and after our fight, above mentioned, in all our practice jumping or on the march, or
riding about, I never had occasion to use the spur,—
indeed, I seldom wore one. A simple " Come, Don," and
he was quick to obey my every wish. He was kind and
tractable with others, but it was a singular fact that, as for
jumping or any other favors, he would do nothing for
anybody but me, not even for my man who took care of
him. Others, including horse-trainers, repeatedly asked
to try him, thinking they could improve his work, but
he drew the line on all; not even a little jump would
he make for any of them. I had been jumping him, one
day, to the delight and admiration of the men. Among
them was a horse-trainer of the Fourth New York, who
asked the privilege of trying him. He mounted and

brought him cantering up to the pole as though he was going over all right, but instead of making the leap he suddenly whirled, almost dumping the trainer, to the infinite amusement of the men; nor could he induce him to make the leap. I mounted again and he went over, back and forth, without the slightest hesitation. I brought him home from the war, and it was a great grief to me that I was unable to keep him as long as he lived. I secured him a good home, where he lived to a dignified old age. One of my household gods is a photograph of Don and myself, with a section of the camp of Hancock's division of the Second Corps for a background, taken at this time, whilst we lay back of Falmouth.

My second adventure that first day on picket duty occurred shortly after I reached the head-quarters of the picket at the Lacey House, directly opposite the city of Fredericksburg. I had seen the new line posted and the old line relieved, when a grizzly bearded old gentleman rode up and inquired for the " Officer of the day." His dress was exceedingly plain. He wore a much-battered slouch hat down over his eyes, and on the shoulders of his blouse, scarcely discernible, was what had been the silver stars of a brigadier-general. I answered his inquiry by saluting, and then recognized General Alfred Sully, long famed as an Indian fighter before the war. He introduced himself as " Corps officer of the day" and my superior officer for this tour of picket duty. The peculiar thing about his presence was his treatment of me. He evidently saw that he had a greenhorn on hand, for the first question he fired at me was, " How many times have you served as picket officer of the day?" I candidly re-

The Winter at Falmouth

plied that this was my first experience. " Your knowledge of the duties of officer of the day is somewhat
limited?" I admitted the fact. " That is all right," said
he with a pleasant smile. " You are just the man I want.
You shall remain with me all day, and I will teach you
all there is about it." I shall never forget that day's
experience with this splendid old officer. I rode with
him over the whole corps line in the morning, and after
that he made his head-quarters at the Lacey House with
me. Our division front, said he, is where an attack is
most to be looked for, and then he went over it carefully
with me, pointing out the most probable points of attack
and how they should be met; what to do at this point
and that, and so on, in a most intelligent and entertaining
manner gave me the practical idea of a picket defence,
out of his long and ample experience as a regular army
officer. It was just what I needed and was of the greatest
value to me. It was practical experience under a superb
instructor. If all the regular army officers I came in
contact with had been as kind and considerate as this
superb Indian fighter, I should have been equally grateful.
Unfortunately, this was not the case. My experience in
this respect may have been exceptional, but the instance
above narrated is the one solitary case in which my duties
brought me in contact with regular army officers that I
did not receive a rebuff, frequently most brutal and in-
sulting. Doubtless the lack of knowledge of army cus-
toms and routine on the part of us volunteer officers was
calculated to try their patience, for they occupied all the
higher executive staff positions, and routine business of
all kinds had to pass their scrutiny.

War from the Inside

But what were they given West Point education and training at the public expense for if not to impart it to those who should be called to fill volunteer positions in times of the country's need? And how should a volunteer, called into the service of his country without a particle of military education, be expected to understand the interminable routine of army red tape? I will dismiss this digression with a single instance of my experience in seeking information from one of the younger West Pointers. It occurred while I was still adjutant and shortly before my promotion. Some special detailed report was called for. There were so many of these wanted, with so many minute and intricate details, that I cannot remember what this particular one was, but they were enough almost to drive a man to drink. This one, I remember, utterly stumped me, and I rode over to Captain Mason, assistant adjutant-general of our brigade, a thoroughly competent officer, for information. He looked at it a moment, then said: "It beats me; but go down to corps head-quarters and you will find Lieutenant ———, a regular army officer, whose business it is to give just such information as you require." I rode there at once and inquired for Lieutenant ———, as directed. The reply was, "Here he is. What in h—l do you want?" Not specially reassured by this inquiry, I handed him the paper and made known my wishes for information. He literally threw it back at me with the reply, "Go to h—l and find out." I replied that from his manner of speech I appeared to be pretty near there now. I went back to Captain Mason and recounted my experience, to his intense disgust, but that was all that ever came of it.

The Winter at Falmouth

We volunteers learned to avoid a regular officer, especially of the young West Point type, as we would a pestilence.

Returning now to my picket duties of that day, a third incident occurred in the afternoon. The captain of the picket came into our office at the Lacey House with the information that there was a hail from the opposite bank of the river with a flag of truce—a small white flag. We all rushed out, and General Sully directed the captain to take a corporal's guard—a corporal and four men—from his reserve, and go down to the water's edge under a like flag and inquire what was wanted. This formality, he said, was necessary to properly recognize their flag of truce, and to guard against a possible fake or bit of treachery. The reply from the other side was that a young woman in Fredericksburg was exceedingly desirous of reaching her home some distance within the Union lines, and would the Union commander receive a communication upon the subject. General Sully replied that he would receive their communication and forward it to head-quarters, whereupon an orderly was sent over in a boat with the communication. He was unarmed, as were those who rowed him over. The letter was despatched to army head-quarters, whilst the orderly and his boatmen were detained at the landing under guard of our detail. They sat down and in an entirely easy and friendly way chatted with our guard. One would not have believed that these men would shed each other's blood instantly the little white flag was lowered. Yet such was the fact. A half-hour brought a reply to the communication. We, of course, saw neither their letter nor the

War from the Inside

reply, but my lady was immediately brought over and escorted by a mounted guard to army head-quarters, an ambulance being utilized for the purpose. She was really a very pretty young woman, and evidently a thorough lady, though a spirit of hauteur made it apparent she was a Southerner through and through. She maintained a perfect composure during the formality of her reception into our lines, for the officer from the rebel lines who escorted her required a receipt from the officer who had been sent down from head-quarters to receive her; and the appearance of a pretty woman in our lines was so unusual an event that Uncle Sam's boys may have been pardoned if they were all anxious to get a square view of the charming vision. This receipt had to be made in duplicate, one for each army, both officers, as well as the young woman, attesting it with their signatures. General Sully more than half suspected she was a rebel spy. If she was, they wisely chose a beauty for the work.

CHAPTER XIV

DURING the remainder of the winter at Falmouth, I was on as field-officer of the day about every fifth day, so that I was much of the time at the Lacey House, and on the picket-line described in the foregoing chapter. The scenes here enacted constituted my chief experience at this time. The Lacey House was famous during the war as being the head-quarters of either the picket lines between the two armies or of commanding officers of portions of both so frequently that it deserves more than a passing notice. It was a large old-time brick mansion, beautifully situated on the bank of the Rappahannock, just opposite Fredericksburg, and was, at the outbreak of the war, the private residence of Colonel Lacey, who was at the time I write a colonel in the rebel army. The house was very large; its rooms almost palatial in size, had been finished in richly carved hardwood panels and wainscoting, mostly polished mahogany. They were now denuded of nearly all such elegant wood-work. The latter, with much of the carved furniture, had been appropriated for firewood. Pretty expensive fuel? Yes, but not nearly so expensive as the discomfort of staying there without a fire, with the temperature just above the freezing-point, and your feet and body wet through from the rain and slush of the storm outside, in which you were

doing picket duty. The only other fuel obtainable was a
few soggy green logs; whether these had been cut from
the old shade trees surrounding its ample grounds or not
I do not know. I more than suspect they had, but the
only way they could be made to burn in the old-fashioned
open fireplaces was to assist the flames with an occasional
piece of dry wood, the supply of which, as long as it
lasted, was from the panels, wainscoting, and furniture
of the house. Later on the interior doors, all of heavy,
elegant hardwood and finished in keeping with the other
appointments of the place, had to go. This may seem at
this distance as vandalism pure and simple. But if the
would-be critic will place himself in the shoes of the
soldier doing picket duty that winter, with all its hardships, and then remember that Colonel Lacey, the owner
of the place, was not only in active rebellion against the
government we were fighting to maintain, but was a
colonel commanding a rebel regiment as a part of that
great rebel army encamped not a rifle-shot away, which
made it necessary for us to do this picket duty, he may
reach the same conclusion as did our men, that it was not
worth while to freeze ourselves in order to preserve this
rebel's property. The large and ample grounds had been
laid out with all the artistic care a landscape gardener
could bestow upon them. Rare plants, shrubs, and trees
from all over the world had been transplanted here in
great variety. They were now feeling the bitter blight
of war. Army wagons and artillery had made sad havoc
of the beautiful grounds, and such of the rare trees and
shrubbery as interfered with a good vision of the operations of the rebels in and around Fredericksburg had

been ruthlessly removed, and this included the larger part of them.

The Christian Commission had its head-quarters in one wing of the house during this winter. It was presided over by Mrs. John Harris, of Philadelphia, a most benevolent and amiable elderly lady. She was assisted by two or three young women, among whom was a daughter of Justice Grier, of the United States Supreme Court. These ladies were engaged in distributing supplies of various kinds, furnished by this association, to the sick and wounded soldiers in the various hospitals. They had an ambulance at their disposal, and one or two orderlies detailed to assist them. Their work was most gracious and helpful, and they were entitled to the greatest credit for their hard and self-sacrificing labors. The red flag of the hospital floated over them, and such protection as it afforded they had; but it may be well understood that this location between two hostile armies, with active hostilities likely to be resumed any moment, and in the midst of a picket force keenly on the alert night and day, was not likely to be selected as a sanitarium for cases of nervous prostration. The men on picket had reason to remember Mrs. Harris, for those located at the Lacey House daily partook of her bounty in the way of hot coffee, and frequently a dish of good hot soup; and the officers stationed there, usually three or four, were regularly invited to her table for all meals. These invitations were sure to be accepted, for they afforded an opportunity for a partially civilized meal. Her meals were always preceded by a " grace" said by herself, while breakfast was followed by a worship service, at which a chapter from the Bible was

War from the Inside

read and prayer offered by her. These prayers I shall never forget—their sweet fervency, in which the soldiers came in for a large share of her earnest requests. This large-hearted, motherly little woman made a host of friends among the boys in blue that winter. But her motherly kindness was occasionally taken advantage of by some of those sons of Belial. One of them told this story of his former tour of duty: The weather was beastly uncomfortable, from rain and snow making a slush and mud, through which they had tramped until thoroughly soaked. They concluded they must have some hot whiskey punch. Mother Harris, they knew, had all the necessary ingredients, but how to get them was the question. One of them feigned a sudden attack of colic, and was all doubled up on the floor, groaning piteously. Mother Harris was told of it. Of course, she rushed in to render assistance. In reply to her inquiries, the rascal could think of but one thing that would help him, and that was whiskey. A bottle was instantly produced, and a dose administered which gave partial relief; and now if he only had some hot water he was sure it would relieve him. A pitcher of steaming hot water was immediately sent in. Then it was found that the strong liquor nauseated him, and one of the other scamps suggested that perhaps a lemon would relieve that, and a nice lemon was instantly produced. They had plenty of sugar themselves, and so from good Mother Harris's benevolent provision for the colic these rascals deliberately brewed a pitcher full of excellent hot whiskey punch. They had to invent a number of additional lies to keep her out of the room, but they were equal to it. She sent her orderlies in, one after
182

the other, to inquire how the patient was progressing, and the boys secured a proper message back by letting them in for a swig. I hope the good old lady never discovered the fraud. I am sure she would not have believed anybody who might have undertaken to enlighten her, for her confidence in her "boys in blue" was so unbounded.

Almost every tour of picket duty revealed some new incident. Our pickets were now posted in full view of those of the enemy, and the river was so narrow that conversation between the pickets could be carried on without difficulty. Peremptory orders were issued forbidding our pickets from replying, or in any manner communicating with them, but it required the greatest care and vigilance on the part of all the officers of the picket to enforce this order. One of their sentries would hail one of ours with some friendly remark, and it was difficult to suppress the desire to reply. If a reply was not forthcoming, a nagging ejaculation, calculated to provoke, would follow, such as, "What's the matter, Yank, are ye deaf?" "Maybe ye are afeared o' those d—d officers." "We 'uns don't give a d— for our officers," and so volley after volley would follow, whilst poor Yank had to continue silently walking his beat. Sometimes the "Johnny" would wind up with a blast of oaths at his silent auditor. Frequently our men would reply if they thought no officer was near to hear; they seemed to feel that it was only decent to be courteous to them. Strange as it may seem, there was a strong disposition to fraternize whenever opportunity offered on the part of the men of both sides. This was manifested daily on this picket-line, not only in talk across the river, but in communication by means of miniature boats. Our men were generally short of tobacco, and the Johnnies had an abundance of this article of the very best quality; on the other hand, our men were " long" on coffee, of which commodity they were " short." So " Johnny" would fix up a trade. " Say, Yank, if I send you over a boat-load of ' backy,' will ye send her back filled with coffee?" If he got an affirmative reply, which he often did, he would place his little boat in the stream with its rudder so fastened that the current would shoot it across a hundred yards or so 'further down. Yank would watch his opportunity, get the boat, take out its precious cargo of tobacco, reload it with coffee, reverse the rudder, and send it back to " Johnny," who was watching for it further down the stream. Newspapers soon were called for by " Johnny," and became a regular part of the cargo of these boats, for the rebels were wild to get our papers. The exchange of coffee and tobacco was a comparatively harmless matter and would probably have been winked at, but the sending of our Northern papers into their line, containing news of every movement of our forces, was a thing that must be prohibited. A large part of the special instructions of all picket officers related to the suppression of this traffic. Scarcely a day passed that we did not confiscate one or more of these boats. The tobacco our men were allowed to take, but the boat and all rebel newspapers had to be sent to army head-quarters. Some of these miniature boats were marvels of beauty, and showed mechanical skill in construction of the highest order. Others were rude " dugouts." They were generally about thirty inches long, six to ten inches wide, and about six inches deep. They were therefore capable of holding quite a quantity. It was a traffic very difficult to suppress, for our men wanted the tobacco and were unwilling to take that without sending back the proper *quid pro quo*. I doubt if it was ever altogether stopped that winter. The desire for tobacco on the part of our men was so great that they would break over, and some of the subordinate officers participated in it. These exchanges generally took place in the very early dawn, when the officer of the day and the officers of the picket were not supposed to be around. The officer of the day was required to make the "rounds" of his picket-line once after midnight, and then if everything was all right he could rest, his officers of the picket being responsible to him for their respective sections of the line. What is known in army regulations as the "grand rounds," a ceremonial visiting of the line by the officer of the day, accompanied by a sergeant and detail, was omitted on the picket-line as too noisy and ostentatious. In its place the officer of the day went over his line as quietly as possible, assuring himself that each man was in his proper place and was alert and doing his duty.

The sleepy time was from two o'clock A.M. until daylight, and this was the time I found it necessary to be on the line. It took from two to four hours to get over the entire line and visit every sentry. The line, as I have stated heretofore, extended from the railroad bridge at Fredericksburg to the village of Falmouth, a distance of two and a half to three miles. In the daytime I could ride over it comfortably, but in the night I had to take it on foot. When these were dark as ink, and rainy, and the ground was slushy and muddy, as it usually was at that time, it was not a very agreeable duty. However, my duty was so much lighter than that of the men (who, though they were only two hours on post at a time, were out in the storm all the while), that I could not complain. The fidelity of our men to duty under these trying circumstances was most remarkable. Twice only that winter did I find a man sleeping on post. In both of these cases the delinquent was scarcely more than a boy, who I really believed told the truth when they said they sat down because unable to stand up any longer, and, of course, instantly fell asleep. I had them relieved and sent back to camp, and did not report their offence.

A disagreeable duty I had to perform occurred one morning just at break of day. I had just returned from my trip over the line and was about entering the Lacey House, when I noticed a man running down towards the water's edge on the other side of the river. On these night tours of duty I wore a large cavalry overcoat with a long cape, which thoroughly concealed my rank and sword. I stepped out to the top of the bank to see what this man was doing, and he hailed me with: " Hello, Yank. I am going to send ye over a nice boat, with tobacco and newspapers. Look out and get her, and send her back with coffee and newspapers, and don't let any of your d—d officers get hold of it. If they catch ye they'll raise h—l with you, and swipe the whole business." I did not say a word, but quietly walked down to where I saw the boat would touch the shore and waited for it. In the mean time he kept up a running fire of admonitions like the above, chiefly directed to the need of watching against the vigilance of our d——d officers. I picked up the boat, took it up the bank, and then threw my coat open, disclosing my sword and my sash as officer of the day. Oh! the profanity and billingsgate that followed beggars description. I thought I had heard swearing before, but never anything to touch this fellow, and I really could not blame him very much. He had simply hailed the wrong man. The man he thought he was hailing, seeing my presence, kept out of the way. The boat was a little beauty, one of the handsomest I ever saw. It contained five or six pounds of the best Virginia plug tobacco and several newspapers from Richmond. I would have been glad to have kept the boat as a souvenir, but had to despatch it to head-quarters with all its contents at once. Of course I never saw it again.

The " Johnnies" were not without their fun, as well as our boys. Several times I was saluted by their pickets as officer of the day. Army regulations require the sentry nearest the picket reserve, on seeing the officer of the day approach, to call out, " Turn out the guard, officer of the day." Thereupon the officer of the picket parades his reserves, which presents arms and is then inspected by the officer of the day. The red sash worn crosswise over the shoulder is the insignia of the officer of the day. Several times that winter, as I was riding along our line, a rebel sentry yelled, " Turn out the guard, officer of the day," and a sergeant paraded his guard, faced towards me across the river, and presented arms. Of course, I lifted my cap in acknowledgment of the compliment, even though it was a bit of deviltry on their part. This indicated a grave want of discipline on the part of their troops.

War from the Inside

I am sure such an act would not have been thought of by our men.

General Burnside was relieved from command of the army on the 26th of January, 1863, and was succeeded by Major-General Joseph Hooker. "Fighting Joe," as he was familiarly called, was justly popular with the army, nevertheless there was general regret at the retirement of Burnside, notwithstanding his ill success. That there was more than the " fates" against him was felt by many, and whether under existing conditions " Fighting Joe" or any one else was likely to achieve any better success was a serious question. However, all felt that the new commander had lots of fight in him, and the old Army of the Potomac was never known to " go back" on such a man. His advent as commander was signalized by a modest order announcing the fact, and matters moved on without a ripple upon the surface. Routine work, drills, and picket duty occupied all our time. Some of our men were required to go on picket duty every other day, so many were off duty from sickness and other causes. Twenty-four hours on picket duty, with only twenty-four hours off between, was certainly very severe duty, yet the men did it without a murmur. When it is understood that this duty required being that whole time out in the most trying weather, usually either rain, sleet, slush, or mud, and constantly awake and alert against a possible attack, one can form an idea of the strain upon physical endurance it involved.

The chief event preceding the Chancellorsville movement was the grand review of the army by President Lincoln and staff. The exact date of this review I do not remember, but it occurred a short time before the movement upon Chancellorsville. Owing to the absence of Colonel Albright and the illness of Lieutenant-Colonel Shreve, the command of the regiment devolved upon me, and I had a funny experience getting ready for it. As a sort of preliminary drill, I concluded I would put the regiment through a practice review on our drill grounds. To do this properly, I had to imagine the presence of a reviewing officer standing before our line at the proper distance of thirty to forty yards. The ceremony involved opening the ranks, which brought the officers to the front of the line, the presenting arms, and dipping the colors, which the reviewing officer, usually a general, acknowledged by lifting his hat and gracefully bowing. I had reached the point in my practice drill where the " present arms" had been executed, and the colors lowered, and had turned to the front myself to complete the ceremony by presenting sword to my imaginary general, when lo! there rose up in front of me, in the proper position, a real reviewing officer in the shape of one of the worst looking army " bums" I ever saw. He assumed the position and dignified carriage of a major-general, lifted his dirty old " cabbage-leaf" cap, and bowed up and down the line with the grace and air of a Wellington, and then he promptly skedaddled. The " boys" caught the situation instantly and were bursting with laughter. Of course I didn't notice the performance, but the effort not to notice it almost used me up. This will illustrate how the army " bummer" never let an opportunity slip for a practical joke, cost what it might. This fellow was a specimen of this genus that was ubiquitous in the army. Every regiment had one or more. They were always dirty and lousy, a sort of tramp, but always on hand at the wrong time and in the wrong place. A little indifferent sort of service could be occasionally worked out of them, but they generally skulked whenever there was business on hand, and then they were so fertile of excuses that somehow they escaped the penalty and turned up again when the "business" was over. Their one specialty was foraging. They were born foragers. What they could not steal was not to be had, and this probably accounts in a measure for their being endured. Their normal occupation was foraging and, incidentally, Sancho Panza like, looking for adventure. They knew more of our movements, and also of those of the enemy, than the commanding general of either. One of the most typical of this class that I knew was a young fellow I had known very, well before the war. He was a shining light in society, occupying a high and responsible business position. His one fault was his good-fellowship and disposition to be convivial when off duty. He enlisted among the first, when the war broke out in 1861, and I did not see him again until one day one of this genus "bummer" strayed into our camp. He stuck his head into my tent and wanted to know how "Fred. Hitchcock was." I had to take a long second look to dig out from this bunch of rags and filth my one-time Beau Brummel acquaintance at home. His eyes were bleared, and told all too surely the cause of the transformation. His brag was that he had skipped every fight since he enlisted. "It's lots more fun," he said, "to climb a tree well in the rear and see the show. It's perfectly safe, you know, and then you

don't get yourself killed and planted. What is the use,"
he argued, " of getting killed and have a fine monument
erected over you, when you can't see it nor make any use
of it after it is done? Let the other fellows do that if
they want to. I've no use for monuments." Poor fellow,
his cynical ideas were his ruin. Better a thousand times
had he been " planted" at the front, manfully doing his
duty, than to save a worthless life and return with the
record of a poltroon, despised by himself and everybody
else.

This review by President Lincoln and the new com-
mander-in-chief, General Hooker, was, from a military,
spectacular point of view, the chief event of our army
experience. It included the whole of the great Army of
the Potomac, now numbering upward of one hundred
and thirty thousand men, probably its greatest numerical
strength of the whole war. Deducting picket details,
there were present on this review, it is safe to say, from
ninety thousand to one hundred thousand men. It was
a remarkable event historically, because so far as I can
learn it was the only time this great army was ever
paraded in line so that it could be seen all together. In
this respect it was the most magnificent military pageant
ever witnessed on this continent, far exceeding in its
impressive grandeur what has passed into history as the
" great review," which preceded the final " muster out"
at the close of the war in the city of Washington. At the
latter not more than ten thousand men could have been
seen at one time, probably not nearly so many, for the eye
could take in only the column which filled Pennsylvania
Avenue from the Capitol to the Treasury Building.

War from the Inside

Whereas, upon our review the army was first drawn up in what is known as three lines of "masses," and one glance of the eye could take in the whole army. Think of it! One hundred thousand men in one sweep of vision! If the word "Selah" in the Psalm means "stop! think! consider!" it would be particularly appropriate here.

A word now about the formation in "lines of masses." Each regiment was formed in column of divisions. To those unfamiliar with military terms, I must explain that this very common formation with large bodies of troops consists in putting two companies together as a division under the command of the senior officer, thus making of a regiment of ten companies a column of five divisions, each two-company front. This was known as "massing" the troops. When so placed in line they were called a line of "masses;" when marching, a column of "masses." It will be seen that the actual frontage of each regiment so formed was the width of two companies only, the other eight companies being formed in like manner in their rear. Now imagine four regiments so formed and placed side by side, fronting on the same line and separated from each other by say fifty feet, and you have a brigade line of masses. The actual frontage of a brigade so formed would be considerably less than that of a single regiment on dress parade. Now take three such brigades, separated from each other by say fifty feet, and you have a division line of masses. Three divisions made up an army corps. The army was formed in three lines of masses, of two corps each, on the large open plain opposite Fredericksburg, to the south and east of where the railroad crossed the river. Each of these lines of masses

The Winter at Falmouth

contained from seventy to eighty regiments of infantry, besides the artillery, which was paraded on the several lines at different intervals. I do not remember seeing any cavalry, and my impression is that this branch of the service was not represented. Some idea may be formed of the magnificence of this spectacle when I state that each of these lines of masses was more than a mile in length, and the depth of the three lines from front to rear, including the spaces between, was not less than four hundred yards, or about one-fifth of a mile. Each of the regiments displayed its two stands of silk colors, one the blue flag representing the State from which it came, the other the national colors. There were here and there a brace of these flags, very conspicuous in their brilliant newness, indicating a fresh accession to the army, but most of them were tattered and torn by shot and shell, whilst a closer look revealed the less conspicuous but more deadly slits and punctures of the minie-balls.

Now place yourself on the right of this army paraded for review and look down the long lines. Try to count the standards as the favoring wind lifts their sacred folds and caressingly shows you their battle scars. You will need to look very closely, lest those miniature penants, far away, whose staffs appear no larger than parlor matches protruding above lines of men, whose forms in the distance have long since merged into a mere bluish gray line, escape your eye. Your numbering will crowd the five hundred mark ere you finish, and you should remember that each of these units represented a thousand men when in the vigor and enthusiasm of patriotic manhood they bravely marched to the front. Only a fifth of them left?

you say. And the others? Ah! the battle, the hospital, the prison-pen, the h-ll of war, must be the answer.

How can words describe the scene? This is that magnificent old battered Army of the Potomac. Look upon it; you shall never behold its like again. There have been and may yet be many armies greater in numbers, and possibly, in all the paraphernalia of war, more showy. There can never be another Army of the Potomac, with such a history. As I gazed up and down those massive lines of living men, felt that I was one of them, and saw those battle-scarred flags kissed by the loving breeze, my blood tingled to my very finger-tips, my hair seemed almost to raise straight up, and I said a thousand Confederacies can't whip us. And here I think I grasped the main purpose of this review. It was not simply to give the President a sight of his " strong right arm," as he fondly called the Army of the Potomac, nor General Hooker, its new commander, an opportunity to see his men and them a chance to see their new chief,—though both of these were included,—but it was to give the army a square look at its mighty self, see how large and how strong it really was, that every man might thereby get the same enthusiasm and inspiration that I did, and know that it simply could not be beaten. The enemy, it is not strange to say, were intensely interested spectators of this whole scene, for the review was held in full view of the whole of their army. No place could have been chosen that would better have accommodated their enjoyment of the picture, if such it was, than that open plain, exactly in their front. And we could see them swarming over Marye's Heights and the lines to the south of it, intently gazing upon us. A scene more resplendent with military pageantry and the soul-stirring accessories of war they will never see again. But did it stir their blood? Yes; but with bitterness only, for they must have seen that the task before them of successfully resisting the onslaughts of this army was impossible. Here was disclosed, undoubtedly, another purpose of this grand review, viz., to let the enemy see with their own eyes how powerful the army was with which they had to contend.

A remarkable feature of this review was the marvellous celerity of its formation. The various corps and subdivisions of the army were started on the march for the reviewing ground so as to reach it at about the same time. It should be remembered that most of them were encamped from four to eight miles away. Aides-de-camp with markers by the score were already in position on the plain when the troops arrived, so that there was almost no delay in getting into position. As our column debouched upon the field, there seemed an inextricable mass of marching columns as far as the eye could see. Could order ever be gotten out of it? Yet, presto! the right of the line fell into position, a series of blue blocks, and then on down to the far left, block after block, came upon the line with unerring order and precision, as though it were a long curling whiplash straightening itself out to the tension of a giant hand. And so with each of the other two lines. All were formed simultaneously. Here was not only perfection of military evolution, but the poetry of rhythmic movement. The three lines were all formed within twenty minutes, ready for the reviewing officers.

War from the Inside

Almost immediately the blare of the trumpets announced the approach of the latter, and the tall form of the President was seen, accompanied by a large retinue, galloping down the first line. Our division was formed, as I recollect, in the first line, about three hundred yards from the right. The President was mounted on a large, handsome horse, and as he drew near I saw that immediately on his right rode his son, Robert Lincoln, then a bright-looking lad of fourteen to fifteen years, and little "Tad" Lincoln, the idol of his father, was on his left. The latter could not have been more than seven or eight years old. He was mounted on a large horse, and his little feet seemed to stick almost straight out from the saddle. He was round and pudgy, and his jolly little body bobbed up and down like a ball under the stiff canter of his horse. I wondered how he maintained his seat, but he was really a better horseman than his father, for just before reaching our regiment there was a little summer stream ravine, probably a couple of yards wide, that had to be jumped. The horses took it all right, but the President landed on the other side with a terrific jounce, being almost unseated. The boys went over flying, little "Tad" in high glee, like a monkey on a mustang.

Of course, a mighty cheer greeted the President as he galloped down the long line. There was something indescribably weird about that huzzah from the throats of these thousands of men, first full, sonorous, and thrilling, and then as it rolled down that attenuated line gradually fading into a minor strain until it was lost in the distance, only to reappear as the cavalcade returned in front of the second line, first the faintest note of a violin, then

The Winter at Falmouth

rapidly swelling into the full volume, to again die away and for the third time reappear and die away as the third line was reviewed. The President was followed by a large staff dressed in full uniform, which contrasted strongly with his own severely plain black. He wore a high silk hat and a plain frock coat. His face wore that peculiar sombre expression we see in all his photographs, but it lighted up into a half-smile as he occasionally lifted his hat in acknowledgment of the cheering of the men.

About one hundred yards in rear of the President's staff came the new commanding general, " Fighting Joe." He was dressed in the full uniform of a major-general, and was accompanied by his chief of staff, Seth Williams —he who had held this position under every commander of the Army of the Potomac thus far—and a large and brilliant staff. There must have been fully twenty officers of various ranks, from his chief of staff, a general, down through all grades to a lieutenant, in this corps of staff officers. It was the first time I had seen General Hooker to know him. His personal appearance did not belie his reputation. He had a singularly strong, handsome face, sat his superb horse like a king, broad-shouldered and elegantly proportioned in form, with a large, fine head, well covered with rather long hair, now as white as the driven snow and flowing in the wind as he galloped down the line, chapeau in hand; he was a striking and picturesque figure. It was evident the head of the army had lost nothing in personal appearance by its recent change. The same cheering marked the appearance of " Fighting Joe" which had greeted the President, as he and staff galloped down and up and down through the three long lines.

Both reviewing cavalcades moved at a brisk gallop, and occupied only about twenty minutes covering the three miles of lines; and then the President and staff took position, for the marching review, some distance in front and about midway of the lines. Instantly the scene was transformed. The first line wheeled into column by brigades successively and, headed by General Hooker and staff, moved rapidly forward. There were but few bands, and the drum corps had been consolidated into division corps. On passing the President, General Hooker took position by his side and remained throughout the remainder of the ceremony. The troops marched in columns of masses, in the same formation they had stood in line; that is, in column of two companies front and only six yards between divisions. This made a very compact mass of troops, quite unusual in reviews, but was necessary in order to avoid the great length of time that in the usual formation would have been required for the passing of this vast body of men. Yet in this close formation the balance of the day was nearly consumed in marching past the President.

It must have been a trying ordeal to him, as he had to lift his hat as each stand of colors successively dipped in passing. Immediately on passing the President, the several brigades were wheeled out of the column and ordered to quarters. I remember that we returned to our camp, over a mile distant, dismissed the men, and then several of us officers rode back to see the continuation of the pageant. When we got back the second line was only

The Winter at Falmouth

well on its way, which meant that only about half the army had passed in review. We could see from fifteen to twenty thousand men in column—that is to say, about one army corps—at a time. The quick, vigorous step, in rhythmical cadence to the music, the fife and drum, the massive swing, as though every man was actually a part of every other man; the glistening of bayonets like a long ribbon of polished steel, interspersed with the stirring effects of those historic flags, in countless numbers, made a picture impressive beyond the power of description. A picture of the ages. How glad I am to have looked upon it. I could not remain to see the end. When finally I was compelled to leave the third line was marching. I can still see that soul-thrilling column, that massive swing, those flaunting colors, that sheen of burnished steel! Majestic! Incomparable!! Glorious!!!

CHAPTER XV

An interesting item in the experience that winter at Falmouth was the celebration of St. Patrick's day by the Irish brigade and their multitude of friends. They were encamped about a mile to the south of our brigade upon a beautiful, broad, open plain between the surrounding hills, which gave them a superb parade and drill-ground. Upon this they had laid out a mile race track in excellent shape, and they had provided almost every conceivable sort of amusement that was possible to army life— matches in running, jumping, boxing, climbing the greased pole, sack races, etc. But the usual pig performance had to be omitted owing to the enforced absence of the pig. The appearance of a live porker would have stampeded the army in a wild chase for fresh meat.

The chief events were horse races. The army abounded in excellent thoroughbreds, private property of officers, and all were anxious to show the mettle of their steeds. Everybody was invited to be present and take such part as he pleased in any of the events. It was a royal gala day to the army; from morning until night there were excitement and side-splitting amusement. Nor was there,

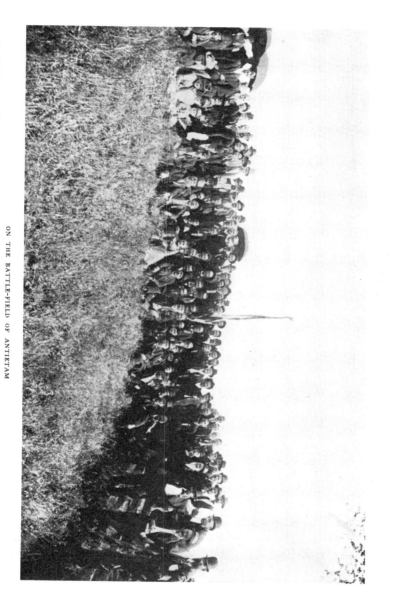

ON THE BATTLE-FIELD OF ANTIETAM

Fourth Reunion of Survivors of 132d Regiment P. V., held Sept. 17, 1891, on the ground occupied by the Regiment during the battle, in front of Sunken Road, near Roulette House

The Battle of Chancellorsville

throughout the whole day, a thing, not even a small fight, that I heard of, to mar the wholesome fun, until towards night our old enemy, John Barleycorn, managed to get in some of his work.

The chief event of the day and the wind-up was a hurdle and ditch race, open to officers only. Hurdles and ditches alternated the course at a distance of two hundred yards, except at the finish, where a hurdle and ditch were together, the ditch behind the hurdle. Such a race was a hare-brained performance in the highest degree; but so was army life at its best, and this was not out of keeping with its surroundings. Excitement was what was wanted, and this was well calculated to produce it.

The hurdles were four and five feet high and did not prove serious obstacles to the jumpers, but the ditches, four and five feet wide and filled with water, proved a *bête noir* to most of the racers. Some twenty-five, all young staff-officers, started, but few got beyond the first ditch. Many horses that took the hurdle all right positively refused the ditch. Several officers were dumped at the first hurdle, and two were thrown squarely over their horses' heads into the first ditch, and were nice-looking specimens as they crawled out of that bath of muddy water. They were unhurt, however, and re-mounted and tried it again, with better success.

The crowning incident of the day occurred at the finish of this race at the combination hurdle and ditch. Out of the number who started, only three had compassed safely all the hurdles and ditches and come to the final leap. The horses were about a length apart each. The first took the hurdle in good shape, but failed to reach the further bank of the ditch and fell over sideways into it, carrying down his rider. Whilst they were struggling to get out, the second man practically repeated the performance and fell on the first pair, and the rear man, now unable to check his horse, spurred him over, only to fall on the others. It was a fearful sight for a moment, and it seemed certain that the officers were killed or suffocated in that water, now thick with mud. But a hundred hands were instantly to the rescue, and in less time than it takes to tell it all were gotten out and, strange to say, the horses were unhurt and only one officer seriously injured, a broken leg only to the bad for the escapade. But neither officers nor horses were particularly handsome as they emerged from that ditch. The incident can be set down as a terrific finale to this first and last army celebration of St. Patrick's day.

The tedium of routine duty occupied our time without specially exciting incident until pleasanter weather towards the middle of April brought rumors of impending army movements again. About April 20 we heard the cavalry under Stoneman were on the move, and this was confirmed the next day, when I saw that general with quite a body of cavalry marching leisurely north. The horses appeared in excellent condition after a winter of partial rest. General Stoneman was a large man, with short gray whiskers and gray hair and a strikingly bronzed red face. This story was told of him anent this movement, that Hooker had told him to do something with his horses; to cross the river at one of the fords above and shake out his cavalry, that it was " about time the army saw a dead cavalryman." Stoneman had replied, asking for materials to build bridges with, and "Fighting Joe" had impatiently replied that he wouldn't "give a d—n for a cavalryman who couldn't make a bridge without materials," meaning who could not cross a river without a bridge.

Soon orders came to supply ourselves with extra ammunition, and be prepared to move with six days' rations at a moment's notice. This settled it that "business" was about to commence again in earnest. What the contemplated movement was we had not the remotest idea, though we knew, of course, it was to be another whack in some form at the Johnnies on the other side of the river. We set about disposing of all surplus baggage which had accumulated for winter quarters, and putting everything in trim for field living once more. We could now see columns of troops in the distance marching north. Was the new movement, then, to be in that direction? This was the topic upon all lips. The desire to know something of what was being done with us was naturally very strong. Where were we going? What were we going to do? Yet a desire that in the nature of things could not be satisfied. One can have no conception of the feeling of going day after day blindly ahead, not knowing whither or why; knowing only that sooner or later you are going to fetch up against a fight, and calculating from your surroundings the probabilities of when.

We felt one satisfaction, however, that this was to be our last campaign as a regiment. Most of our men had enlisted in the July previous for nine months, and their time was now practically out; but, to their credit be it said, they would not raise this question during an active movement. There were troops who threw down their arms on the eve of battle and refused to go into action because their time was out. Such action has been severely criticised, and I think uncharitably. After a man has honorably and patriotically served his full time and is entitled to his discharge, it would seem pretty hard to force him to go into battle and be killed or wounded. Nevertheless, as a matter of fact, nearly this whole campaign was overtime for most of our regiment, yet the question was not raised.

On April 28 our corps broke camp and joined the column northward. The winter's rest had brought some accessions to our ranks from the sick and wounded, though the severe picket duty and the excessively damp weather had given us a large sick list. We had, to start with, upward of three hundred and seventy-five men, to which was added some twenty-five or thirty from the sick list, who came up to us on the march. It is a curious fact that many men left sick in camp, unable to march when the regiment leaves, will get themselves together after the former has been gone a few hours and pull out to overtake it. I saw men crying like children because the surgeon had forbidden them going with the regiment. The loneliness and homesickness, or whatever you please to call it, after the regiment has gone are too much for them. They simply cannot endure it, and so they strike out and follow. They will start by easy marches, and they generally improve in health from the moment they start. Courage and nerve are both summoned for

The Battle of Chancellorsville

the effort, and the result is that at the end of the second or third day they rejoin the regiment and report for duty. This does not mean that they were not really sick, but that will power and exercise have beaten the disease. I have heard many a sick man say he would rather die than be left behind.

We marched about six miles the first day, much of our route being through a wooded country, some of it so wet and spongy that corduroy roads had to be built for the wagons and artillery. The army can, as a rule, move as rapidly as it can move its artillery and supply trains, and no faster. Of course, for short distances and special expeditions, where circumstances require, both cavalry and infantry move very rapidly, ignoring the wagon trains and artillery; but on a general campaign this is impossible, and so where the ground is bad these must be helped along. In a wooded country the usual method is by corduroy road. Extra details are made to assist the pioneer corps, who cut down young saplings three to six inches in diameter and about six feet in length and lay them side by side on the ground, which is roughly levelled to receive them. They do not make a handsome road to speed over, but they bear up the artillery and army schooners, and that is all that is wanted of them.

The second day we crossed the Rappahannock at United States ford on a pontoon bridge. There had been a sharp skirmish here when the first troops crossed a couple of days before, and a battery of artillery was still in position guarding the crossing. We now began to experience once more the unmistakable symptoms of approaching battle,—sharp spurts of cannonading at irregular intervals some distance to the south and west of us, with the hurry of marching troops, ambulances and stretcher corps towards the front; more or less of army débris scattered about, and the nervous bustle everywhere apparent. We reached the famous Chancellorsville House shortly after midnight. This was an old-time hostelry, situated on what was called the Culpeper plank-road. It stood with two or three smaller houses in a cleared square space containing some twenty or thirty acres, in the midst of the densest forest of trees and undergrowth I ever saw. We had marched all day on plank and corduroy roads, through this wild tanglewood forest, most of the time in a drizzling rain, and we had been much delayed by the artillery trains, and it was after midnight when we reached our destination. The distance marched must have been twelve or more miles, and our men became greatly fatigued towards the last.

It was my first experience with the regiment on the march in the field in my new position as major. As adjutant my place had been with the colonel at the head of the column. Now my duties required me to march in the rear and keep up the stragglers. After nightfall it became intensely dark, and at each rest the men would drop down just where they were and would be instantly sound asleep. Whether they dropped down into mud or not made little difference to many of them, for they were soaking wet and were so exhausted that they did not care. My troubles began when the " forward" was sounded, to arouse these seeming logs and get them on their feet once more and started. All who were practically exhausted had drifted to the rear and were on my hands. We had

The Battle of Chancellorsville

a provost guard in the rear, whose duty it was to bring up every man and permit no straggling, but they were in almost as bad a plight as the rest of the regiment. To arouse these sleeping men I had occasionally to resort to a smart blow with the flat of my sword and follow it up with the most energetic orders and entreaties. An appeal to their pluck and nerve was generally sufficient, and they would summon new courage and push manfully on. My own condition was scarcely better than that of the men. I rode that night considerable distances between our halts for rest, sitting bolt upright in my saddle fast asleep. I had all day alternated with some of the men in marching whilst they rode, and was not only thoroughly tired, but wet through. The march was much more trying to us because of our unseasoned condition owing to the long winter's exemption from this exercise. Furthermore, we had been marching towards the firing, and were under the nervous strain always incident to operations in the presence of the enemy. Nothing will quicker exhaust men than the nervous tension occasioned by the continued firing which indicates the imminence of a battle.

At daylight we were aroused and under arms again. We found we were at the head-quarters of the army. The Chancellorsville House, which had been vacated by its occupants, was used for office purposes, and much of the open space around it was occupied by the tents of General Hooker and staff and hospital tents. Of the latter there were three or four pitched so as to connect with each other, and over them was flying the yellow flag of the corps hospital. The First and Third Divisions of our Second Corps were massed in this Chancellorsville square,

beside Pettit's battery. Our brigade now consisted of
the Fourth New York, First Delaware, and our regiment.
The first named was sent off on some guard duty, which
left Colonel Albright, of our regiment, the senior officer
in command of the brigade. The ominous rattle of musketry not far away became momentarily more pronounced, and ambulances and stretcher-carriers were passing back and forth to the hospitals, carrying wounded
men. The dead body of a regular army captain was soon
brought back from the front, where Sykes's division of
regulars was sharply engaged. I do not know the name
of this captain, but he was a fine-looking young officer.
He had been killed by a minie-ball squarely through his
forehead.

We were marching out the plank-road as they brought
this body in. Passing out of the clearing, the woods and
undergrowth each side the road was so dense that we
could not see into it a half-dozen steps. We had gone
possibly a quarter of a mile when we were overtaken by
a staff-officer, who in whispers ordered us to turn back,
regardless of orders from the front, and get back to the
Chancellorsville House as rapidly as possible, and to do
so absolutely noiselessly; that a heavy force of rebels
were in the woods on both sides of us, and we were in
great danger of being cut to pieces and captured. We
obeyed, and he rapidly worked his way to the front of
the brigade and succeeded very quickly in getting us all
safely out. We formed line near the Chancellorsville
House and were resting on our arms when I noticed
another brigade going down that same road from which
we had just been so hurriedly gotten out. The circum-

stance was so strange that I inquired what brigade it was, and learned that it was Colonel (afterwards Governor) James A. Beaver's brigade of Hancock's division of our corps. They had been gone but a short time when the rebels opened upon them from both sides of the road, and they were very roughly handled. Colonel Beaver was soon brought back, supposed mortally wounded. I saw him as he was brought to the rear. It was said he was shot through the body. Afterwards, whilst he was governor, I mentioned the circumstance to him, and asked how he succeeded in fighting off the last enemy at that time. He said he then fully believed his wound was mortal. The bullet had struck him nearly midway of his body and appeared to have passed through and out of his back, and he was bleeding freely. He was brought to the hospital, where the corps surgeon—his own family physician at home—found him, and with an expression of countenance indicating the gravest fear proceeded to examine his wound. Suddenly, with a sigh of relief, he exclaimed: " Colonel, you are all right; the ball has struck a rib and followed it around and out." It was one of the hundreds of remarkable freaks performed by those ugly minie-balls during the war. Why that brigade should have been allowed to march into that ambuscade, from which we had so narrowly escaped, I could not understand. It was one of the early *faux pas* of that unfortunate comedy, rather tragedy of errors,—battle.

In view of the events of the next two days, it will be interesting to recall the somewhat windy order published to the army by General Hooker on the morning of the 1st of May, the date of the first day's battle, on which the

War from the Inside

events narrated in the last chapter occurred. This is the order:

HEAD-QUARTERS ARMY OF THE POTOMAC,
CAMP NEAR FALMOUTH, VA., April 30, 1863.

It is with heartfelt satisfaction the commanding general announces to the army that the operations of the last three days have determined that our enemy must either ingloriously fly or come out from behind his defences and give us battle on our own ground, when certain destruction awaits him.

*　　*　　*　　*　　*　　*　　*　　*

By command of Major-General Hooker.

S. WILLIAMS,
Asst. Adjt.-Gen'l.

My recollection recalls a phrase in this order reading something like this: " We have got the enemy where God Almighty can't save him, and he must either ingloriously," etc. I have been surprised not to find it in the records, and my memory is not alone in this respect, for a lieutenant-colonel of Portland, Me., in his account of this battle alludes to Hooker's blasphemous order.

The purpose of this order was to encourage the men and inspire them with the enthusiasm of forthcoming victory. But when we consider that the portion of the army operating around Chancellorsville was at that very moment apparently as thoroughly caged up in a wilderness of almost impenetrable undergrowth, which made it impossible to move troops, and into which one could not see a dozen feet, as though they were actually behind iron bars, it will be seen how little ground there was for encouragement. I can think of no better comparison of the situation than to liken it to a fleet of ships enveloped in a dense fog endeavoring to operate against another having the advantage of the open.

The Battle of Chancellorsville

It will be remembered that when this movement commenced the Army of the Potomac numbered from one hundred and twenty thousand to one hundred and thirty thousand men, about double the opposing rebel force. Hooker divided this army, taking with him four corps, numbering probably seventy thousand men, to operate from Chancellorsville towards Fredericksburg, and leaving three corps, about fifty thousand men, under Sedgwick, to move upon the latter place from below. The purpose was to get Lee's army between these two forces and crush him. All historians of this battle agree that up to a certain point Hooker's strategy was most admirable. General Pleasanton, who commanded our cavalry forces in that action, says that up to a certain point the movement on Chancellorsville was one of the most brilliant in the annals of war. He put that point at the close of Thursday, April 30. He had made a full reconnoissance of all that country and had informed General Hooker of the nature of the ground, that for a depth of from four to five miles it was all unbroken tanglewood of the densest undergrowth, in which it was impossible to manœuvre an army or to know anything of the movements of the enemy; that beyond this wilderness the country was open and well adapted to military movements, and he had taken occasion to urge upon him the importance of moving forward at once, so as to meet the enemy in open ground, but his information and advice, he tells us, fell upon leaden ears.

Lee had, up to this time, no information of the movement upon Chancellorsville, having been wholly occupied with Sedgwick at Fredericksburg. The former was therefore a complete surprise to him. The "golden moment," according to Pleasanton, to move forward anᵈ carry the battle out into the open, where the army could have been handled and would have had a chance, was on that day, as instantly the movement was disclosed, the enemy, being familiar with every foot of the country, would detach a sufficient force to operate in the open, and along the edge of the wilderness could keep us practically bottled up there and beat us in detail; and that is precisely what seems to have been done. The inexplicable question is, Why did fighting "Joe Hooker," with seventy thousand as good troops as ever fired a gun, sit down in the middle of that tanglewood forest and allow Lee to make a monkey of him while Sedgwick was doing such magnificent work below?

Two distinguished participants in all these events holding high commands, namely, General Alfred Pleasanton, quoted above, and General Doubleday, commanding First Division, First Army Corps, have written articles upon this battle, agreeing on the feasibility and brilliancy of the movement, but by inference and things unsaid have practically left the same question suspended in the air. It is possible the correct answer should not now be given.

To return to our own doings, on that Friday, 1st of May, our division was drawn up in line of battle in front of the Chancellorsville House, and we were permitted to rest on our arms. This meant that any moment we might be expected to move forward. The battle was now on in earnest. Heavy firing was heard some miles below us, which was Sedgwick's work at Fredericksburg. Nearer by there was cannonading and more or less severe mus-

The Battle of Chancellorsville

ketry firing. Ambulances and stretcher-carriers were constantly coming back from the front with wounded soldiers, taking them to the field hospital, which was just in our rear, and we could see the growing piles of amputated legs and arms which were thrown outside with as little care as if they were so many pieces of wood. We were evidently waiting for something, nobody seemed to know what. Everything appeared to be " at heads." Our corps and division commanders, Couch, Hancock, and French, with their staffs, were in close proximity to the troops, and all seemed to be in a condition of nervous uncertainty. What might be progressing in those black woods in front, was the question. A nearer volley of musketry would start everybody up, and we would stand arms in hand, as if expecting the unseen enemy to burst through the woods upon us. Then the firing would slacken and we would drop down again for a time.

In the mean time shells were screeching over us continually, and an occasional bullet would whiz uncomfortably near. The nervous strain under such conditions may be imagined. This state of affairs continued all through Friday night and most of Saturday. Of course, sleep was out of the question for any of our officers. On Thursday and Friday nights the men got snatches of sleep, lying on their arms, between the times all were aroused against some fresh alarm.

On Saturday some beef cattle were driven up and slaughtered in the open square in front of our lines, and the details were progressing with the work of preparing the meat for issue when the storm of disaster of Saturday afternoon burst upon us and their work was rudely interrupted. We had anxious premonitions of this impending storm for some hours. Captain Pettit, who commanded the famous battery of that name, which was posted immediately in our rear, had spent much of his time in the forenoon of Saturday high up in a tall tree which stood just in front of the Chancellorsville House and close to our line, with his field glass reconnoitring. Several times he had come down with information that heavy bodies of the enemy were massing for a blow upon our front and where he believed they would strike. This information, we were told, he imparted to Hooker's chief of staff, and begged permission to open at long range with his rifled guns, but no attention was paid to him. I saw him up the tree and heard some of his ejaculating, which indicated that he was almost wild with apprehension of what was coming. Once on coming down he remarked to General Hancock that we would " catch h—l in less than an hour." The latter seemed to be thoroughly alive to the situation and exceedingly anxious, as were Couch and French, to do something to prepare for what was coming, yet nothing more was done until suddenly the firing, which had been growing in volume and intensity and gradually drawing nearer, developed in a storm of musketry of terrific fury immediately in our right front, apparently not more than three hundred yards away.

We could not see a thing. What there might be between us and it, or whether it was the onslaught of the enemy or the firing of our troops, we knew not. But we had not long to wait. Soon stragglers, few in numbers, began to appear, emerging from the woods into our clearing, and then more of them, these running, and then

The Battle of Chancellorsville

almost at once an avalanche of panic-stricken, flying men without arms, without knapsacks, many bareheaded, swearing, cursing, a wild, frenzied mob tearing to the rear. Instantly they began to appear, General Couch, commanding our corps, took in the situation and deployed two divisions to catch and hold the fugitives. Part of the Third Corps was also deployed on our left. We were ordered to charge bayonets and permit no man to pass through our ranks. We soon had a seething, howling mob of Dutchmen twenty to thirty feet in depth in front of our line, holding them back on the points of our bayonets, and still they came. Every officer of our division, with drawn sword and pistol, was required to use all possible endeavor to hold them, and threatening to shoot the first man who refused to stand as ordered. General French and staff were galloping up and down our division line assisting in this work.

In the mean time another line of battle was rapidly thrown in between these fugitives and the woods to stay the expected advance of the enemy. This was the famous break of the Eleventh Corps, starting with Blenker's division and finally extending through the whole corps, some fifteen thousand men. It seemed as though the whole army was being stampeded. We soon had a vast throng of these fugitives dammed up in our front, a terrible menace to the integrity of our own line as well as of all in our rear. We were powerless to do anything should the enemy break through, and were in great danger of being ourselves swept away and disintegrated by this frantic mob. All this time the air was filled with shrieking shells from our own batteries as well as those of the enemy, doing, however, little damage beyond adding to the terror of the situation. The noise was deafening. Pandemonium seemed to reign supreme in our front. Our line, as well as that of the Third Corps on our left, was holding firm as a rock. I noticed a general officer, I thought it was General Sickles, was very conspicuous in the vigor of his efforts to hold the line. A couple of fugitives had broken through his line and were rapidly going to the rear. I heard him order them to halt and turn back. One of them turned and cast a look at him, but paid no further attention to his order. He repeated the order in stentorian tones, this time with his pistol levelled, but it was not obeyed, and he fired, dropping the first man dead in his tracks. He again ordered the other man to halt, and it was sullenly obeyed. These men seemed to be almost stupid, deaf to orders or entreaty in their frenzy.

An incident in our own front will illustrate. I noticed some extra commotion near our colors and rushed to see the cause. I found an officer with drawn sword threatening to run the color-sergeant through if he was not allowed to pass. He was a colonel and evidently a German. My orders to him to desist were answered with a curse, and I had to thrust my pistol into his face, with an energetic threat to blow his head off if he made one more move, before he seemed to come to his senses. I then appealed to him to see what an example he as an officer was setting, and demanded that he should get to work and help to stem the flight of his men rather than assist in their demoralization. To his credit be it said, he at once regained his better self, and thenceforth did splendid work up and down amongst these German fugitives, and later on, when they were moved to the rear, he rendered very material assistance. I did not learn who he was, but he was a splendid-looking officer and spoke both English and German fluently.

One may ask why those men should have lost their heads so completely. To answer the question intelligently, one needs to put oneself into their place. The facts as we were told at the time were: That the Eleventh Corps, which contained two divisions of German troops, under Schurz and Blenker (I think Steinwehr commanded the latter division in this action), was posted on the right of Hooker's line in the woods, some distance in front and to the right of the Chancellorsville House. That at the time Stonewall Jackson made his famous atttack, above referred to, he caught one of those divisions " napping"—off their guard. They had stacked their guns and knapsacks, and were back some twenty yards, making their evening coffee, when suddenly the rebel skirmishers burst through the brush upon them, followed immediately by the main line, and before they realized it were between these troops and their guns. Consternation reigned supreme in an instant and a helter-skelter flight followed. Jackson followed up this advantage with his usual impetuosity, and although the other divisions of the Eleventh made an effort to hold their ground, this big hole in the line was fatal to them and all were quickly swept away. Of course, the division and brigade commanders were responsible for that unpardonable carelessness. No valid excuse can be made for such criminal want of watchfulness, especially for troops occupying a front line, and which had

War from the Inside

heard, or should have heard, as we a half mile farther in the rear had, all the premonitions of the coming storm. But it was an incident showing the utter folly of the attempt to maintain a line of battle in the midst of a dense undergrowth, through which nothing could be seen. It is exceedingly doubtful whether they could have held their line against Jackson's onset under those conditions had they been on the alert, for he would have been on and over them almost before they could have seen him. To resist such an onset needs time to deliver a steady volley and then be ready with the bayonet.

It was towards six o'clock in the evening when this flying mob struck our lines, and darkness had fallen before we were rid of them and something like order had been restored. In the mean time it certainly seemed as if everything was going to pieces. I got a little idea of what a panic-stricken army means. The fearful thing about it was, we knew it was terribly contagious, and that with all the uncertainties in that black wilderness from which this mob came and the pandemonium in progress all about us, it might seize our own troops and we be swept away to certain destruction in spite of all our efforts. It is said death rides on horseback with a fleeing army. Nothing can be more horrible. Hence a panic must be stopped, cost what it may. Night undoubtedly came to our rescue with this one.

One of the most heroic deeds I saw done to help stem the fleeing tide of men and restore courage was not the work of a battery, nor a charge of cavalry, but the charge of a band of music! The band of the Fourteenth Connecticut went right out into that open space between our

The Battle of Chancellorsville

new line and the rebels, with shot and shell crashing all about them, and played " The Star-Spangled Banner," the " Red, White, and Blue," and " Yankee Doodle," and repeated them for fully twenty minutes. They never played better. Did that require nerve? It was undoubtedly the first and only band concert ever given under such conditions. Never was American grit more finely illustrated. Its effect upon the men was magical. Imagine the strains of our grand national hymn, " The Star-Spangled Banner," suddenly bursting upon your ears out of that horrible pandemonium of panic-born yells, mingled with the roaring of musketry and the crashing of artillery. To what may it be likened? The carol of birds in the midst of the blackest thunder-storm? No simile can be adequate. Its strains were clear and thrilling for a moment, then smothered by that fearful din, an instant later sounding bold and clear again, as if it would fearlessly emphasize the refrain, " Our flag is still there."

CHAPTER XVI

THE BATTLE OF CHANCELLORSVILLE—CONTINUED

RECURRING again to the incident of the band playing out there between the two hostile lines in the midst of that panic of the Eleventh Corps, it was a remarkable circumstance that none of them were killed. I think one or two were slightly wounded by pieces of exploding shells, and one or two of their instruments carried away scars from that scene. The rebels did not follow up their advantage, as we expected, probably owing to the effective work of our batteries, otherwise they would all have been either killed or captured. None of the enemy came into our clearing that I saw. We must have corralled upward of eight thousand of our demoralized men. Some had their arms, most of them had none, which confirmed the story of their surprise narrated in the last chapter. They were marched to the rear under guard, and thus the further spread of the panic was avoided.

It was now dark and the firing ceased, but only for a few moments, for the two picket-lines were posted so close together, neither knowing exactly where the other was, that both were exceedingly nervous; and the slightest movement, the stepping of a picket, the scurry of a rabbit, would set the firing going again. First it would be the firing of a single musket, then the quick rattle of a half-dozen, then the whole line with the reserves, for all were on the line together there; and then the batteries, of which there were now at least a half-dozen massed right around us, would open with terrific vigor, all firing into the darkness, whence the enemy was supposed to be coming. This continued at short intervals all night long.

After the mob of fugitives had been disposed of, our division had formed in line of battle directly in front of the Chancellorsville House, supporting the provisional line which had been hurriedly thrown in to cover the break of the Eleventh Corps, and we were " resting (?) on our arms." At each of these alarms every man was instantly on his feet, with guns at a " ready." General French and staff were close to us, and General Couch and his staff only a few feet away. All were exceedingly nervous and keenly on the alert. It was a night of terrific experience long to be remembered.

The nervous strain upon all was simply awful. We knew that the Eleventh Corps had been stampeded by the impetuous charge of Stonewall Jackson, and we felt sure he would seek to reap the fruits of the break he had made by an effort to pierce our centre, and this we would have to meet and repel when it came. We did not then know that in the general mix-up of that fateful afternoon that able and intrepid leader had himself fallen and was then dying. This fact, fortunate for us, undoubtedly accounts for the failure of the expected onset to materialize. We could probably have held him, for we had two divisions of the Second Corps and part of the Third Corps in double lines, all comparatively fresh, and before midnight the First Corps was in position on our right. But the slaughter would have been horrible.

War from the Inside

After midnight these outbursts became less frequent, and we officers lay down with the men and tried to sleep. I do not think any of our general officers or their staffs even sat down that whole night, so apprehensive were they of the descent of the rebels upon our position. I said in the last chapter that on Saturday morning some beef cattle were slaughtered near our line for issue to our division; that the work of distribution had not been completed before the panic came, and then these carcasses of beef were between ours and the rebel line on "debatable ground." This was too much for some of our men, and two or three crawled out to them during the night and helped themselves to such cuts as they could make from our side. One party next day told of being surprised by hearing cutting on the other side of the beef, and found, on investigating, that a "Johnny" was there, when the following colloquy took place:

"Hello, Johnny, are ye there?"

"Yes, Yank; too bad to let this 'fresh' spoil. I say, Yank, lend me your knife, mine's a poor one. We 'uns and you 'uns is all right here. Yank, I'll help you if you'll help me, and we'll get all we want."

The knife was passed over, and these two foes helped each other in that friendly darkness. How much actual truth there was in this story I do not know, but I do know that there was considerable fresh beef among the men in the morning, and it was not at all unlikely that the Johnnies also profited by the presence of that "fresh" between the lines. Soldiers of either army would run almost any risk to get a bit of fresh beef.

The next morning we were ordered to pile up our

The Battle of Chancellorsville

knapsacks and make a breastwork of them for such protection as they might afford, in anticipation of the still
expected attack. We managed to make a cup of coffee
and eat a hardtack without getting off our guard for an
instant, and about ten o'clock the First Brigade, now
Carroll's, and ours, consisting of two regiments only, the
First Delaware and ours, under command of our Colonel
Albright, were ordered forward into the woods to the
right of the Chancellorsville House. This was the opening of the third day's battle. We moved forward in
excellent line until we struck the edge of the woods. The
moment the crackling of the brush under our feet apprised
the enemy of our advance we received a heavy volley,
which must have been very hurriedly delivered, for it
passed over our heads, not a man being hit, I think. The
morning was lowering and misty and the air very light,
so that the smoke made by the rebel volley, not more
than fifty yards away, hung like a chalk line and indicated
their exact position. The sudden retirement of our lieutenant-colonel at this point placed the command of the
regiment on me, and I shouted to the men to aim below
that line of smoke and then gave the order, fire by battalion, and we emptied our guns as one man, reloaded,
and receiving no reply to our volley, moved forward
through the thick brush and undergrowth. We soon
came upon the rebel line, and a dreadful sight it was.
The first officer I saw was a rebel captain, an Irishman.
He ejaculated, " We're all killed! We're all killed!" and
offered to surrender. The commanding officer must have
suffered the fate of his men. Most of them were either
killed or wounded. The hundred or so living promptly

threw down their arms, and Colonel Albright sent them to the rear under guard. This Irish captain vouchsafed the remark sotto voce that he was glad to be captured, that he'd been trying to get out of the d—n Confederacy for a year. Our battalion volley had exactly reached its mark and had done fearful execution. There must have been more than two hundred lying there either dead or wounded, marking their line of battle. This was the only instance in my war experience where we delivered a volley as a battalion. The usual order of firing in line of battle is by " file," each man firing as rapidly as he can effectively, without regard to any other man. The volley they had delivered at us was a battalion volley, and it would have effectively disposed of our advance had it been well delivered. Fortunately for us, it was not, and their smoke-line gave us the opportunity to deliver a very effective counter-stroke. It had to be quickly done, we were so close together. There was no time to meditate. It was us or them. Instantly I resolved to give them all we could, aiming well under their line of smoke, and take our chances with the bayonet if necessary. The order was calmly given and the volley was coolly delivered. I have never heard a better one. The value of coolness in delivering and the effectiveness of such a volley were clearly demonstrated in this instance.

We again moved forward, working our way through the tangled undergrowth, and had gained probably five or six hundred yards when we encountered another line, and sharp firing began on both sides. We could see the enemy dodging behind trees and stumps not more than one hundred yards away. We also utilized the same

The Battle of Chancellorsville

shelter, and therefore suffered comparatively little. Suddenly I found bullets beginning to come from our left and rear as well as from our front. Two of these bullets had been aimed at me as I stood behind a small tree on our line. The first knowledge I had of them was from the splinters of bark in my face from the tree, first one and then the other in quick succession as the bullets struck, not more than three inches from my head. They were fairly good shots. I was thankful they were no better. But now I had to move a couple of companies to the left to meet this flank attack. It did not prove a serious matter, and the enemy was quickly driven back. The same thing was tried shortly after on our right flank, and was again disposed of the same way. They were probably groups of sharpshooters hunting for our officers. One of them, I happened to know, never went back, for I saw one of our sergeants kill him. I was at that moment standing by him, when he clapped his hand to his ear and exclaimed, " That was a ' hot one,' " as a bullet just ticked it. " There is the devil who did it. See him behind that bush?" and with that he aimed and fired. The fellow rolled over dead.

We soon had the better of this fighting and our opponents withdrew. We seemed now to be isolated. We must have been nearly a half mile from where we entered the woods. We could not see nor hear of any troops on our immediate right or left. Colonel Albright came back to consult as to what was best to be done now. The brush and undergrowth were exceedingly dense. What there might be on our right or left we could not know without sending skirmishers out. The colonel said his orders

15

225

were to advance and engage the enemy. No orders had come to him since our advance commenced, two hours and more before. We had met and beaten two lines of the enemy. Should we continue the advance or retire and get further orders? My advice was to retire; that with our small force, not more than five hundred men, isolated in that dense wood, we were liable to be gobbled up. The colonel agreed with this view and ordered the line faced about and marched to the rear. I mention this consultation over the situation because here we were, two young men, who knew almost nothing about military matters beyond obeying orders, suddenly called upon to exercise judgment in a critical situation. Bravery suggested push ahead and fight. To retire savored of overprudence. Nevertheless, it seemed to us we had no business remaining out there without connection with other troops on either right or left, and this decided the colonel to order the retreat.

We moved back in line of battle in excellent order and quite leisurely, having no opposition and, so far as we knew, no troops following us. We came out into the clearing just where we had entered the woods two hours before. But here we met a scene that almost froze our blood. During our absence some half-dozen batteries, forty or more guns, had been massed here. Hurried earthworks had been thrown up, covering the knapsacks our brigade had left there when we advanced. These guns were not forty yards away and were just waiting the order to open on those woods right where we were. As we emerged from the brush, our colors, fortunately, were a little in advance, and showed through before the line appeared. Their timely appearance, we were told, saved us from being literally blown to pieces by those batteries. A second later the fatal order would have been given and our brigade would have been wiped out of existence by our own guns!

As we came out of the woods an aide galloped down to us, his face perfectly livid, and in a voice portraying the greatest excitement shouted to Colonel Albright: " What in h—l and d-mnation are you doing here? Get out of here! Those woods are full of rebel troops, and we are just waiting to open on them." Albright replied very coolly, " Save your ammunition. There is not a rebel within a half mile, for we have just marched back that distance absolutely unmolested. Why haven't you sent us orders? We went in here two hours ago, and not an order have we received since." He replied, " We have sent a dozen officers in to you with orders, and they all reported that you had been captured." Albright answered, " They were a lot of cowards, for there hasn't been a minute since we advanced that an officer could not have come directly to us. There is something wrong about this. I will go and see General Hooker." And directing me to move the troops away from the front of those guns, he started for General Hooker's head-quarters, only a short distance away. As I was passing the right of that line of batteries a voice hailed me, and I turned, and there stood one of my old Scranton friends, Captain Frank P. Amsden, in command of his battery. Said he, as he gripped my hand, " Boy, you got out of those woods just in time. Our guns are double-shotted with grape and canister; the word ' fire' was just on my lips when your colors appeared." I saw his gunners standing with their hands on the lanyards. After forty years my blood almost creeps as I recall that narrow escape.

We now moved to the rear across the plank-road from the Chancellorsville House in the woods, where we supported Hancock's line. Colonel Albright soon returned from his visit to Hooker's head-quarters. His account of that visit was most remarkable, and was substantially as follows: " I scratched on the flap of the Hooker head-quarters' tent and instantly an officer appeared and asked what was wanted. I said I must see General Hooker, that I had important information for him. He said, ' You cannot see General Hooker; I am chief of staff; any information you have for the commanding general should be given to me.' I said, ' I must see General Hooker,' and with that pushed myself by him into the tent, and there lay General Hooker, apparently dead drunk. His face and position gave every indication of that condition, and I turned away sick and disgusted." It was subsequently stated that General Hooker was unconscious at that time from the concussion of a shell. That he was standing on the porch of the Chancellorsville House, leaning against one of its supports, when a shell struck it, rendering him unconscious. The incident narrated above occurred about one P.M. on Sunday, May 3. The army was practically without a commander from this time until after sundown of that day, when General Hooker reappeared and in a most conspicuous manner rode around between the lines of the two armies. If he was physically disabled, why was not the fact made known at once to the next officer in rank, whose duty it would have been to have assumed command of the army, and if possible stem the tide of defeat now rapidly overwhelming us? A half-day of most precious time would have been saved. That this was not done I happen to know from the following circumstances.

In our new position we were only about fifty yards behind General Hancock's line. The head-quarters at this time of General Couch, commanding our corps; of General French, commanding our division, and of General Hancock were all at the right of our regiment, behind our line. These generals and their staffs were resting, as were our troops, and they were sitting about, only a few feet away from us. We therefore heard much of their conversation. Directly General Howard joined them. I well remember his remarks concerning the behavior of his corps on the previous afternoon. His chagrin was punctured with the advice of old French to shoot a few dozen of them for example's sake. Naturally, the chief subject of their conversation related to the present situation. It was perfectly clear they regarded it as very critical. We could hear heavy cannonading in the distance towards Fredericksburg. Several times Hancock broke out with a savage oath as he impatiently paced up and down, swinging his sword. "They are knocking Sedgwick to pieces. Why don't we go forward?" or a similar ejaculation, and then, "General Couch, why do you not assume command and order us forward? It is your duty." (The latter was next in rank to Hooker.)

To which General Couch replied, "I cannot assume

command." French and Howard agreed with Hancock, but Couch remained imperturbable, saying, "When I am properly informed that General Hooker is disabled and not in command, I shall assume the duty which will devolve upon me." And so hour after hour passed of inactivity at this most critical juncture. They said it was plain Lee was making simply a show of force in our front whilst he had detached a large part of his army and was driving Sedgwick before him down at Fredericksburg. Now, why this period of inactivity whilst Sedgwick was being punished? Why this interregnum in the command? When Colonel Albright returned from his call at Hooker's tent, narrated above, he freely expressed his opinion that Hooker's condition was as stated above. His views were then generally believed by those about head-quarters, and this was understood as the reason why the next officer in rank was not officially notified of his chief's disability and the responsibility of the command placed upon him. Nothing was then said about the concussion of a shell. It is profoundly to be hoped that Colonel Albright's impression was wrong, and that the disability was produced, as alleged, by concussion of a shell. If so, there was a very grave dereliction of duty on the part of his chief of staff in not imparting the fact immediately to General Couch, the officer next in rank, and devolving the command upon him.

In our new position on the afternoon of Sunday, the third day's battle, we were subjected to a continuous fire of skirmishers and sharpshooters, without the ability of replying. We laid up logs for a barricade and protected ourselves as well as we could. Several were wounded

The Battle of Chancellorsville

during the afternoon, among them Captain Hall, of Company I. His was a most singular wound. We were all lying prone upon the ground, when suddenly he spoke rather sharply and said he had got a clip on his knee. He said it was an insignificant flesh wound, but his leg was benumbed. He tried to step on it, but could not bear his weight on it, and very soon it became exceedingly painful, and his ankle swelled to double its natural size. He was taken back to one of the hospitals, where it was found a minie-ball had entered his leg above the knee and passed down between the bones to the ankle, where it was removed. This practically ended the service of one of the youngest of our captains, a brave and brilliant young officer.

Towards night a cold, drizzling rain set in, which chilled us to our bones. We could not have any fires, not even to make our coffee, for fear of disclosing our position to the enemy. For four days now we had been continuously under the terrible nervous strain incident to a battle and practically without any rest or sleep. During this time we had no cooked food, nothing but hardtack and raw pork and coffee but once. This condition began to tell upon us all. I had been under the weather when the movement began, and was ordered by our surgeon to remain behind, but I said no, not as long as I could get around. Now I found my strength had reached its limit, and I took that officer's advice, with the colonel's orders, and went back to the division field hospital to get under cover from the rain and get a night's sleep if possible.

I found a half-dozen hospital tents standing together as one hospital, and all full to overflowing with sick and wounded men. Our brigade surgeon, a personal friend, was in charge. He finally found a place for me just under the edge of one of the tents, where I could keep part of the rain off. He brought me a stiff dose of whiskey and quinine, the universal war remedy, and I drank it and lay down, and was asleep in less time than it takes me to write it.

About midnight the surgeon came and aroused me with the information that the army was moving back across the river, and that all in the hospital who could march were ordered to make their way back as best they could; that of the others the ambulances would carry all they could and the others would be left. This was astounding information. My first impulse was, of course, to return to my regiment, but the doctor negatived that emphatically by saying, " You are under my orders here, and my instructions are to send you all directly back to the ford and across the river; and then the army is already on the march, and you might as well attempt to find a needle in a haystack as undertake to find your regiment in these woods in this darkness." If his first reason had not been sufficient, the latter one was quite convincing. I realized at once the utter madness of any attempt to reach the regiment, at the same time that in this night tramp back over the river, some eight miles, I had a job that would tax my strength to the utmost. The doctor had found one of the men of our regiment who was sick, and bidding us help each other started us back over the old plank-road.

How shall I describe the experiences of that night's tramp? The night was intensely dark and it was raining

232

The Battle of Chancellorsville

hard. The plank-road was such only in name. What few remnants remained of the old planks were rotten and were a constant menace to our footing. I must have had more than a dozen falls during that march from those broken planks, until face, arms, and legs were a mass of bruises. We were told to push forward as rapidly as we could to keep ahead of the great rabble of sick and wounded which was to follow immediately. This we tried to do, though the road was now crowded with the occupants of the other hospitals already on their way. These men were all either sick or wounded, and were making their way with the greatest difficulty, most of them in silence, but there was an occasional one whose tongue gave expression to every possible mishap in outbursts of the most shocking profanity. There were enough of these to make the night hideous.

Our road was a track just wide enough to admit a single wagon through the densest jungle of timber and undergrowth I ever saw. I cannot imagine the famed jungles of Africa more dense or impenetrable, and it seemed to be without end as we wearily plodded on hour after hour, now stepping into a hole and sprawling in the mud, again stumbling against a stolid neighbor and being in turn jostled by him, with an oath for being in his way. Many a poor fellow fell, too exhausted to rise, and we were too nearly dead to do more than mechanically note the fact.

Towards morning a quartette of men overtook us carrying a man on their shoulders. As they drew near us one of the forward pair stumbled and fell, and down came the body into the mud with a swash. If the body was not dead, the fall killed it, for it neither moved nor uttered a sound. With a fearful objurgation they went on and left it, and we did not have life enough left in us to make any investigation. It was like the case of a man on the verge of drowning seeing others perishing without the ability to help. It was a serious question whether we could pull ourselves through or should be obliged to drop in our tracks, to be run over and crushed or trampled to death, as many a poor fellow was that night. We had not an ounce of strength, nor had any of the hundreds of others in our condition, to bestow on those who could not longer care for themselves. Here it was every man for himself. This night's experience was a horrible nightmare.

It was long after daylight when we crawled out of those woods and reached United States ford. Here a pontoon bridge had been thrown over, and a double column of troops and a battery of artillery were crossing at the same time. We pushed ourselves into the throng, as to which there was no semblance of order, and were soon on the other side. On the top of the bluff, some one hundred feet above the river, on our side, we noticed a hospital tent, and we thought if we could reach that we might find shelter and rest, for it was still raining and we were drenched to the skin, and so cold that our faces were blue and our teeth chattered. A last effort landed us at this hospital. Alas for our hopes! it was crowded like sardines in a box with others who in like condition had reached it before us. I stuck my head in the tent. One glance was enough. The surgeon in charge, in answer to our mute appeal, said, " God help you, boys; I

The Battle of Chancellorsville

cannot. But here is a bottle of whiskey, take a good drink; it will do you good." We took a corking dose, nearly half the bottle, and lay down, spoon fashion, my comrade and I, by the side of that tent in the rain and slept for about an hour, until the stimulus of the liquor passed off and the cold began again to assert itself, when we had to start on again. I have never had any use for liquors in my life, and the use of them in any form as a beverage I consider as nothing else than harmful in the highest degree, yet I have always felt that this big dose of whiskey saved my life. Could we have had a good cup of hot coffee at that time it would possibly have been better, but we might as well have looked for lodgings in the Waldorf-Astoria as for coffee at that time and place. Imagine my feelings during all this night as I reflected that I had a good horse, overcoat, and gum blanket some-where,—yes, somewhere, back, or wherever my regiment might be,—and here I was soaking wet, chilled to the bones and almost dead from tramping.

We got word at the Ford that the troops were to go back to their old camps, and there was nothing for us to do but to make our way back there as best we might. Soon after we started Colonel (afterwards Judge Dana, of Wilkes-Barre) Dana's regiment passed. The colonel hailed me and kindly inquired why I happened to be there by myself on foot, said I looked most wretched, and in-sisted on my taking another bracer from a little emergency stock he had preserved. I had been but a few months out of his law office, from which I had been admitted to the bar. His kindly attentions under these limited cir-cumstances were very cheering and helpful. We were all day covering the eight or more miles back to camp. But early in the day the rain ceased, the sun came out, we got warmed up marching, and after some hours our clothes became sufficiently dry to be more comfortable, so that when we reached camp in the evening our condition was much improved. This was due in part probably as much to the relief from the awful nervous strain of the battle and the conditions through which we had passed in that wilderness as to rest and the changed weather. When we reached this side of the river that nervous strain ceased. We were sure that fighting was over, at least for the present. We found the regiment had been in camp some hours ahead of us. Our corps was probably on the march when we left the hospital, and had preceded us all the way back. I found my horse had brought back one of our wounded men, and this was some compensation for my own loss.

We had been gone on this campaign from the 29th of April until the 5th of May, and such a week! How much that was horrible had been crowded into it. For variety of experiences of the many dreadful sides of war, that week far exceeded any other like period of our service. The fighting was boy's play compared with either Antietam or Fredericksburg, yet for ninety-six hours continuously we were under the terrible nervous strain of battle. Our losses in this action were comparatively light, 2 men killed, 2 officers wounded (one of whom died a few days later), and 39 men wounded, and one man missing; total loss, 44, or about fifteen per cent. of the number we took into action. This missing man I met at the recent reunion of our regiment. He was picked up from our skirmish

The Battle of Chancellorsville

line by that flanking party of rebels on the third day's fight described in my last. The circumstance will show how close the rebels were upon us before we discovered them. Our skirmishers could not have been more than a dozen yards in advance of our main line, yet the thicket was so dense that the enemy was on him before he fairly realized it. He said he was placed with a lot of other prisoners and marched to the rear some distance, under guard, when a fine-looking Confederate officer rode up to them. He was told it was General Lee. He said he wore long, bushy whiskers and addressed them with a cheery,—

" Good-morning, boys. What did you come down here for? a picnic? You didn't think you could whip us men of the South, did you?"

One of the prisoners spoke up in reply,—

" Yes, d—n you, we did, and we will. You haven't won this fight yet, and Joe Hooker will lick h—l out of you and recapture us before you get us out of these woods."

The general laughed good-naturedly at the banter his questions had elicited, and solemnly assured them that there were not men enough in the whole North to take Richmond. Our man was probably misinformed as to who their interlocutor was. General Lee did not wear long, bushy whiskers, and was at that time probably down directing operations against Fredericksburg. This was probably Jeb Stuart, who had succeeded Jackson in command of that wing of the rebel army.

Our prisoner fared much better than most prisoners, for it was his good fortune to be exchanged after twenty-three days' durance, probably owing to the expiration of his term of service. Although the actual dates of enlistment of our men were all in July and their terms therefore expired, the government insisted upon holding us for the full period of nine months from the date of actual muster into the United States service, which would not be completed until the 14th of May. We had, therefore, eight days' service remaining after our return from the battle of Chancellorsville, and we were continued in all duties just as though we had months yet to serve. Our principal work was the old routine of picket duty again. Our friends, the enemy, were now quick to tantalize our pickets with the defeat at Chancellorsville. Such remarks as these were volleyed at us:

"We 'uns give you 'uns a right smart lickin' up in them woods."

"How d'ye like Virginny woods, Yank?"

And then they sang to us:

"Ain't ye mighty glad to get out the wilderness?"

A song just then much in vogue. Another volunteered the remark, as if to equalize the honors in some measure, "If we did wallop you 'uns, you 'uns killed our best general." "We feel mighty bad about Stonewall's death," and so their tongues would run on, whether our men replied or not.

CHAPTER XVII

THE MUSTER OUT AND HOME AGAIN

On the 14th of May we received orders to proceed to Harrisburg for muster out. There was, of course, great rejoicing at the early prospect of home scenes once more. We walked on air, and lived for the next few days in fond anticipation. We were the recipients of any amount of attention from our multitude of friends in the division. Many were the forms of leave-taking that took place. It was a great satisfaction to realize that in our comparatively brief period of service we had succeeded in winning our way so thoroughly into the big hearts of those veterans. The night before our departure was one of the gladdest and saddest of all our experience. The Fourteenth Connecticut band, that same band which had so heroically played out between the lines when the Eleventh Corps broke on that fateful Saturday night at Chancellorsville, came over and gave us a farewell serenade. They played most of the patriotic airs, with " Home, Sweet Home," which I think never sounded quite so sadly sweet, and suggestively wound up with " When Johnny Comes Marching Home." Most of the officers and men of the brigade were there to give us a soldier's good-by, and Major-General Couch, commanding our corps (the Second), also paid us the compliment of a visit and made a pleasant little speech to the men who were informally grouped around head-quarters, commending our behavior in three of the greatest battles of the war.

It had been our high honor, he said, to have had a part in those great battles, and though new and untried we had acquitted ourselves with great credit and had held our ground like veterans. He expressed the fervent hope that our patriotism would still further respond to the country's needs, and that we would all soon again be in the field. Our honors were not yet complete. General French, commanding our division, issued a farewell order, a copy of which I would have been glad to publish, but I have not been able to get it. It was, however, gratifying in the extreme. He recounted our bravery under his eye in those battles and our efficient service on all duty, and wound up by saying he felt sure that men with such a record could not long remain at home, but would soon again rally around their country's flag. Of General Couch, our corps commander, we had seen but little, and were therefore very pleasantly surprised at his visit. Of General French, bronzed and grizzly bearded, we had seen much; all our work had been under his immediate supervision. He was a typical old regular, and many were the cuffs and knocks we received for our inexperience and shortcomings, all, however, along the lines of discipline and for our good, and which had really helped to make soldiers of us. These incidents showed that each commanding general keeps a keen eye on all his regiments, and no one is quicker to detect and appreciate good behavior than they. We felt especially pleased with the praises of General French, because it revealed the other side of this old hero's character. Rough in exterior and manner of speech, he was a strong character and a true hero.

His position at the breaking out of the war will illustrate this. He was a Southerner of the type of Anderson and Farragut. When so many of his fellows of the regular army, under pretext of following their States, went over into rebellion and treason, he stood firm and under circumstances which reflect great credit upon him. He had been in Mexico and had spent a life on the frontier, and had grown old and gray in the service, reaching only the rank of captain. When the war finally came he was in command of a battery of artillery stationed some three hundred and fifty miles up the Rio Grande, on the border of Mexico. He was cut off from all communication with Washington, and the commander of his department, the notorious General David E. Twiggs, had gone over to the Confederacy. He was, therefore, thoroughly isolated. Twiggs sent him a written order to surrender his battery to the rebel commander of that district. His characteristic reply was, that he would " see him and the Confederacy in hell first;" that he was going to march his battery into God's country, and if anybody interfered with his progress they might expect a dose of shot and shell they would long remember. None of them felt disposed to test his threat, and so he marched his battery alone down through that rebel country those three hundred and fifty miles and more into our lines at the mouth of the Rio Grande, bringing off every gun and every dollar's worth of government property that he could carry, and what he could not carry he destroyed. He was immediately ordered north with his battery and justly rewarded with a brigadier-general's commission.

Early on the morning of the 15th we broke camp and bade farewell to that first of the world's great armies, the grand old Army of the Potomac. Need I say that, joyous as was our home-going, there was more than a pang at the bottom of our hearts as we severed those heroic associations? A last look at the old familiar camp, a wave of the hand to the friendly adieus of our comrades, whose good-by glances indicated that they would gladly have exchanged places with us; that if our hearts were wrung at going, theirs were, too, at remaining; a last march down those Falmouth hills, another and last glance at those terrible works behind Fredericksburg, and we passed out of the army and out of the soldier into the citizen, for our work was now done and we were soldiers only in name.

As our train reached Belle-plain, where we were to take boat for Washington, we noticed a long train of ambulances moving down towards the landing, and were told they were filled with wounded men, just now brought off the field at Chancellorsville. There were upward of a thousand of them. It seems incredible that the wounded should have been left in those woods during these ten to twelve days since the battle. How many hundreds perished during that time for want of care nobody knows, and, more horrible still, nobody knows how many poor fellows were burned up in the portions of those woods that caught fire from the artillery. But such is war. Dare any one doubt the correctness of Uncle Billy Sherman's statement that "War is hell!"

The Muster Out and Home Again

Reaching Washington, the regiment bivouacked a single night, awaiting transportation to Harrisburg. During this time discipline was relaxed and the men were permitted to see the capital city. The lieutenant-colonel and I enjoyed the extraordinary luxury of a good bath, a square meal, and a civilized bed at the Metropolitan Hotel, the first in five long months. Singular as it may seem, I caught a terrific cold as the price I paid for it. The next day we were again back in Camp Curtin, at Harrisburg, with nothing to do but to make out the necessary muster rolls, turn in our government property,—guns, accoutrements, blankets, etc., and receive our discharges. This took over a week, so that it was the 24th of May before we were finally discharged and paid off. Then the several companies finally separated.

If it had been hard to leave our comrades of the Army of the Potomac, it was harder to sever the close comradeship of our own regiment, a relationship formed and cemented amidst the scenes that try men's souls, a comradeship born of fellowship in privation, danger, and suffering. I could hardly restrain my tears as we finally parted with our torn and tattered colors, the staff of one of which had been shot away in my hands. We had fought under their silken folds on three battle-fields, upon which we had left one-third of our number killed and wounded, including a colonel and three line officers and upward of seventy-five men killed and two hundred and fifteen wounded. Out of our regiment of one thousand and twenty-four men mustered into the service August 14, 1862, we had present at our muster out six hundred and eighteen. We had lost in battle two hundred and ninety-five in killed and wounded and one hundred and eleven from physical disability, sickness, etc., and all in the short space of nine months. Of the sixteen nine-months regiments formed in August, 1862, the One Hundred and Thirtieth and ours were the only regiments to actively participate in the three great battles of Antietam, Fredericksburg, and Chancellorsville, and we lost more men than either of the others.

I should mention a minor incident that occurred during our stay in Harrisburg preparing for muster out. A large number of our men had asked me to see if I could not get authority to re-enlist a battalion from the regiment. I was assured that three-fourths of the men would go back with me, provided they could have a two weeks' furlough. I laid the matter before Governor Curtin. He said the government should take them by all means; that here was a splendid body of seasoned men that would be worth more than double their number of new recruits; but he was without authority to take them, and suggested that I go over to Washington and lay the matter before the Secretary of War. He gave me a letter to the latter and I hurried off. I had no doubt of my ability to raise an entire regiment from the great number of nine-months men now being discharged. I repaired to the War Department, and here my troubles began. Had the lines of sentries that guarded the approach to the armies in the field been half as efficient as the cordon of flunkies that barred the way to the War Office, the former would have been beyond the reach of any enemy. At the entrance my pedigree was taken, with my credentials and a statement of my business. I was finally permitted to sit down

The Muster Out and Home Again

in a waiting-room with a waiting crowd. Occasionally a senator or a congressman would break the monotony by pushing himself in whilst we cultivated our patience by waiting. Lunch time came and went. I waited. Several times I ventured some remarks to the attendant as to when I might expect my turn to come, but he looked at me with a sort of far-off look, as though I could not have realized to whom I was speaking. Finally, driven to desperation, after waiting more than four hours, I tried a little bluster and insisted that I would go in and see somebody. Then I was assured that the only official about the office was a Colonel ———, acting assistant adjutant-general. I might see him.

"Yes," I said, "let me see him, anybody!"

I was ushered into the great official's presence. He was a lieutenant-colonel, just one step above my own rank. He was dressed in a faultless new uniform. His hair was almost as red as a fresh red rose and parted in the middle, and his pose and dignity were quite worthy of the national snob hatchery at West Point, of which he was a recent product.

"Young man," said he, with a supercilious air, "what might your business be?"

I stated that I had brought a letter from His Excellency, Governor Curtin, of Pennsylvania, to the Secretary of War, whom I desired to see on important business.

"Where is your letter, sir?"

"I gave it up to the attendant four hours ago, who, I supposed, took it to the Secretary."

"There is no letter here, sir! What is your business? You cannot see the Secretary of War."

I then briefly stated my errand. His reply was,—

" Young man, if you really desire to serve your country, go home and enlist."

Thoroughly disgusted, I retired, and so ended what might have saved to the service one of the best bodies of men that ever wore a government uniform, and at a time when the country was sorely in need of them.

A word now of the personnel of the One Hundred and Thirty-second Regiment and I am done. Dr. Bates, in his history of the Pennsylvania troops, remarks that this regiment was composed of a remarkable body of men. This judgment must have been based upon his knowledge of their work. Every known trade was represented in its ranks. Danville gave us a company of iron workers and merchants, Catawissa and Bloomsburg, mechanics, tradesmen, and farmers. From Mauch Chunk we had two companies, which included many miners. From Wyoming and Bradford we had three companies of sturdy, intelligent young farmers intermingled with some mechanics and tradesmen. Scranton, small as she was then, gave us two companies, which was scarcely a moiety of the number she sent into the service. I well remember how our flourishing Young Men's Christian Association was practically suspended because its members had gone to the war, and old Nay Aug Hose Company, the pride of the town, in which many of us had learned the little we knew of drill, was practically defunct for want of a membership which had " gone to the war." Of these two Scranton companies, Company K had as its basis the old Scranton City Guard, a militia organization which, if not large, was thoroughly well drilled and made up of most excellent material. Captain Richard Stillwell, who commanded this company, had organized the City Guard and been its captain from the beginning. The other Scranton company was perhaps more distinctively peculiar in its personnel than either of the other companies. It was composed almost exclusively of Delaware, Lackawanna & Western Railroad shop and coal men, and was known as the Railroad Guards. In its ranks were locomotive engineers, firemen, brakemen, trainmen, machinists, telegraph operators, despatchers, railroad-shop men, a few miners, foremen, coal-breaker men, etc. Their captain, James Archbald, Jr., was assistant to his father as chief engineer of the road, and he used to say that with his company he could survey, lay out, build and operate a railroad. The first sergeant of that company, George Conklin, brother of D. H. Conklin, chief despatcher of the Delaware, Lackawanna & Western, and his assistant, had been one of the first to learn the art of reading telegraph messages by ear, an accomplishment then quite uncommon. His memory had therefore been so developed that after a few times calling his company roll he dispensed with the book and called it alphabetically from memory. Keeping a hundred names in his mind in proper order we thought quite a feat. Forty years later, at one of our reunions, Mr. Conklin, now superintendent of a railroad, was present. I asked him if he remembered calling his company roll from memory.

"Yes," said he, "and I can do it now, and recall every face and voice," and he began and rattled off the names of his roll. He said sometimes in the old days the boys would try to fool him by getting a comrade to answer for them, but they could never do it, he would detect the different voice instantly.

Now, as I close this narrative, shall I speak of the gala day of our home-coming? I can, of course, only speak of the one I participated in, the coming home to Scranton of Companies I and K and the members of the field and staff who lived here. This, however, will be a fair description of the reception each of the other companies received at their respective homes. Home-coming from the war! Can we who know of it only as we read appreciate such a home-coming? That was forty-one years ago the 25th of last May. Union Hall, on Lackawanna Avenue, midway between Wyoming and Penn, had been festooned with flags, and in it a sumptuous dinner awaited us. A committee of prominent citizens, our old friends, not one of whom is now living, met us some distance down the road. A large delegation of Scranton's ladies were at the hall to welcome and serve us, and of these, the last one, one of the mothers and matrons, has just passed into the great beyond. Many of those of our own age, the special attraction of the returning " boys," have also gone, but a goodly number still remain. They will recall this picture with not a little interest, I am sure. If perchance cheeks should be wet and spectacles moistened as they read, it will be but a reproduction of the emotions of that beautiful day more than forty years ago. No soldier boys ever received a more joyous or hearty welcome. The bountiful repast was hurriedly eaten, for anxious mothers, wives, sisters, and sweethearts were there, whose claim upon their returning " boy in blue" for holier and tenderer relationship was paramount.

The Muster Out and Home Again

Amidst all these joyous reunions, were there no shadows? Ah, yes. In the brief period of nine months our regiment had lost forty per cent. of its membership. Company I had gone to the front with one hundred and one stalwart officers and men, and but sixty-eight came back with the company. Of the missing names, Daniel S. Gardner, Moses H. Ames, George H. Cator, Daniel Reed, Richard A. Smith, and John B. West were killed in battle or died of wounds soon after; Orville Sharp had died in the service. The others had succumbed to the hardships of the service and been discharged. Of the same number Company K took into the service, sixty-six came home with the company. Sergeant Martin L. Hower, Richard Davis, Jacob Eschenbach, Jephtha Milligan, Allen Sparks, Obadiah Sherwood, and David C. Young had been killed in battle or died of wounds; Thomas D. Davis, Jesse P. Kortz, Samuel Snyder, James Scull, Solon Searles, and John W. Wright had died in the service. The most conspicuous figure in the regiment, our colonel, Richard A. Oakford, had been the first to fall. So that amidst our rejoicings there were a multitude of hearts unutterably sad. Will the time ever come when " the bitter shall not be mingled with the sweet" and tears of sorrow shall not drown the cup of gladness? Let us hope and pray that it may; and now, as Father Time tenderly turns down the heroic leaf of the One Hundred and Thirty-second Pennsylvania Volunteers, let us find comfort in the truth,

" Dulce et decorum est, pro patria mori."

APPENDIX

THE following are copies of the muster-out rolls of the Field and Staff and the several companies of the One Hundred and Thirty-second Regiment, Pennsylvania Volunteers, taken originally from Bates's History, and compared and corrected from the original rolls in the Adjutant-General's office, at Harrisburg, Pa. Several corrections have been made from the personal recollections of officers and men whom I have been able to consult. There are doubtless errors in the original rolls, owing to the paucity of records in the hands of those whose duty it was to make them at the time of muster-out, owing to resignations and other casualties. Some of these officers were new in the command, and complete records were not in their hands. It will be remembered that the whole period of service of the One Hundred and Thirty-second was occupied in the three strenuous campaigns of Antietam, Fredericksburg, and Chancellorsville, during which regimental and company baggage, which included official records, were seldom seen, and in many cases were entirely lost. For example, at the battle of Chancellorsville on the fateful 3d of May, we had lain in line of battle behind our knapsacks piled up in twos, as a little protection from bullets. When we were ordered forward, so quick was the movement, that these knapsacks, and officers' luggage as well, were ordered to be left. When, two hours later, on our return we reached this ground, we found our knapsacks were at the bottom of an earth-work which had been hurriedly thrown up during our absence, over which a line of batteries thrust the frowning muzzles of their guns. With one or two exceptions (where the officer commanding the company happened to have it in his pocket), the company rolls were lost in the knapsacks of the first sergeant, whose duty it was to carry it. Thereupon new rolls had to be made up, and of course mostly from memory. Under all these circumstances, the wonder is that there are not more errors in them. Almost at the last moment did I learn that I could include these rolls in my book, without exceeding its limits under the contract price. During this time I have en-

251

Appendix

deavored at considerable expense and labor to get them correct, but even so, I cannot hope that they are more than approximately complete. Nothing can be more sacred or valuable to the veteran and his descendants than his war record. The difficulty with these rolls will be found I fear not so much in what is so briefly stated, but in what has been inadvertently omitted, and which was necessary to a complete record. There are a number of desertions. I have given them as they are on the rolls. It is possible that some of these men may have dropped out of the column from exhaustion on the march, fallen sick and had been taken to some hospital and died without identification. Failing to report at roll-call and being unaccounted for, they would be carried on the company rolls as "absent without leave," until prolonged absence without information would compel the adding of the fearful word "deserted." There were instances where men taken sick made their way home without leave and were marked deserters. After recovering from a severe case of "army fever" they returned again to duty. This was in violation of discipline, and under the strict letter of the law they were deserters, but they saved the government the cost of their nursing, and, what is more, probably saved their lives and subsequent service by their going. I mention these things so that where the record appears harsh, the reader may know that possibly, if all the facts had been known, it might have been far different.

FIELD AND STAFF.

RICHARD A. OAKFORD, colonel, mustered in Aug. 22, 1862; killed at Antietam, Sept. 17, 1862.

VINCENT M. WILCOX, colonel, mustered in Aug. 26, 1862; promoted from lieutenant-colonel September, 1862; discharged on surgeon's certificate Jan. 24, 1863.

CHARLES ALBRIGHT, colonel, mustered in Aug. 22, 1862; promoted from major to lieutenant-colonel September, 1862, to colonel Jan. 24, 1863; mustered out with regiment May 24, 1863.

JOSEPH E. SHREVE, lieutenant-colonel, promoted from captain Co. A to major September, 1862, to lieutenant-colonel Jan. 24, 1863; mustered out with regiment May 24, 1863.

FREDERICK L. HITCHCOCK, major, mustered in Aug. 22, 1862; promoted from adjutant Jan. 24, 1863; twice wounded at Fredericksburg Dec. 13, 1862; mustered out with regiment May 24, 1863.

AUSTIN F. CLAPP, adjutant, promoted from corporal Co. K to

Appendix

sergeant-major Nov. 1, 1862; to adjutant Jan. 24, 1863; mustered out with regiment May 24, 1863.

CLINTON W. NEAL, quartermaster, mustered in Aug. 13, 1862; promoted from Co. E Aug. 22, 1862; mustered out with regiment May 24, 1863.

JAMES W. ANAWALT, surgeon (major), mustered in Sept. 22, 1862; mustered out with regiment May 24, 1863.

GEORGE K. THOMPSON, assistant surgeon (first lieutenant), mustered in Aug. 19, 1862; mustered out with regiment May 24, 1863.

GEORGE W. HOOVER, assistant surgeon (first lieutenant), mustered in Sept. 3, 1862; mustered out with regiment May 24, 1863.

A. H. SCHOONMAKER, chaplain (first lieutenant), mustered in Sept. 20, 1862; mustered out with regiment May 24, 1863.

THOMAS MAXWELL, sergeant-major, promoted to sergeant-major from Co. A Aug. 22, 1862; promoted to first lieutenant Co. A Nov. 1, 1862. (See Co. A.)

FRANK J. DEEMER, sergeant-major, mustered in Aug. 14, 1862; promoted from Co. K Jan. 24, 1863; mustered out with regiment May 24, 1863.

ELMORE H. WELLS, quartermaster-sergeant, mustered in Aug. 15, 1862; promoted from Co. B Aug. 26, 1862; owing to prolonged sickness in hospital returned to Co. Jan. 1, 1863. (See Co. B.)

BROOKS A. BASS, quartermaster-sergeant, mustered in Aug. 15, 1862; promoted from Co. I Jan. 1, 1863; mustered out with regiment May 24, 1863.

JOHN F. SALMON, commissary-sergeant, mustered in Aug. 13, 1862; promoted from Co. G Aug. 15, 1862; died at Harper's Ferry, Va., Oct. 16, 1862.

WILLIAM W. COOLBAUGH, commissary-sergeant, mustered in Aug. 15, 1862; promoted from Co. K Oct. 17, 1862; transferred to company Dec. 25, 1862. (See Co. K.)

ALONZO R. CASE, commissary-sergeant, mustered in Aug. 11, 1862; promoted from sergeant Co. C Dec. 25, 1862; mustered out with regiment May 24, 1863.

HORACE A. DEANS, hospital steward, mustered in Aug. 15, 1862; promoted from Co. I Oct. 1, 1862; transferred to ranks April 1, 1863. (See Co. I.)

MOSES G. CORWIN, hospital steward, mustered in Aug. 14, 1862; promoted from Co. K April 6, 1863; mustered out with regiment May 24, 1863.

Appendix

COMPANY A.

JOSEPH E. SHREVE, captain, mustered in Aug. 15, 1862; promoted to major. See Field and Staff.

CHARLES C. NORRIS, captain, mustered in Aug. 15, 1862; promoted from second lieutenant Nov. 1, 1862; mustered out with company May 24, 1863.

GEORGE W. VANGILDER, first lieutenant, mustered in Aug. 15, 1862; discharged on surgeon's certificate Oct. 26, 1862.

THOMAS MAXWELL, first lieutenant, mustered in Aug. 14, 1862; promoted from sergeant-major Nov. 1, 1862; mustered out with regiment.

---

* Bates's History, Pennsylvania Volunteers, places here the name of " Charles A. Meylert, second lieutenant, promoted from private, Co. K, Feb. 23, 1863, missing since that date." Co. K's roll notes the transfer of this man to Co. A. His name is not on the original roll of Co. A, and is therefore omitted here. The following note received from Captain Charles C. Norris, Co. A, explains:

PHILADELPHIA, July 12, 1904.

Colonel F. L. HITCHCOCK, Scranton, Pa.

MY DEAR COLONEL: . . . I have a copy of the muster-out roll of Co. A, to which I have referred. . . . I would also state that Charles A. Meylert does not appear on the muster-out roll, nor was he at any time carried on the roll of Co. A. . . . On the march from Harper's Ferry to Warrenton, Va., about Nov. 1, 1862, Co. A held an election for officers to fill vacancies caused by the promotion of Captain Shreve to be major of the regiment. The following were elected: Chas. C. Norris, captain; Thomas Maxwell, first lieutenant, and Edward W. Roderick, second lieutenant. The result of this election was forwarded through head-quarters to Governor Curtin. The commissions were not sent on until some time in December, 1862. Colonel Albright, commanding the regiment, sent for me one day and told me he had received a commission for Charles A. Meylert as second lieutenant of Co. A; that it was an outrage upon Co. A, and that he would send it back to Governor Curtin with a letter, which I believe he did, the result of which was Roderick's commission was issued in accordance with his election, and he was mustered in, and Meylert's commission was revoked.

Appendix

ED. W. RODERICK, second lieutenant, mustered in Aug. 14, 1862; promoted from private; mustered out with company.

DAVID SHUTT, first sergeant, mustered in Aug. 14, 1862; promoted from sergeant March 1, 1863; mustered out with company May 24, 1863.

J. M. HASSENPLUG, sergeant, mustered in Aug. 14, 1862; killed at Antietam, Md., Sept. 17, 1862.

JOHN S. WARE, sergeant, mustered in Aug. 14, 1862; promoted from corporal March 1, 1863; mustered out with company May 24, 1863.

ISAAC D. CREWITT, sergeant, mustered in Aug. 14, 1862; promoted from corporal March 1, 1863; mustered out with company May 24, 1863.

MICHAEL KESSLER, sergeant, mustered in Aug. 14, 1862; promoted from private March 6, 1863; wounded at Fredericksburg, Va., Dec. 13, 1862; mustered out with company May 24, 1863.

GEORGE LOVETT, sergeant, mustered in Aug. 14, 1862; promoted from private Feb. 1, 1863; mustered out with company May 24, 1863.

JACOB H. MILLER, sergeant, mustered in Aug. 14, 1862; discharged, Jan. 30, 1863, at Washington, for wounds received at Antietam, Va., Sept. 17, 1862.

JOSEPH H. NEVINS, sergeant, mustered in Aug. 14, 1862; discharged on surgeon's certificate March 6, 1863, at Baltimore, Md.

DANIEL VANROUK, sergeant, mustered in Aug. 14, 1862; killed at Antietam, Md., Sept. 17, 1862.

JACOB REDFIELD, corporal, mustered in Aug. 15, 1862; promoted from private Sept. 18, 1862; wounded at Chancellorsville, Va., May 3, 1863; mustered out with company May 24, 1863.

JAMES WILLIAMS, corporal, mustered in Aug. 14, 1862; promoted from private Oct. 15, 1862; mustered out with company May 24, 1863.

CONRAD S. ATEN, corporal, mustered in Aug. 14, 1862; promoted from private Dec. 3, 1862; mustered out with company May 24, 1863.

As the commanding officer of Co. A, I never received any official notice or record of Meylert's commission or muster into service; hence his name was never entered upon my company roll. How Bates came to place his name upon my roll, I do not know.

I am yours truly,

CHAS. C. NORRIS.

Appendix

GEORGE SNYDER, corporal, mustered in Aug. 14, 1862; absent, sick, at muster-out.

ALEX. HUNTINGTON, corporal, mustered in Aug. 14, 1862; promoted from private Feb. 1, 1863; mustered out with company May 24, 1863.

SAMUEL STALL, corporal, mustered in Aug. 14, 1862; promoted from private Feb. 1, 1863; mustered out with company May 24, 1863.

HENRY VINCENT, corporal, mustered in Aug. 14, 1862; promoted from private March 6, 1863; mustered out with company May 24, 1863.

JOHN HARIG, corporal, mustered in Aug. 14, 1862; promoted from private March 6, 1863; mustered out with company May 24, 1863.

CHARLES FLICK, corporal, mustered in Aug. 14, 1862; discharged at Baltimore, Md., Dec. 6, 1862, of wounds received at Antietam Sept. 17, 1862.

NATHAN F. LIGHTNER, corporal, mustered in Aug. 14, 1862; discharged at Newark, N. J., on surgeon's certificate Dec. 8, 1862.

WM. C. McCORMICK, corporal, mustered in Aug. 14, 1862; discharged March 1, 1863; wounds received at Fredericksburg, Va., Dec. 13, 1862.

HENRY L. SHICK, musician, mustered in Aug. 14, 1862; mustered out with company May 24, 1863.

AMOS APPLEMAN, private, mustered in Aug. 14, 1862; mustered out with company May 24, 1863.

SYLVESTER W. ARNWINE, private, mustered in Aug. 14, 1862; wounded at Antietam, Md., Sept. 17, 1862; mustered out with company May 24, 1863.

HENRY ADAMS, private, mustered in Aug. 14, 1862; died Sept. 22 of wounds received at Antietam, Md., Sept. 17, 1862.

ARTHUR W. BEAVER, private, mustered in Aug. 15, 1862; mustered out with company May 24, 1863.

JACOB J. BOOKMILLER, private, mustered in Aug. 14, 1862; wounded at Chancellorsville, Va., May 3, 1863; mustered out with company May 24, 1863.

FRANKLIN G. BLEE, private, mustered in Aug. 14, 1862; mustered out with company May 24, 1863.

JEREMIAH BLACK, private, mustered in Aug. 14, 1862; mustered out with company May 24, 1863.

WILLIAM H. CARROLL, private, mustered in Aug. 14, 1862;

Appendix

wounded at Chancellorsville, Va., May 3, 1863; mustered out with company May 24, 1863.

SAMUEL E. COOPER, private, mustered in Aug. 14, 1862; deserted Oct. 22, 1862; left at Bolivar Heights, Va.; sick, failed to return to company.

FRANKLIN DEVINE, private, mustered in Aug. 14, 1862; mustered out with company May 24, 1863.

WILLIAM DAVIS, private, mustered in Aug. 14, 1862; mustered out with company May 24, 1863.

SAMUEL V. DYE, private, mustered in Aug. 14, 1862; discharged at Philadelphia on surgeon's certificate April 8, 1863.

WILLIAM EARP, JR., private, mustered in Aug. 14, 1862; wounded at Fredericksburg, Va., Dec. 13, 1862; mustered out with company May 24, 1863.

JAMES S. EASTON, private, mustered in Aug. 14, 1862; mustered out with company May 24, 1863.

HIRAM EGGERT, private, mustered in Aug. 14, 1862; mustered out with company May 24, 1863.

JOSEPH FEIDEL, private, mustered in Aug. 15, 1862; mustered out with company May 24, 1863.

SAMUEL FLICKINGER, private, mustered in Aug. 14, 1862; mustered out with company May 24, 1863.

JOHN B. A. FOIN, private, mustered in Aug. 14, 1862; mustered out with company May 24, 1863.

JAMES FOSTER, private, mustered in Aug. 14, 1862; mustered out with company May 24, 1863.

C. W. FITZSIMMONS, private, mustered in Aug. 14, 1862; mustered out with company May 24, 1863.

JOHN L. FIELDS, private, mustered in Aug. 15, 1862; mustered out with company May 24, 1863.

GEORGE FRANCIS, private, mustered in Aug. 14, 1862; discharged at Harrisburg on surgeon's certificate Nov. 15, 1862.

THOMAS GOODALL, private, mustered in Aug. 14, 1862; mustered out with company May 24, 1863.

SAMUEL GULICKS, private, mustered in Aug. 14, 1862; mustered out with company May 24, 1863.

JOHN GIBSON, private, mustered in Aug. 14, 1862; killed at Antietam, Md., Sept. 17, 1862.

JOSEPH HALE, private, mustered in Aug. 14, 1862; mustered out with company May 24, 1863.

Appendix

GEORGE E. HUNT, private, mustered in Aug. 14, 1862; mustered out with company May 24, 1863.

ADAM HORNBERGER, private, mustered in Aug. 14, 1862; mustered out with company May 24, 1863.

D. HENDRICKSON, private, mustered in Aug. 14, 1862; mustered out with company May 24, 1863.

SAMUEL HILLNER, private, mustered in Aug. 14, 1862; killed at Antietam, Md., Sept. 17, 1862.

HIRAM HUMMEL, private, mustered in Aug. 14, 1862; killed at Antietam, Md., Sept. 17, 1862.

THOMAS JONES, private, mustered in Aug. 14, 1862; mustered out with company May 24, 1863.

THOMAS JAMES, private, mustered in Aug. 14, 1862; mustered out with company May 24, 1863.

W. J. W. KLASE, private, mustered in Aug. 14, 1862; mustered out with company May 24, 1863.

DANIEL J. P. KLASE, private, mustered in Aug. 14, 1862; killed at Antietam, Md., Sept. 17, 1862.

CONRAD LECHTHALER, private, mustered in Aug. 14, 1862; left sick at Warrenton, Va., Nov. 14, 1862; reported discharged; no official notice received.

SAMUEL LANGER, private, mustered in Aug. 14, 1862; mustered out with company May 24, 1863.

JOHN LEICHOW, private, mustered in Aug. 14, 1862; discharged Oct. 28, 1862, for wounds received at Antietam, Md., Sept. 17, 1862.

JACOB LONG, private, mustered in Aug. 14, 1862; killed at Antietam, Md., Sept. 17, 1862.

WATKIN MORGAN, private, mustered in Aug. 14, 1862; mustered out with company May 24, 1863.

LEVI M. MILLER, private, mustered in Aug. 14, 1862; mustered out with company May 24, 1863.

JACOB W. MOYER, private, mustered in Aug. 14, 1862; mustered out with company May 24, 1863.

LEONARD MAYER, private, mustered in Aug. 14, 1862; mustered out with company May 24, 1863.

CORNELIUS C. MOYER, private, mustered in Aug. 14, 1862; mustered out with company May 24, 1863.

JOHN MORRIS, private, mustered in Aug. 14, 1862; wounded at Antietam, Md., Sept. 17, 1862; mustered out with company May 24, 1863.

Appendix

JOHN MCCOY, private, mustered in Aug. 14, 1862; mustered out with company May 24, 1863.

JAMES MCKEE, private, mustered in Aug. 15, 1862; deserted Aug. 16, 1862, from Harrisburg.

WM. B. NEESE, private, mustered in Aug. 14, 1862; wounded at Antietam, Md., Sept. 17, 1862; mustered out with company May 24, 1863.

JAMES M. PHILLIPS, private, mustered in Aug. 14, 1862; mustered out with company May 24, 1863.

JOHN P. REASER, private, mustered in Aug. 14, 1862; mustered out with company May 24, 1863.

SIMON REIDY, private, mustered in Aug. 14, 1862; mustered out with company May 24, 1863.

ISAAC RANTZ, private, mustered in Aug. 14, 1862; mustered out with company May 24, 1863.

DAVID H. RANK, private, mustered in Aug. 14, 1862; discharged on surgeon's certificate Jan. 29, 1863.

WM. A. RINGLER, private, mustered in Aug. 14, 1862; discharged May 5, 1863, for wounds received at Antietam, Md., September 17, 1862.

JONATHAN RICE, private, mustered in Aug. 14, 1862; killed at Fredericksburg, Va., Dec. 13, 1862.

WILLIAM STEWART, private, mustered in Aug. 14, 1862; mustered out with company May 24, 1863.

EDWARD D. SMITH, private, mustered in Aug. 14, 1862; mustered out with company May 24, 1863.

WILLIAM SUNDAY, private, mustered in Aug. 14, 1862; mustered out with company May 24, 1863.

AUGUST SCHRIEVER, private, mustered in Aug. 14, 1862; mustered out with company May 24, 1863.

JOHN STINE, private, mustered in Aug. 14, 1862; mustered out with company May 24, 1863.

EDWIN L. SMITH, private, mustered in Aug. 14, 1862; mustered out with company May 24, 1863.

OLIVER B. SWITZER, private, mustered in Aug. 14, 1862; mustered out with company May 24, 1863.

SHARP M. SNYDER, private, mustered in Aug. 14, 1862; mustered out with company May 24, 1863.

AARON SECHLER, private, mustered in Aug. 14, 1862; mustered out with company May 24, 1863.

Appendix

ARCHIBALD VANDLING, private, mustered in Aug. 14, 1862; discharged at Harrisburg on surgeon's certificate Nov. 28, 1862.

ANGUS WRIGHT, private, mustered in Aug. 14, 1862; mustered out with company May 24, 1863.

ANDREW WAUGH, private, mustered in Aug. 14, 1862; mustered out with company May 24, 1863.

JOHN WALLACE, private, mustered in Aug. 14, 1862; left sick in hospital at Harper's Ferry, Va.; reported discharged; no official notice received.

SAMUEL WOTE, private, mustered in Aug. 14, 1862; mustered out with company May 24, 1863.

MATTHEW R. WRIGHT, private, mustered in Aug. 14, 1862; killed at Fredericksburg, Va., Dec. 13, 1862.

JAMES D. WRAY, private, mustered in Aug. 14, 1862; deserted Sept. 19, 1862.

COMPANY B.

SMITH W. INGHAM, captain, mustered in Aug. 14, 1862; resigned on surgeon's certificate at Georgetown, Sem. Hospital, Feb. 5, 1863.

GEORGE H. EASTMAN, captain, mustered in Aug. 14, 1862; promoted from first lieutenant Feb. 8, 1863; wounded at Chancellorsville, Va., May 3, 1863; mustered out with company May 24, 1863.

ANSON G. CARPENTER, first lieutenant, mustered in Aug. 14, 1862; promoted from second lieutenant Feb. 8, 1863; mustered out with company May 24, 1863.

DeWITT C. KITCHEN, second lieutenant, mustered in Aug. 11, 1862; promoted to first sergeant Sept. 18, 1862; to second lieutenant Feb. 8, 1863; mustered out with company May 24, 1863.

JOHN D. SMITH, first sergeant, mustered in Aug. 11, 1862; promoted to sergeant Nov. 1, 1862; to first sergeant Feb. 8, 1863; mustered out with company May 24, 1863.

GEORGE D. WARNER, sergeant, mustered in Aug. 11, 1862; killed at Antietam, Md., Sept. 17, 1862; buried in National Cemetery, Sec. 26, Lot A, Grave 14.

JONAS H. FARR, sergeant, mustered in Aug. 11, 1862; promoted from corporal Sept. 18, 1862; mustered out with company May 24, 1863.

FREEMAN H. DIXON, sergeant, mustered in Aug. 11, 1862; captured at Antietam, Md., Sept. 17, 1862; promoted from corporal Feb. 8, 1863; mustered out with company May 24, 1863.

Appendix

Julian W. Stellwell, sergeant, mustered in Aug. 11, 1862; promoted to corporal Sept. 12, 1862; to sergeant Feb. 8, 1863; mustered out with company May 24, 1863.

Abner Lewis, sergeant, mustered in Aug. 11, 1862; promoted from private Nov. 1, 1862; mustered out with company May 24, 1863.

John H. Teneyck, sergeant, mustered in Aug. 11, 1862; killed at Antietam, Md., Sept. 17, 1862; buried in National Cemetery, Sec. 26, Lot A, Grave 15.

John B. Overfield, corporal, mustered in Aug. 11, 1862; wounded at Fredericksburg, Va., Dec. 13, 1862; mustered out with company May 24, 1863.

John W. Reynolds, corporal, mustered in Aug. 11, 1862; promoted to corporal Sept. 12, 1862; mustered out with company May 24, 1863.

Calvin L. Briggs, corporal, mustered in Aug. 11, 1862; promoted to corporal Feb. 8, 1863; wounded at Chancellorsville, Va., May 3, 1863; mustered out with company May 24, 1863.

Hansom H. Carrier, corporal, mustered in Aug. 11, 1862; promoted to corporal Feb. 8, 1863; wounded at Chancellorsville, Va., May 3, 1863; mustered out with company May 24, 1863.

Isaac Polmatien, corporal, mustered in Aug. 11, 1862; promoted to corporal Feb. 8, 1862; wounded at Chancellorsville, Va., May 3, 1863; mustered out with company May 24, 1863.

Daniel W. Smith, corporal, mustered in Aug. 11, 1862; mustered out with company May 24, 1863.

George N. Colvin, corporal, mustered in Aug. 11, 1862; promoted to corporal Feb. 8, 1863; mustered out with company May 24, 1863.

Porter Carpenter, corporal, mustered in Aug. 11, 1862; promoted to corporal Feb. 8, 1863; mustered out with company May 24, 1863.

James N. Gardner, corporal, mustered in Aug. 11, 1862; discharged on surgeon's certificate Nov. 23, 1862.

Otis Gilmore, corporal, mustered in Aug. 11, 1862; wounded at Antietam, Md., Sept. 17, 1862; discharged at Ascension Hospital, Washington, D. C., on surgeon's certificate December 23, 1862.

Decatur Hewett, corporal, mustered in Aug. 11, 1862; deserted April 11, 1863.

Appendix

ANDREW J. LEWIS, musician, mustered in Aug. 14, 1862; prisoner of war from May 3 to May 22, 1863; mustered out with company May 24, 1863.

ROBERT L. REYNOLDS, musician, mustered in Aug. 11, 1862; prisoner of war from May 3 to May 22, 1863; mustered out with company May 24, 1863.

ELIAS ATON, private, mustered in Aug. 11, 1862; mustered out with company May 24, 1863.

LOREN BALL, private, mustered in Aug. 11, 1862; prisoner of war from May 3 to May 22, 1863; mustered out with company May 24, 1863.

JOHN R. BRIGGS, private, mustered in Aug. 14, 1862; mustered out with company May 24, 1863.

WILLARD E. BULLOCK, private, mustered in Aug. 11, 1862; wounded at Antietam, Md., Sept. 17, 1862; mustered out with company May 24, 1863.

JOSEPH BILLINGS, private, mustered in Aug. 11, 1862; mustered out with company May 24, 1863.

SAMUEL BISHOP, private, mustered in Aug. 11, 1862; killed at Fredericksburg, Va., Dec. 13, 1862.

THOMAS J. CHASE, private, mustered in Aug. 11, 1862; absent in hospital since Sept. 6, 1862; mustered out with company May 24, 1863.

LEVI CONKLIN, private, mustered in Aug. 11, 1862; mustered out with company May 24, 1863.

THOMAS A. CASTLE, private, mustered in Aug. 11, 1862; mustered out with company May 24, 1863.

GEORGE A. CARNEY, private, mustered in Aug. 11, 1862; wounded at Antietam, Md., Sept. 17, 1862; mustered out with company May 24, 1863.

SETH A. COBB, private, mustered in Aug. 11, 1862; wounded at Antietam, Md., Sept. 17, 1862; mustered out with company May 24, 1863.

OLIVER E. CLARK, private, mustered in Aug. 11, 1862; mustered out with company May 24, 1863.

ADELBERT COLVIN, private, mustered in Aug. 11, 1862; discharged at Harwood Hospital, Washington, on surgeon's certificate Sept. 25, 1862.

BENJAMIN V. COLE, private, mustered in Aug. 11, 1862; killed at Antietam, Md., Sept. 17, 1862.

Appendix

Jerome E. Detrick, private, mustered in Aug. 11, 1862; mustered out with company May 24, 1863.

James C. Degraw, private, mustered in Aug. 11, 1862; mustered out with company May 24, 1863.

Ezra Dean, private, mustered in Aug. 11, 1862; discharged at Harwood Hospital, Washington, on surgeon's certificate Sept. 29, 1862.

Charles Evans, private, mustered in Aug. 11, 1862; killed at Antietam, Md., Sept. 17, 1862.

John F. Evans, private, mustered in Aug. 11, 1862; died at Acquia Creek, Va., Dec. 13, 1862; buried in Military Asylum Cemetery, Washington, D. C.

Sylvester Farnham, private, mustered in Aug. 11, 1862; mustered out with company May 24, 1863.

Elisha Farnham, private, mustered in Aug. 11, 1862; wounded with loss of arm at Antietam, Md., Sept. 17, 1862; discharged on surgeon's certificate Jan. 1, 1863.

Dennis D. Gardner, private, mustered in Aug. 11, 1862; mustered out with company May 24, 1863.

Alonzo E. Gregory, private, mustered in Aug. 11, 1862; killed at Antietam, Md., Sept. 17, 1863.

Philander Grow, private, mustered in Aug. 11, 1862; died near Falmouth, Va., Dec. 17, 1862.

Leslie E. Hawley, private, mustered in Aug. 11, 1862; left sick at Harper's Ferry Oct. 30, 1862, discharged but received no official notice.

Samuel Hooper, private, mustered in Aug. 11, 1862; mustered out with company May 24, 1863.

Thomas M. Hines, private, mustered in Aug. 11, 1862; mustered out with company May 24, 1863.

Harvey B. Howe, private, mustered in Aug. 11, 1862; discharged at Acquia Creek Hospital on surgeon's certificate Feb. 1, 1863.

Peter B. Hanyon, private, mustered in Aug. 11, 1862; discharged at Convalescent Camp Hospital on surgeon's certificate Feb. 15, 1863.

George M. Harding, private, mustered in Aug. 11, 1862; wounded at Fredericksburg, Va., Dec. 13, 1862; discharged at hospital, Washington, on surgeon's certificate March 10, 1863.

Benjamin H. Hanyon, private, mustered in Aug. 11, 1862; deserted Sept. 17, 1862; left in Smoketown Hospital.

Appendix

STEPHEN T. INGHAM, private, mustered in Aug. 14, 1862; mustered out with company May 24, 1863.

HORACE JACKSON, private, mustered in Aug. 11, 1862; mustered out with company May 24, 1863.

JUDSON A. JAYNE, private, mustered in Aug. 11, 1862; mustered out with company May 24, 1863.

MARTIN V. KENNEDY, private, mustered in Aug. 11, 1862; mustered out with company May 24, 1863.

SILAS G. LEWIS, private, mustered in Aug. 11, 1862; mustered out with company May 24, 1863.

FRANCIS M. LEWIS, private, mustered in Aug. 11, 1862; wounded at Fredericksburg, Va., Dec. 13, 1862, and at Chancellorsville, Va., May 3, 1863; mustered out with company May 24, 1863.

EZRA A. LAWBERT, private, mustered in Aug. 11, 1862; mustered out with company May 24, 1863.

ALVAH LETTEEN, private, mustered in Aug. 11, 1862; discharged at Fort Wood Hospital, N. Y. Harbor, on surgeon's certificate March 4, 1863.

ALBANUS LITTLE, private, mustered in Aug. 11, 1862; wounded at Antietam, Md., Sept. 17, 1862; absent at muster-out.

URIAH MOTT, private, mustered out with company May 24, 1863.

EMMET J. MATHEWSON, private, mustered in Aug. 11, 1862; mustered out with company May 24, 1863.

CHARLES W. MARTIN, private, mustered in Aug. 11, 1862; discharged at Hammond's Hospital, Point Pleasant, Md., on surgeon's certificate Jan. 6, 1863.

WILSON D. MINOR, private, mustered in Aug. 11, 1862; wounded at Antietam, Md., Sept. 17, 1862; discharged on surgeon's certificate Nov. 1, 1862.

THOMAS S. MOORE, private, mustered in Aug. 11, 1862; died at Georgetown, D. C., Oct. 14, 1862.

OLIVER C. NEWBERG, private, mustered in Aug. 11, 1862; discharged at Patent Office, 400 F, Washington, D. C., on surgeon's certificate Jan. 11, 1863.

HORACE O'NEAL, private, mustered in Aug. 11, 1862; mustered out with company May 24, 1863.

HENRY ORNT, private, mustered in Aug. 11, 1862; killed at Antietam, Md., Sept. 17, 1862.

ELISHA PEDRICK, private, mustered in Aug. 11, 1862; wounded at Antietam, Md., Sept. 17, 1862.

Appendix

BYRON PREVOST, private, mustered in Aug. 11, 1862; wounded at Antietam, Md., Sept. 17, 1862; mustered out with company May 24, 1863.

CHARLES PLATTENBURG, private, mustered in Aug. 11, 1862; mustered out with company May 24, 1863.

RUFUS F. PARRISH, private, mustered in Aug. 11, 1862; wounded at Antietam, Md., Sept. 17, 1862; discharged on surgeon's certificate Feb. 25, 1863.

REUBEN PLATTENBURG, private, mustered in Aug. 11, 1862; died at Washington, D. C., March 12, 1863.

WILLIAM H. REYNOLDS, private, mustered in Aug. 11, 1862; wounded at Antietam, Md., Sept. 17, 1862; deserted Oct. 20, 1862; returned January 13, 1863; mustered out with company May 24, 1863.

ALBERT G. REYNOLDS, private, mustered in Aug. 11, 1862; mustered out with company May 24, 1863.

OLIVER E. REYNOLDS, private, mustered in Aug. 11, 1862; mustered out with company May 24, 1863.

PERRY T. ROUGHT, private, mustered in Aug. 11, 1862; mustered out with company May 24, 1863.

WASHINGTON L. ROUGHT, private, mustered in Aug. 11, 1862; discharged at Washington on surgeon's certificate Feb. 12, 1863.

MILOT ROBERTS, private, mustered in Aug. 11, 1862; died Sept. 20 of wounds received at Antietam, Md., Sept. 17, 1862.

ESICK SMITH, private, mustered in Aug. 11, 1862; mustered out with company May 24, 1863.

JEREMIAH STANTON, private, mustered in Aug. 11, 1862; mustered out with company May 24, 1863.

DAVIS C. SMITH, private, mustered in Aug. 11, 1862; left in hospital near Falmouth May 15, 1863; absent at muster-out.

WILLIAM SHOEMAKER, private, mustered in Aug. 11, 1862; mustered out with company May 24, 1863.

ASA SMERD, private, mustered in Aug. 11, 1862; left sick at Belle Plains Landing Dec. 6, 1862; absent sick at muster-out.

HARMAN STARK, private, mustered in Aug. 11, 1862; wounded at Antietam, Md., Sept. 17, 1862; mustered out with company May 24, 1863.

WESLEY J. STARK, private, mustered in Aug. 11, 1862; deserted Nov. 20, 1862; returned March 12, 1863; mustered out with company May 24, 1863.

Appendix

BURTON SHOEMAKER, private, mustered in Aug. 11, 1862; discharged at New York on surgeon's certificate Jan. 6, 1863.

JOHN H. SMITH, private, mustered in Aug. 11, 1862; killed at Antietam, Md., Sept. 17, 1862; buried in National Cemetery, Sec. 26, Lot A, Grave 16.

JOSEPH W. STANTON, private, mustered in Aug. 11, 1862; left sick at Harper's Ferry Oct. 30, 1862; deserted from hospital.

JACOB A. THOMAS, private, mustered in Aug. 11, 1862; mustered out with company May 24, 1863.

UTLEY TURNER, private, mustered in Aug. 14, 1862; discharged at Philadelphia on surgeon's certificate Jan. 6, 1863.

HENRY B. TURNER, private, mustered in Aug. 11, 1862; killed at Antietam, Md., Sept. 17, 1862.

W. B. VANARSDALE, private, mustered in Aug. 11, 1862; mustered out with company May 24, 1863.

ANDREW M. WANDLE, private, mustered in Aug. 11, 1862; captured at Sniker's Gap, Va., Nov. 4, 1862, prisoner of war from Nov. 4 to Dec. 24, 1862; mustered out with company May 24, 1863.

JOHN WALL, private, mustered in Aug. 11, 1862; mustered out with company May 24, 1863.

* ELMORE H. WELLS, private, mustered in Aug. 14, 1862; promoted to quartermaster-sergeant of regiment Aug. 26, 1862; returned to company Jan. 1, 1863; mustered out with company.

HIRAM E. WORDEN, private, mustered in Aug. 11, 1862; mustered out with company May 24, 1863.

COMPANY C.

HERMAN TOWNSEND, captain, mustered in Aug. 13, 1862; discharged on surgeon's certificate Jan. 10, 1863.

CHARLES M. McDOUGAL, captain, mustered in Aug. 13, 1862; promoted from first lieutenant Jan. 10, 1863; wounded at Fredericksburg, Va., Dec. 13, 1862; mustered out with company May 24, 1863.

JAMES A. ROGERS, first lieutenant, mustered in Aug. 11, 1862; promoted from sergeant to first sergeant Sept. 18, 1862; to first lieutenant Jan. 10, 1863; mustered out with company May 24, 1863.

ANSON C. CRANMER, second lieutenant, mustered in Aug. 13, 1862; killed at Antietam, Md., Sept. 17, 1862.

---

* Prolonged illness from typhoid fever.

Appendix

LEVI D. LANDON, second lieutenant, mustered in Aug. 11, 1862; promoted from first sergeant Sept. 18, 1862; mustered out with company May 24, 1863.

RUSSELL J. ROSS, first sergeant, mustered in Aug. 11, 1862; promoted from corporal Jan. 11, 1863; mustered out with company May 24, 1863.

DEWITT TEAVER, sergeant, mustered in Aug. 11, 1862; mustered out with company May 24, 1863.

AMOS W. VANFLEET, sergeant, mustered in Aug. 11, 1862; promoted from corporal Sept. 18, 1862; mustered out with company May 24, 1863.

ANDREW E. WATTS, sergeant, mustered in Aug. 11, 1862; promoted to corporal Sept. 18, 1862; to sergeant Jan. 11, 1863; mustered out with company May 24, 1863.

SAMUEL W. WILCOX, sergeant, mustered in Aug. 11, 1862; promoted from corporal Oct. 1, 1862; mustered out with company May 24, 1863.

JOHN C. CRAVEN, sergeant, mustered in Aug. 11, 1862; discharged on surgeon's certificate Feb. 5, 1863.

ALONZO R. CASE, sergeant, mustered in Aug. 11, 1862; promoted to commissary-sergeant Dec. 25, 1862. (See Field and Staff.)

H. W. PARKHURST, corporal, mustered in Aug. 11, 1862; absent, sick, at muster-out.

JOHN A. BLOOM, corporal, mustered in Aug. 11, 1862; mustered out with company May 24, 1863.

JOHN MCCLURE, corporal, mustered in Aug. 11, 1862; promoted to corporal Jan. 11, 1863; wounded at Chancellorsville, Va., May 3, 1863; mustered out with company May 24, 1863.

LUCIEN BOTHWELL, corporal, mustered in Aug. 11, 1862; promoted to corporal Jan. 11, 1863; mustered out with company May 24, 1863.

ELIJAH R. HICKOK, corporal, mustered in Aug. 11, 1862; promoted to corporal March 1, 1863; mustered out with company May 24, 1863.

WALLACE BIDDLE, corporal, mustered in Aug. 11, 1862; discharged on surgeon's certificate Feb. 15, 1863.

SAMUEL E. BLANCHARD, corporal, mustered in Aug. 11, 1862; discharged on surgeon's certificate Feb. 16, 1863.

MELVILLE F. EPHLINE, musician, mustered in Aug. 11, 1862; mustered out with company May 24, 1863.

Appendix

WILLIAM SPENCER, musician, mustered in Aug. 11, 1862; mustered out with company May 24, 1863.

ALLEN M. AYRES, private, mustered in Aug. 11, 1862; wounded at Antietam, Md., Sept. 17, 1862; absent sick at muster-out.

HARRISON B. BENSON, private, mustered in Aug. 11, 1862; mustered out with company May 24, 1863.

GEORGE BENNETT, private, mustered in Aug. 11, 1862; mustered out with company May 24, 1863.

MANNING BAILEY, private, mustered in Aug. 11, 1862; mustered out with company May 24, 1863.

AMOS S. BOOTHE, private, mustered in Aug. 11, 1862; absent sick at muster-out.

JAMES A. BARNES, private, mustered in Aug. 11, 1862; mustered out with company May 24, 1863.

JEREMIAH BAILEY, private, mustered in Aug. 11, 1862; discharged on surgeon's certificate Nov. 24, 1862.

SAMUEL H. BARTLETT, private, mustered in Aug. 11, 1862; died at Falmouth, Va., Feb. 4, 1863.

OLIVER BLANCHARD, private, mustered in Aug. 11, 1862; died Sept. 24 of wounds received at Antietam, Md., Sept. 17, 1862; buried in National Cemetery, Sec. 26, Lot A, Grave 181.

LEROY J. CEASE, private, mustered in Aug. 11, 1862; mustered out with company May 24, 1863.

THOMAS D. CROSS, private, mustered in Aug. 11, 1862; mustered out with company May 24, 1863.

NATHAN S. DENMARK, private, mustered in Aug. 11, 1862; mustered out with company May 24, 1863.

LEWIS DARLING, private, mustered in Aug. 11, 1862; mustered out with company May 24, 1863.

SIMEON ELLIOTT, private, mustered in Aug. 11, 1862; mustered out with company May 24, 1863.

SYLVESTER M. GREEN, private, mustered in Aug. 11, 1862; mustered out with company May 24, 1863.

JOHN GRAUTEER, private, mustered in Aug. 11, 1862; mustered out with company May 24, 1863.

OSCAR C. GRISWOLD, private, mustered in Aug. 11, 1862; mustered out with company May 24, 1863.

AMBROSE S. GRAY, private, mustered in Aug. 11, 1862; mustered out with company May 24, 1863.

Appendix

MARTIN W. GRAY, private, mustered in Aug. 11, 1862; discharged on surgeon's certificate Dec. 22, 1862.

HENRY H. HOAGLAND, private, mustered in Aug. 11, 1862; mustered out with company May 24, 1863.

JASPER N. HOAGLAND, private, mustered in Aug. 11, 1862; mustered out with company May 24, 1863.

ISAAC N. HARVEY, private, mustered in Aug. 11, 1862; mustered out with company May 24, 1863.

GEORGE W. HARVEY, private, mustered in Aug. 11, 1862; mustered out with company May 24, 1863.

JOHN J. HOWLAND, private, mustered in Aug. 11, 1862; mustered out with company May 24, 1863.

TRUMAN HARRIS, private, mustered in Aug. 11, 1862; mustered out with company May 24, 1863.

SOLON J. HICKOK, private, mustered in Aug. 11, 1862; mustered out with company May 24, 1863.

STEPHEN C. HICKOK, private, mustered in Aug. 11, 1862; mustered out with company May 24, 1863.

CHARLES O. HAZLETON, private, mustered in Aug. 11, 1862; discharged on surgeon's certificate April 20, 1863.

WILLIAM HAMILTON, private, mustered in Aug. 11, 1862; discharged on surgeon's certificate Feb. 15, 1863.

FRANCIS HARRIS, private, mustered in Aug. 11, 1862; died at Le Roy, Pa., Jan. 18, 1863.

JOHN C. HURLBURT, private, mustered in Aug. 11, 1862; killed at Fredericksburg, Va., Dec. 13, 1862.

SETH HOWLAND, private, mustered in Aug. 11, 1862; killed at Chancellorsville, Va., May 3, 1863.

ANDREW E. HOAGLAND, private, mustered in Aug. 11, 1862; killed at Fredericksburg, Va., Dec. 13, 1862.

WILLIAM W. HAXTON, private, mustered in Aug. 11, 1862; deserted Sept. 17, 1862.

SILICK JUNE, private, mustered in Aug. 11, 1862; mustered out with company May 24, 1863.

FREDERICK KERRICK, private, mustered in Aug. 11, 1862; discharged on surgeon's certificate Feb. 4, 1863.

ROSCOE S. LOOMIS, private, mustered in Aug. 11, 1862; mustered out with company May 24, 1863.

DAVID P. LINDLEY, private, mustered in Aug. 11, 1862; mustered out with company May 24, 1863.

Appendix

SAMUEL LINDLEY, private, mustered in Aug. 11, 1862; prisoner of war; date not given; mustered out with company May 24, 1863.

IRA LINDLEY, private, mustered in Aug. 11, 1862; discharged April 29, 1863; expiration of term.

LEVI R. LESTER, private, mustered in Aug. 11, 1862; died at Washington, D. C., Feb. 9, 1863; buried in Military Asylum Cemetery.

LEWIS M. LEONARD, private, mustered in Aug. 11, 1862; killed at Fredericksburg, Va., Dec. 13, 1862.

GEORGE MALLORY, private, mustered in Aug. 11, 1862; discharged on surgeon's certificate Nov. 28, 1862.

CHARLES L. MILES, private, mustered in Aug. 11, 1862; died near Falmouth, Va., May 12, 1863.

LYMAN R. NEWELL, private, mustered in Aug. 11, 1862; discharged on surgeon's certificate Feb. 15, 1863.

STEPHEN A. RANDALL, private, mustered in Aug. 11, 1862; mustered out with company May 24, 1863.

JOHN H. NEWELL, private, mustered in Aug. 11, 1862; discharged Oct. 29, 1862, on surgeon's certificate of disability.

JOHN RANDALL, private, mustered in Aug. 11, 1862; mustered out with company May 24, 1863.

CHARLES M. ROGERS, private, mustered in Aug. 11, 1862; mustered out with company May 24, 1863.

JUDSON A. ROYSE, private, mustered in Aug. 11, 1862; mustered out with company May 24, 1863.

DeWITT C. ROBINSON, private, mustered in Aug. 11, 1862; mustered out with company May 24, 1863.

JEREMIAH ROCKWELL, private, mustered in Aug. 11, 1862; discharged on surgeon's certificate March 23, 1863.

LYNDS A. SPENCER, private, mustered in Aug. 11, 1862; mustered out with company May 24, 1863.

JAMES SOPER, private, mustered in Aug. 11, 1862; mustered out with company May 24, 1863.

JOHN B. STREETS, private, mustered in Aug. 11, 1862; mustered out with company May 24, 1863.

GEO. C. SHOEMAKER, private, mustered in Aug. 11, 1862; mustered out with company May 24, 1863.

JOHN SCHNADER, private, mustered in Aug. 11, 1862; mustered out with company May 24, 1863.

Appendix

SOLOMON STONE, private, mustered in Aug. 11, 1862; prisoner of war; mustered out with company May 24, 1863.

LEWIS SELLARD, private, mustered in Aug. 11, 1862; mustered out with company May 24, 1863.

WILLIAM SMITH, private, mustered in Aug. 11, 1862; discharged on surgeon's certificate Feb. 9, 1863.

DANIEL W. SMITH, private, mustered in Aug. 11, 1862; discharged on surgeon's certificate Feb. 26, 1863.

NATHAN J. SPENCER, private, mustered in Aug. 11, 1862; discharged on surgeon's certificate April 2, 1863.

JAMES M. SNADER, private, mustered in Aug. 11, 1862; discharged on surgeon's certificate Nov. 28, 1862.

LUKE P. STREETER, private, mustered in Aug. 11, 1862; discharged on surgeon's certificate Oct. 12, 1862.

JEREMIAH SMITH, private, mustered in Aug. 11, 1862; died near Falmouth, Va., Jan. 8, 1863.

CHARLES B. THOMAS, private, mustered in Aug. 11, 1862; killed at Fredericksburg, Va., Dec. 13, 1862.

GEORGE M. VAN DYKE, private, mustered in Aug. 11, 1862; mustered out with company May 24, 1863

E. G. VAN DYKE, private, mustered in Aug. 11, 1862; prisoner of war; mustered out with company May 24, 1863.

LANING N. VARGASON, private, mustered in Aug. 11, 1862; mustered out with company May 24, 1863.

SEVELLON A. WILCOX, private, mustered in Aug. 11, 1862; mustered out with company May 24, 1863.

JEFFERSON A. WITHERALL, private, mustered in Aug. 11, 1862; mustered out with company Aug. 24, 1863.

CHARLES WALTER, private, mustered in Aug. 11, 1862; mustered out with company May 24, 1863.

CHAUNCEY W. WHEELER, private, mustered in Aug. 11, 1862; mustered out with company May 24, 1863.

MERTON C. WRIGHT, private, mustered in Aug. 11, 1862; discharged Sept. 11, 1862, on surgeon's certificate.

JOSEPH N. WRIGHT, private, mustered in Aug. 11, 1862; discharged Sept. 11, 1862, on surgeon's certificate.

ROSWELL A. WALKER, private, mustered in Aug. 11, 1862; died at Belle Plain, Va., Dec. 7, 1862.

Appendix

COMPANY D.

CHARLES H. CHASE, captain, mustered in Aug. 14, 1862; resigned Dec. 6, 1862.

W. H. CARNOCHAN, captain, mustered in Aug. 14, 1862; promoted from second lieutenant Nov. 29, 1862; mustered out with company May 24, 1863.

CHARLES E. GLADDING, first lieutenant, mustered in Aug. 14, 1862; mustered out with company Nov. 24, 1863.

J. W. BROWN, second lieutenant, mustered in Aug. 14, 1862; discharged Aug. 20, 1862, to date Aug. 14, 1862.

F. MARION WELLS, second lieutenant, mustered in Aug. 12, 1862; promoted from first sergeant Dec. 6, 1862; wounded with loss of leg at Chancellorsville, Va., May 3, 1863; absent in hospital at muster-out; died a few days later.

WILLIAM C. COBB, first sergeant, mustered in Aug. 13, 1862; promoted to first sergeant Feb. 6, 1863; mustered out with company May 24, 1863.

ALVAH L. COOPER, sergeant, mustered in Aug. 12, 1862; promoted from corporal Feb. 6, 1863; mustered out with company May 24, 1863.

LERT BALLARD, sergeant, mustered in Aug. 12, 1862; mustered out with company May 24, 1863.

ALBERT LONG, sergeant, mustered in Aug. 12, 1862; promoted from corporal Jan. 29, 1863; mustered out with company May 24, 1863.

ALBERT S. COBB, sergeant, mustered in Aug. 12, 1862; promoted from corporal Feb. 6, 1863; mustered out with company May 24, 1863.

DANIEL GRACE, corporal, mustered in Aug. 12, 1862; promoted to corporal April 16, 1863; mustered out with company May 24, 1863.

ALONZO ROSS, corporal, mustered in Aug. 12, 1863; promoted to corporal April 16, 1863; mustered out with company May 24, 1863.

ALBERT PRESTON, corporal, mustered in Aug. 12, 1862; wounded at Fredericksburg, Va., Dec. 13, 1862; promoted to corporal Feb. 4, 1863; mustered out with company.

JAMES F. CARMAN, corporal, mustered in Aug. 12, 1863; promoted to corporal Jan. 7, 1863; mustered out with company.

ALBERT O. SCOTT, corporal, mustered in Aug. 12, 1862; wounded

Appendix

at Fredericksburg, Va., Dec. 13, 1862; promoted to corporal Feb. 6, 1863; mustered out with company.

FURMAN BULLOCK, corporal, mustered in Aug. 12, 1862; promoted to corporal Feb. 6, 1863; mustered out with company.

SAMUEL HARKNESS, corporal, mustered in Aug. 12, 1862; mustered out with company May 24, 1863.

JOHN C. McMAHON, corporal, mustered in Aug. 12, 1862; discharged on surgeon's certificate Oct. 14, 1862.

ELIHU B. CHASE, corporal, mustered in Aug. 12, 1862; discharged on surgeon's certificate Oct. 14, 1862.

L. N. BURNHAM, corporal, mustered in Aug. 12, 1862; died Nov. 14, 1862, of wounds received at Antietam, Md., Sept. 17, 1862; buried at Chester, Pa.

HUBBARD H. WILLIAMS, corporal, mustered in Aug. 12, 1862; deserted at Washington, D. C., Nov. 10, 1862; returned May 1, 1865; discharged by General Order June 12, 1865.

NATHANIEL MATTOCK, musician, mustered in Aug. 12, 1862; mustered out with company May 24, 1863.

DANIEL H. MOORE, musician, mustered in Aug. 12, 1862; discharged on surgeon's certificate Jan. 6, 1863.

STEPHEN T. HALL, wagoner, mustered in Aug. 15, 1862; promoted to corporal Aug. 15, 1862; reduced to ranks Feb. 6, 1863; mustered out with company.

JOHN B. ALEXANDER, private, mustered in Aug. 12, 1862; mustered out with company May 24, 1863.

JULIAN L. ANDRUS, private, mustered in Aug. 12, 1862; mustered out with company May 24, 1863.

NATHAN E. BAILEY, private, mustered in Aug. 12, 1862; mustered out with company May 24, 1863.

CHARLES BOYCE, private, mustered in Aug. 12, 1862; mustered out with company May 24, 1863.

DARIUS BULLOCK, private, mustered in Aug. 12, 1862; mustered out with company May 24, 1863.

JOSEPH BOUGHTON, private, mustered in Aug. 12, 1862; wounded at Fredericksburg, Va., Dec. 13, 1862; mustered out with company.

WARREN S. BIXLEY, private, mustered in Aug. 12, 1862; mustered out with company May 24, 1863.

ELLIS H. BEST, private, mustered in Aug. 12, 1862; mustered out with company May 24, 1863.

Appendix

GEORGE BENNETT, private, mustered in Aug. 12, 1862; mustered out with company May 24, 1863.

AARON W. BAILEY, private, mustered in Aug. 12, 1862; discharged on surgeon's certificate Jan. 20, 1863.

OLIVER E. BLAKESLEE, private, mustered in Aug. 12, 1862; died at Washington, D. C., Jan. 23, 1863; pneumonia.

ORRIN G. BLAKESLEE, private, mustered in Aug. 12, 1862; died at Harper's Ferry, Va., Nov. 19, 1862.

WARREN S. BAILEY, private, mustered in Aug. 12, 1862; deserted Oct. 3, 1862, at Harper's Ferry.

RICHARD W. CANEDY, private, mustered in Aug. 12, 1862; mustered out with company May 24, 1863.

WILLIAM M. CLARK, private, mustered in Aug. 12, 1862; mustered out with company May 24, 1863.

DANIEL CARMAN, private, mustered in Aug. 12, 1862; mustered out with company May 24, 1863.

CHARLES O. DARK, private, mustered in Aug. 12, 1862; mustered out with company May 24, 1863.

CHRISTOPHER DENMARK, private, mustered in Aug. 12, 1862; wounded at Fredericksburg, Va., Dec. 13, 1862; mustered out with company May 24, 1863.

REUBEN DUDLEY, private, mustered in Aug. 12, 1862; discharged on surgeon's certificate March 1, 1863.

PETER FULLER, private, mustered in Aug. 13, 1862; wounded at Chancellorsville, Va., May 3, 1863; in hospital at muster-out.

GEORGE FIELDS, private, mustered in Aug. 12, 1862; wounded at Antietam, Md., Sept. 17, 1862; mustered out with company May 24, 1863.

LEANDER L. GREGORY, private, mustered in Aug. 12, 1862; mustered out with company May 24, 1863.

GEORGE C. GEROULD, private, mustered in Aug. 12, 1862; died Oct. 14 of wounds received at Antietam, Md., Sept. 17, 1862.

RICHARD M. HOWLAND, private, mustered in Aug. 12, 1862; mustered out with company May 24, 1863.

GEORGE W. HOWLAND, private, mustered in Aug. 12, 1862; mustered out with company May 24, 1863.

JEROME S. HILL, private, mustered in Aug. 12, 1862; mustered out with company May 24, 1863.

GEORGE W. HARDY, private, mustered in Aug. 12, 1862; mustered out with company May 24, 1863.

Appendix

MARTIN HARKNESS, private, mustered in Aug. 12, 1862; discharged on surgeon's certificate Dec. 16, 1862.

BENJAMIN F. JONES, private, mustered in Aug. 12, 1862; mustered out with company May 24, 1863.

LEWIS W. JONES, private, mustered in Aug. 12, 1862; mustered out with company May 24, 1863.

RICHARD M. JOHNSON, private, mustered in Aug. 12, 1862; deserted Sept. 14, 1862.

ALVAH M. KENT, private, mustered in Aug. 12, 1862; mustered out with company May 24, 1863.

THOMAS LEE, private, mustered in Aug. 12, 1862; mustered out with company May 24, 1863.

LEWIS LAURENT, private, mustered in Aug. 12, 1862; mustered out with company May 24, 1863.

FESTUS LYON, private, mustered in Aug. 12, 1862; mustered out with company May 24, 1863.

WILLIAM A. MORES, private, mustered in Aug. 12, 1862; mustered out with company May 24, 1863.

JOSEPH F. MORLEY, private, mustered in Aug. 12, 1862; mustered out with company May 24, 1863.

GOPHAR MORGAN, private, mustered in Aug. 12, 1862; discharged on surgeon's certificate Nov. 20, 1862.

ABNER MILLER, private, mustered in Aug. 13, 1862; discharged on surgeon's certificate Dec. 31, 1862.

JOHN McGREGOR, private, mustered in Aug. 12, 1862; wounded at Antietam, Md., Sept. 17, 1862; mustered out with company May 24, 1863.

GEORGE W. McALISTER, private, mustered in Aug. 12, 1862; mustered out with company May 24, 1863.

JAMES N. McALISTER, private, mustered in Aug. 12, 1862; deserted Sept. 14, 1862; returned March 31, 1863; mustered out with company May 24, 1863.

MICHAEL E. McINTOSH, private, mustered in Aug. 12, 1862; prisoner of war from Nov. 14 to Dec. 14, 1862; mustered out with company May 24, 1863.

ORRIN P. McALLISTER, private, mustered in Aug. 12, 1862; discharged on surgeon's certificate Dec. 18, 1862.

SAMUEL R. McMAHON, private, mustered in Aug. 12, 1862; killed at Fredericksburg, Va., Dec. 13, 1862.

ISAAC P. McINTYRE, private, mustered in Aug. 12, 1862; died

Appendix

near Falmouth, Va., Dec. 22, of wounds received at Fredericksburg, Va., Dec. 13, 1862.

WILLIAM F. NEWELL, private, mustered in Aug. 12, 1862; mustered out with company May 24, 1863.

HENRY A. NEWELL, private, mustered in Aug. 12, 1862; mustered out with company May 24, 1863.

CHESTER NORTHROP, private, mustered in Aug. 12, 1862; mustered out with company May 24, 1863.

WILLIAM PEET, private, mustered in Aug. 12, 1862; absent in hospital at muster-out.

JAMES PATTERSON, private, mustered in Aug. 13, 1862; mustered out with company May 24, 1863.

RICHARD W. PHILLIPS, private, mustered in Aug. 13, 1862; mustered out with company May 24, 1863.

HOMER T. RHODES, private, mustered in Aug. 13, 1862; mustered out with company May 24, 1863.

HENRY J. RUSSELL, private, mustered in Aug. 12, 1862; mustered out with company May 24, 1863.

S. CHENEY ROBY, private, mustered in Aug. 12, 1862; mustered out with company May 24, 1863.

NEHEMIAH ROBINSON, private, mustered in Aug. 12, 1862; deserted at Frederick City, Md., Sept. 14, 1862.

CHARLES N. SMITH, private, mustered in Aug. 12, 1862; mustered out with company May 24, 1863.

BYRON B. SLADE, private, mustered in Aug. 13, 1862; mustered out with company May 24, 1863.

NORMAN C. SHEPHERD, private, mustered in Aug. 13, 1862; mustered out with company May 24, 1863.

EDWARD C. STRONG, private, mustered in Aug. 13, 1862; discharged on surgeon's certificate Feb. 7, 1863.

BARLOW SMITH, private, mustered in Aug. 12, 1862; died at Harper's Ferry, Va., Nov. 12, 1862.

CONRAD SCHANTZ, private, mustered in Aug. 13, 1862; deserted at Harrisburg Aug. 15, 1862.

J. O. VAN BUSKERK, private, mustered in Aug. 13, 1862; discharged on surgeon's certificate Feb. 6, 1863.

JOSEPH S. WILCOX, private, mustered in Aug. 13, 1862; mustered out with company May 24, 1863.

BARNUM WILCOX, private, mustered in Aug. 13, 1862; mustered out with company May 24, 1863.

Appendix

NORMAN WILCOX, private, mustered in Aug. 12, 1862; wounded at Chancellorsville, Va., May 3, 1863; mustered out with company May 24, 1863.

NATHAN WILCOX, private, mustered in Aug. 12, 1862; wounded at Fredericksburg, Va., Dec. 13, 1862, and at Chancellorsville, Va., May 3, 1863; mustered out with company May 24, 1863.

IRA V. WILLIAMS, private, mustered in Aug. 12, 1862; wounded at Chancellorsville, Va., May 3, 1863; mustered out with company May 24, 1863.

CHARLES W. WHIPPLE, private, mustered in Aug. 13, 1862; wounded at Fredericksburg, Va., Dec. 13, 1862; mustered out with company May 24, 1863.

CHARLES WILLIAMS, private, mustered in Aug. 13, 1862; discharged on surgeon's certificate Oct. 14, 1862.

EZRA H. WELCH, private, mustered in Aug. 13, 1862; died at Belle Plain, Va., Dec. 4, 1862.

W. H. WOODWORTH, private, mustered in Aug. 13, 1862; died at Falmouth, Va., Jan. 9, 1863.

MARTIN WEST, private, mustered in Aug. 13, 1862; deserted October, 1862.

COMPANY E.

MICHAEL WHITMOYER, captain, mustered in Aug. 15, 1862; mustered out with company May 24, 1863.

ANDREW C. MENSCH, first lieutenant, mustered in Aug. 15, 1862; mustered out with company May 24, 1863.

D. RAMSEY MELICK, second lieutenant, mustered in Aug. 15, 1862; mustered out with company May 24, 1863.

WILLIAM A. BARTON, first sergeant, mustered in Aug. 13, 1862; mustered out with company May 24, 1863.

WILLIAM H. GILMORE, sergeant, mustered in Aug. 13, 1862; mustered out with company May 24, 1863.

WILLIAM J. RENN, sergeant, mustered in Aug. 13, 1862; mustered out with company May 24, 1863.

CHARLES P. SLOAN, sergeant, mustered in Aug. 13, 1862; promoted from corporal Jan. 10, 1863; mustered out with company May 24, 1863.

ISAAC N. KLINE, sergeant, mustered in Aug. 13, 1862; promoted from corporal Jan. 10, 1863; mustered out with company May 24, 1863.

Appendix

BENJAMIN F. JOHNSTON, corporal, mustered in Aug. 13, 1862; mustered out with company May 24, 1863.

CLARK KRESSLER, corporal, mustered in Aug. 13, 1862; mustered out with company May 24, 1863.

HENRY M. JOHNSTON, corporal, mustered in Aug. 13, 1862; mustered out with company May 24, 1863.

EPHRAIM N. KLINE, corporal, mustered in Aug. 13, 1862; mustered out with company May 24, 1863.

EDWARD C. GREEN, corporal, mustered in Aug. 14, 1862; promoted to corporal Nov. 10, 1862; mustered out with company May 24, 1863.

JOHN N. HUGHES, corporal, mustered in Aug. 13, 1862; promoted to corporal Jan. 10, 1863.; mustered out with company May 24, 1863.

JAMES B. FORTNER, corporal, mustered in Aug. 13, 1862; promoted to corporal Jan. 10, 1863; mustered out with company May 24, 1863.

SAMUEL WOOD, corporal, mustered in Aug. 13, 1862; promoted to corporal Feb. 25, 1863; mustered out with company May 24, 24, 1863.

WILLIAM C. ROBINSON, corporal, mustered in Aug. 13, 1862; discharged at Harper's Ferry on surgeon's certificate Oct. 26, 1862.

JAMES P. MELICK, corporal, mustered in Aug. 13, 1862; died at Washington, D. C., Dec. 28, of wounds received at Fredericksburg, Va., Dec. 13, 1862.

CLINTON W. NEAL, corporal, mustered in Aug. 13, 1862; promoted to quartermaster Aug. 22, 1862. (See Field and Staff.)

JOHN STALEY, musician, mustered in Aug. 13, 1862; mustered out with company May 24, 1863.

AZIMA V. HOWER, musician, mustered in Aug. 13, 1862; discharged on surgeon's certificate Jan. 29, 1863.

TILLMAN FAUX, wagoner, mustered in Aug. 13, 1862; mustered out with company May 23, 1863.

LAFAYE APPLEGATE, private, mustered in Aug. 13, 1862; mustered out with company May 24, 1863.

LEONARD BEAGLE, private, mustered in Aug. 13, 1862; mustered out with company May 24, 1863.

HIRAM H. BRODT, private, mustered in Aug. 13, 1862; mustered out with company May 24, 1863.

Appendix

JACOB W. BOMBOY, private, mustered in Aug. 14, 1862; mustered out with company May 24, 1863.

JAMES S. BOMBOY, private, mustered in Aug. 13, 1862; mustered out with company May 24, 1863.

EDWARD W. COLEMAN, private, mustered in Aug. 13, 1862; mustered out with company May 24, 1863.

JAMES W. COOK, private, mustered in Aug. 13, 1862; mustered out with company May 24, 1863.

JAMES CADMAN, private, mustered in Aug. 13, 1862; mustered out with company May 24, 1863.

PETER O. CRIST, private, mustered in Aug. 13, 1862; mustered out with company May 24, 1863.

HENRY CROOP, private, mustered in Aug. 13, 1862; discharged on surgeon's certificate Oct. 8, 1862.

THOMAS CAROTHERS, private, mustered in Aug. 13, 1862; discharged on surgeon's certificate Feb. 15, 1863.

ABEL DEILY, private, mustered in Aug. 13, 1862; mustered out with company May 24, 1863.

JOHN MOORE EVES, private, mustered in Aug. 13, 1862; mustered out with company May 24, 1863.

JOHN F. ECK, private, mustered in Aug. 13, 1862; mustered out with company May 24, 1863.

MOSES J. FRENCH, private, mustered in Aug. 14, 1862; mustered out with company May 24, 1863.

CLOD'Y S. M. FISHER, private, mustered in Aug. 13, 1862; wounded at Antietam, Md., Sept. 17, 1862; mustered out with company May 24, 1863.

CHARLES A. FOLK, private, mustered in Aug. 13, 1862; mustered out with company May 24, 1863.

ROBERT GILLASPY, private, mustered in Aug. 13, 1862; mustered out with company May 24, 1863.

JOHN P. GUILDS, private, mustered in Aug. 13, 1862; mustered out with company May 24, 1863.

CLINTON C. HUGHES, private, mustered in Aug. 13, 1862; mustered out with company May 24, 1863.

HENRY C. HARTMAN, SR., private, mustered in Aug. 13, 1862; mustered out with company May 24, 1863.

C. H. HENDERSHOT, private, mustered in Aug. 13, 1862; mustered out with company May 24, 1863.

Appendix

WILLIAM H. HUNTER, private, mustered in Aug. 13, 1862; mustered out with company May 24, 1863.

HENRY C. HARTMAN, JR., private, mustered in Aug. 13, 1862; mustered out with company May 24, 1863.

SAMUEL HARDER, private, mustered in Aug. 13, 1862; prisoner from Dec. 13, 1862, to May 22, 1863; mustered out with company May 24, 1863.

ADAM HEIST, private, mustered in Aug. 13, 1862; mustered out with company May 24, 1863.

GEORGE W. HOWELL, private, mustered in Aug. 13, 1862; mustered out with company May 24, 1863.

SAMUEL HARP, private, mustered in Aug. 13, 1862; discharged on surgeon's certificate Feb. 13, 1863.

ISAIAH S. HARTMAN, private, mustered in Aug. 13, 1862; died Oct. 16 of wounds received at Antietam, Md., Sept. 17, 1862.

JESSE M. HOWELL, private, mustered in Aug. 14, 1862; died near Falmouth, Va., Jan. 8, 1863.

JOSEPH S. HAYMAN, private, mustered in Aug. 13, 1862; deserted Aug. 30, 1862.

SAMUEL R. JOHNSON, private, mustered in Aug. 13, 1862; mustered out with company May 24, 1863.

HIRAM F. KLINE, private, mustered in Aug. 13, 1862; mustered out with company May 24, 1863.

THOMAS O. KLINE, private, mustered in Aug. 13, 1862; mustered out with company May 24, 1863.

SAMUEL C. KRICKBAUM, private, mustered in Aug. 13, 1862; mustered out with company May 24, 1863.

AMOS Y. KISNER, private, mustered in Aug. 13, 1862; mustered out with company May 24, 1863.

GEORGE M. KLINE, private, mustered in Aug. 13, 1862; mustered out with company May 24, 1863.

AUGUSTUS M. KURTZ, private, mustered in Aug. 13, 1862; mustered out with company May 24, 1863.

FRANCIS M. LUTZ, private, mustered in Aug. 13, 1862; mustered out with company May 24, 1863.

ISAAC M. LYONS, private, mustered in Aug. 13, 1862; mustered out with company May 24, 1863.

JOSEPH W. LYONS, private, mustered in Aug. 13, 1862; absent sick in hospital since Oct. 30, 1862; mustered out with company May 24, 1863.

Appendix

JOSEPH LAWTON, private, mustered in Aug. 13, 1862; mustered out with company May 24, 1863.

JOHN LAWTON, private, mustered in Aug. 13, 1862; mustered out with company May 24, 1863.

WILLIAM LAZARUS, private, mustered in Aug. 13, 1862; killed at Antietam, Md., Sept. 17, 1862.

DANIEL MARKLEY, private, mustered in Aug. 13, 1862; mustered out with company May 24, 1863.

LEMUEL MOOD, private, mustered in Aug. 13, 1862; mustered out with company May 24, 1863.

CHARLES MUFFLEY, private, mustered in Aug. 13, 1862; mustered out with company May 24, 1863.

CLARK PRICE, private, mustered in Aug. 13, 1862; mustered out with company May 24, 1863.

LEVI H. PRIEST, private, mustered in Aug. 13, 1862; mustered out with company May 24, 1863.

OLIVER PALMER, private, mustered in Aug. 13, 1862; mustered out with company May 24, 1863.

JOSEPH PENROSE, private, mustered in Aug. 13, 1862; missed in action at Fredericksburg, Va., Dec. 13, 1862.

DAVID RUCKLE, private, mustered in Aug. 13, 1862; mustered out with company May 24, 1863.

JOSIAH REEDY, private, mustered in Aug. 13, 1862; wounded at Fredericksburg, Va., Dec. 13, 1862; mustered out with company May 24, 1863.

JOHN ROADARMEL, private, mustered in Aug. 13, 1862; mustered out with company May 24, 1863.

ISAAC ROADARMEL, private, mustered in Aug. 13, 1862; mustered out with company May 24, 1863.

JEREMIAH REESE, private, mustered in Sept. 3, 1862; captured at Chancellorsville, Va.; prisoner from May 3 to May 22, 1863; mustered out with company May 24, 1863.

JONATHAN W. SNYDER, private, mustered in Aug. 13, 1862; mustered out with company May 24, 1863.

CHARLES W. SNYDER, private, mustered in Aug. 13, 1862; mustered out with company May 24, 1863.

JOSIAH STILES, private, mustered in Aug. 13, 1862; absent, sick in hospital since Sept. 16, 1862.

FREDERICK M. STALEY, private, mustered in Aug. 13, 1862; mustered out with company May 24, 1863.

Appendix

GEORGE W. STERNER, private, mustered in Aug. 13, 1862; mustered out with company May 24, 1863.

HENRY H. SANDS, private, mustered in Aug. 13, 1862; mustered out with company May 24, 1863.

WILLIAM C. SHAW, private, mustered in Aug. 13, 1862; absent, sick, at muster-out.

JAMES F. TRUMP, private, mustered in Aug. 14, 1862; mustered out with company May 24, 1863.

SAMUEL M. VANHORNE, private, mustered in Aug. 13, 1862; died at Washington, D. C., Feb. 16, 1863; buried in Harmony Burial Grounds, D. C.

PHILIP WATTS, private, mustered in Aug. 13, 1862; mustered out with company May 24, 1863.

AMASA WHITENITE, private, mustered in Aug. 13, 1862; wounded at Antietam, Md., Sept. 17, 1862; mustered out with company May 24, 1863.

GOTTLIEB WAGONER, private, mustered in Aug. 13, 1862; mustered out with company May 24, 1863.

GAYLORD WHITMOYER, private, mustered in Aug. 13, 1862; discharged on surgeon's certificate Feb. 17, 1863.

SAMUEL YOUNG, private, mustered in Aug. 13, 1862; mustered out with company May 24, 1863.

FRANKLIN J. R. ZELLARS, private, mustered in Aug. 13, 1862; mustered out with company May 24, 1863.

COMPANY F.

GEORGE W. WILHELM, captain, mustered in Aug. 15, 1862; discharged Dec. 5, 1862.

JACOB D. LACIAR, captain, mustered in Aug. 15, 1862; wounded at Antietam, Md., Sept. 17, 1862; promoted from second lieutenant Jan. 5, 1863; mustered out with company May 24, 1863.

THOMAS MUSSELMAN, first lieutenant, mustered in Aug. 15, 1862; wounded at Fredericksburg, Va., Dec. 13, 1862; mustered out with company May 24, 1863.

JOHN KERNS, second lieutenant, mustered in Aug. 15, 1862; promoted from corporal to sergeant Sept. 22, 1862; to second lieutenant Jan. 5, 1863; mustered out with company May 24, 1863.

OLIVER BRENEISER, first sergeant, mustered in Aug. 15, 1862; wounded at Antietam, Md., Sept. 17, and at Fredericksburg, Va.,

Appendix

Dec. 13, 1862; promoted to corporal Sept. 22, 1862, to first sergeant Jan. 5, 1863; mustered out with company May 24, 1863.

JACOB MILLER, sergeant, mustered in Aug. 15, 1862; mustered out with company May 24, 1863.

JOHN HOFF, sergeant, mustered in Aug. 15, 1862; promoted from corporal Nov. 22, 1862; mustered out with company May 24, 1863.

CHARLES MACK, sergeant, mustered in Aug. 15, 1862; promoted from corporal March 1, 1863; mustered out with company May 24, 1863.

JOHN SHERRY, sergeant, mustered in Aug. 15, 1862; mustered out with company May 24, 1863.

OLIVER F. MUSSELMAN, sergeant, mustered in Aug. 15, 1862; killed at Antietam, Md., Sept. 17, 1862.

F. C. WINTEMUTE, corporal, mustered in Aug. 15, 1862; promoted to corporal Aug. 18, 1862; mustered out with company May 24, 1863.

DAVID M. JONES, corporal, mustered in Aug. 15, 1862; mustered out with company May 24, 1863.

ALBERT E. SHEETS, corporal, mustered in Aug. 15, 1862; mustered out with company May 24, 1863.

WILLIAM MINER, corporal, mustered in Aug. 15, 1862; mustered out with company May 24, 1863.

WILLIAM R. REX, corporal, mustered in Aug. 15, 1862; promoted to corporal Nov. 22, 1862; mustered out with company May 24, 1863.

LEWIS TRAINER, corporal, mustered in Aug. 15, 1862; promoted to corporal Nov. 22, 1862; mustered out with company May 24, 1863.

JOHN SCHULTZ, corporal, mustered in Aug. 15, 1862; wounded at Antietam, Md., Sept. 17, 1862; promoted to corporal Jan. 2, 1863; mustered out with company May 24, 1863.

JOSEPH SCHADEL, corporal, mustered in Aug. 15, 1862; died at Belle Plain, Va., Nov. 28, 1862.

GEORGE W. DURYEA, corporal, mustered in Aug. 15, 1862; deserted Aug. 16, 1862, from Camp Curtin.

EDWIN SEYFRIED, musician, mustered in Aug. 15, 1862; discharged on surgeon's certificate Feb. 25, 1863.

BAR'T ARMBRUSTER, private, mustered in Aug. 15, 1862; mustered out with company May 24, 1863.

Appendix

DAVID ARNER, private, mustered in Aug. 15, 1862; mustered out with company May 24, 1863.

WILLIAM ALLEN, private, mustered in Aug. 15, 1862; captured at Fredericksburg, Va., Dec. 13, 1862; mustered out with company May 24, 1863.

AUGUST BELSNER, private, mustered in Aug. 15, 1862; wounded at Chancellorsville, Va., May 3, 1863; mustered out with company May 24, 1863.

THOMAS BAKER, private, mustered in Aug. 15, 1862; mustered out with company May 24, 1863.

DANIEL BARTLEY, private, mustered in Aug. 15, 1862; deserted Sept. 12, 1862, near Rockville, Md.

STEPHEN CUNFER, private, mustered in Aug. 15, 1862; mustered out with company May 24, 1863.

THOMAS CHRISTINE, private, mustered in Aug. 15, 1862; mustered out with company May 24, 1863.

JOSEPH L. CLEWELL, private, mustered in Aug. 15, 1862; died at Harper's Ferry, Va., Oct. 1 of wounds received at Antietam, Md., Sept. 17, 1862.

CHAS. S. DREISBACH, private, mustered in Aug. 15, 1862; mustered out with company May 24, 1863.

JOSEPH B. DREISBACH, private, mustered in Aug. 15, 1862; mustered out with company May 24, 1863.

JOSEPH DRUMBORE, private, mustered in Aug. 15, 1862; discharged Jan. 13, 1863, for wounds received at Antietam, Md., Sept. 17, 1862.

PETER EVERTS, private, mustered in Aug. 15, 1862; mustered out with company May 24, 1863.

WILLIAM EVERTS, private, mustered in Aug. 15, 1862; wounded at Fredericksburg, Va., Dec. 13, 1862; mustered out with company May 24, 1863.

JONATHAN ECK, private, mustered in Aug. 15, 1862; mustered out with company May 24, 1863.

SAMUEL EVERTS, private, mustered in Aug. 15, 1862; discharged on surgeon's certificate Feb. 13, 1863.

OWEN C. FULLWEILER, private, mustered in Aug. 15, 1862; absent, sick, at muster-out.

AMON FRITZ, private, mustered in Aug. 15, 1862; wounded at Fredericksburg, Va., Dec. 13, 1862; mustered out with company May 24, 1863.

Appendix

LEWIS FREDERICK, private, mustered in Aug. 15, 1862; mustered out with company May 24, 1863.

WILLIAM FRANTZ, private, mustered in Aug. 15, 1862; wounded at Antietam, Md., Sept. 17, 1862; absent, sick, at muster-out.

AARON H. GUMBARD, private, mustered in Aug. 15, 1862; mustered out with company May 24, 1863.

HENRY GROW, private, mustered in Aug. 15, 1862; mustered out with company May 24, 1863.

GEORGE H. GEARHARD, private, mustered in Aug. 15, 1862; discharged March 10, 1863, for wounds received at Fredericksburg, Va., Dec. 13, 1862.

SAMUEL GROW, private, mustered in Aug. 15, 1862; died Dec. 21 of wounds received at Fredericksburg, Va., Dec. 13, 1862; buried at Alexandria; Grave 630.

JOSEPH HONTZ, private, mustered in Aug. 15, 1862; wounded at Antietam, Md., Sept. 17, 1862; mustered out with company May 24, 1863.

OLIVER HOFF, private, mustered in Aug. 15, 1862; mustered out with company May 24, 1863.

FREDERICK HOSLER, private, mustered in Aug. 15, 1862; mustered out with company May 24, 1863.

JOHN W. HOTTENSTEIN, private, mustered in Aug. 15, 1862; mustered out with company May 24, 1863.

GEORGE HOUSER, private, mustered in Aug. 15, 1862; mustered out with company May 24, 1863.

SEBASTIAN HON, private, mustered in Aug. 15, 1862; mustered out with company May 24, 1863.

JOHN HILLS, private, mustered in Aug. 15, 1862; deserted Aug. 16, 1862, from Camp Curtin.

ALEX. JOHNSON, private, mustered in Aug. 15, 1862; mustered out with company May 24, 1863.

SAMUEL KEENE, private, mustered in Aug. 15, 1862; mustered out with company May 24, 1863.

EDWIN KEMMERER, private, mustered in Aug. 15, 1862; mustered out with company May 24, 1863.

JOHN KISTLER, private, mustered in Aug. 15, 1862; wounded, with loss of arm, at Fredericksburg, Va., Dec. 13, 1862; discharged, date unknown.

DANIEL KRESSLEY, private, mustered in Aug. 15, 1862; discharged on surgeon's certificate Jan. 15, 1863.

Appendix

SAMUEL D. LYNN, private, mustered in Aug. 15, 1862; wounded at Fredericksburg, Va., Dec. 13, 1862; mustered out with company May 24, 1863.

LEVI M. LEVY, private, mustered in Aug. 15, 1862; discharged on surgeon's certificate Feb. 25, 1863.

JOHN LENTS, private, mustered in Aug. 15, 1862; died Jan. 2, 1863, of wounds received at Fredericksburg, Va., Dec. 13, 1862.

FRANCIS H. MOSER, private, mustered in Aug. 15, 1862; mustered out with company May 24, 1863.

MONROE MARTIN, private, mustered in Aug. 15, 1862; mustered out with company May 24, 1863.

ALEXANDER MILLS, private, mustered in Aug. 15, 1862; discharged on surgeon's certificate Sept. 29, 1862.

CHARLES F. MOYER, private, mustered in Aug. 15, 1862; died Sept. 22 of wounds received at Antietam, Md., Sept. 17, 1862.

SAMUEL MCCANCE, private, mustered in Aug. 15, 1862; mustered out with company May 24, 1863.

DANIEL MCGEE, private, mustered in Aug. 15, 1862; mustered out with company May 24, 1863.

JACOB NOTESTEIN, private, mustered in Aug. 15, 1862; mustered out with company May 24, 1863.

VALENTINE NEUMOYER, private, mustered in Aug. 15, 1862; mustered out with company May 24, 1863.

MOSES NEYER, private, mustered in Aug. 15, 1862; mustered out with company May 24, 1863.

JAMES E. NACE, private, mustered in Aug. 15, 1862; died Jan. 2, 1863, of wounds received at Fredericksburg, Va., Dec. 13, 1862.

ENOS OLWERSTEFLER, private, mustered in Aug. 15, 1862; wounded at Fredericksburg, Va., Dec. 13, 1862; mustered out with company May 24, 1863.

CHAS. A. PATTERSON, private, mustered in Aug. 15, 1862; mustered out with company May 24, 1863.

JACOB RODFINK, private, mustered in Aug. 15, 1862; mustered out with company May 24, 1863.

LEOPOLD RICE, private, mustered in Aug. 15, 1862; mustered out with company May 24, 1863.

JACOB RIDLER, private, mustered in Aug. 15, 1862; mustered out with company May 24, 1863.

AARON REX, private, mustered in Aug. 15, 1862; wounded at Antietam Sept. 17, 1862; died at Smoketown, Md., Nov. 11, 1862.

Appendix

CHAS. W. RAMALEY, private, mustered in Aug. 15, 1862; died at Windmill Point, Va., Jan. 27, 1863.

PAUL SOLT, private, mustered in Aug. 15, 1862; mustered out with company May 24, 1863.

WILLIAM S. SIEGFRIED, private, mustered in Aug. 15, 1862; mustered out with company May 24, 1863.

JOSIAH SANDEL, private, mustered in Aug. 15, 1862; mustered out with company May 24, 1863.

SAMUEL STEIGERWALT, private, mustered in Aug. 15, 1862; mustered out with company May 24, 1863.

LEWIS STEIGERWALT, private, mustered in Aug. 15, 1862; wounded at Fredericksburg, Va., Dec. 13, 1862; mustered out with company May 24, 1863.

CHARLES SINKER, private, mustered in Aug. 15, 1862; wounded at Antietam, Md., Sept. 17, 1862; mustered out with company May 24, 1863.

JACOB STROUSE, private, mustered in Aug. 15, 1862; wounded at Fredericksburg, Va., Dec. 13, 1862; mustered out with company May 24, 1863.

OTTO STERNER, private, mustered in Aug. 15, 1862; died March 25, 1863, of wounds received at Fredericksburg, Va., Dec. 13, 1862.

FRANCIS SOLT, private, mustered in Aug. 15, 1862; died Sept. 14, 1862, at Frederick City, Md.

HENRY WERNSTEIN, private, mustered in Aug. 15, 1862; mustered out with company May 24, 1863.

COMPANY G.

ROBERT A. ABBOTT, captain, mustered in Aug. 15, 1862; discharged Jan. 13, 1863, for wounds received at Antietam, Md., Sept. 17, 1862.

ISAAC HOWARD, captain, mustered in Aug. 15, 1862; promoted from private to first sergeant Jan. 1, 1863, to captain Jan. 14, 1863; mustered out with company May 24, 1863.

JOHN C. DOLAN, first lieutenant, mustered in Aug. 15, 1862; wounded at Antietam, Md., Sept. 17, 1862; discharged on surgeon's certificate Jan. 30, 1863.

WILLIAM H. FULTON, first lieutenant, mustered in Aug. 15, 1862; promoted from sergeant March 17, 1863; mustered out with company May 24, 1863.

EDMUND H. SALKELD, second lieutenant, mustered in Aug. 15,

Appendix

1862; discharged March 17, 1863, for wounds received at Fredericksburg, Md., Dec. 13, 1862.

JOHN WEISS, second lieutenant, mustered in Aug. 15, 1862; promoted from sergeant March 17, 1863; mustered out with company May 24, 1863.

CHARLES SIMONS, first sergeant, mustered in Aug. 15, 1862; promoted from corporal Feb. 12, 1863; mustered out with company May 24, 1863.

THEOP. WILLIAMS, first sergeant, mustered in Aug. 15, 1862; promoted from private to sergeant, to first sergeant Nov. 13, 1862; killed at Fredericksburg, Va., Dec. 13, 1862.

JOHN I. C. WILLIAMS, sergeant, mustered in Aug. 15, 1862; wounded at Antietam, Md., Sept. 17, 1862; mustered out with company May 24, 1863.

JOSHUA BUTLER, sergeant, mustered in Aug. 15, 1862; promoted from corporal Jan. 14, 1863; mustered out with company May 24, 1863.

WILLIAM RADCLIFF, sergeant, mustered in Aug. 15, 1862; promoted to corporal Feb. 16, 1863; to sergeant March 17, 1863; mustered out with company May 24, 1863.

CHARLES WEISS, sergeant, mustered in Aug. 15, 1862; promoted to corporal, to sergeant Feb. 15, 1863; mustered out with company May 24, 1863.

JOHN GRAVER, sergeant, mustered in Aug. 15, 1862; discharged on surgeon's certificate Sept. 9, 1862.

GEORGE RASE, sergeant, mustered in Aug. 15, 1862; deserted Sept. 5, 1862, at Camp Whipple.

JOHN OSBORN, corporal, mustered in Aug. 15, 1862; wounded, with loss of leg, at Chancellorsville, Va., May 3, 1863; discharged, date not given.

DAVID GABRET, corporal, mustered in Aug. 15, 1862; mustered out with company May 24, 1863.

WILLIAM J. SPRINGER, corporal, mustered in Aug. 15, 1862; mustered out with company May 24, 1863.

JOHN LESLIE, corporal, mustered in Aug. 15, 1862; mustered out with company May 24, 1863.

HUGH COLLAN, corporal, mustered in Aug. 13, 1862; promoted to corporal Feb. 26, 1863; mustered out with company May 24, 1863.

PETER LEASER, corporal, mustered in Aug. 15, 1862; promoted to corporal Feb. 26, 1863; mustered out with company May 24, 1863.

Appendix

WILLIAM H. NOBLE, corporal, mustered in Aug. 15, 1862; discharged on surgeon's certificate Feb. 4, 1863.

ELIJAH YOUTZ, musician, mustered in Aug. 15, 1862; discharged on surgeon's certificate Dec. 22, 1862.

CHARLES ABNER, private, mustered in Aug. 15, 1862; mustered out with company May 24, 1863.

JOSEPH BACKERT, private, mustered in Aug. 15, 1862; mustered out with company May 24, 1863.

GEORGE BUCK, private, mustered in Aug. 15, 1862; deserted August 16, 1862, at Camp Curtin.

JOSEPH CONLEY, private, mustered in Aug. 15, 1862; mustered out with company May 24, 1863.

PETER CASSADY, private, mustered in Aug. 15, 1862; mustered out with company May 24, 1863.

WILLIAM CALLAHAN, private, mustered in Aug. 15, 1862; mustered out with company May 24, 1863.

WILLIAM DAVIS, private, mustered in Aug. 15, 1862; mustered out with company May 24, 1863.

BERNARD DEMPSEY, private, mustered in Aug. 15, 1862; mustered out with company May 24, 1863.

JAMES DERBYSHIRE, private, mustered in Aug. 15, 1862; mustered out with company May 24, 1863.

MICHAEL DOUGHERTY, private, mustered in Aug. 15, 1862; mustered out with company May 24, 1863.

W. M. DARLINGTON, private, mustered in Aug. 15, 1862; died at Washington, D. C., of wounds received at Fredericksburg, Va., Dec. 13, 1862.

PATRICK ELLIOTT, private, mustered in Aug 15, 1862; mustered out with company May 24, 1863.

JOHN EARLEY, private, mustered in Aug. 15, 1862; discharged on surgeon's certificate Jan. 31, 1863.

JOHN EPHLIN, private, mustered in Aug. 15, 1862; killed at Fredericksburg, Va., Dec. 31, 1862.

PATRICK FLEMING, private, mustered in Aug. 15, 1862; mustered out with company May 24, 1863.

CONRAD FRY, private, mustered in Aug. 15, 1862; discharged Dec. 9 for wounds received at Antietam, Md., Sept. 17, 1862.

ANDREW FLOYD, private, mustered in Aug. 15, 1862; died near Falmouth, Va., March 2, 1863.

Appendix

CHARLES HOLMES, private, mustered in Aug. 15, 1862; mustered out with company May 24, 1863.

WILLIAM HAY, private, mustered in Aug. 15, 1862; mustered out with company May 24, 1863.

MORGAN JENKINS, private, mustered in Aug. 15, 1862; mustered out with company May 24, 1863.

CHRISTIAN KLINGLE, private, mustered in Aug. 15, 1862; mustered out with company May 24, 1863.

MATTHEW KELLEY, private, mustered in Aug. 15, 1862; mustered out with company May 24, 1863.

WILLIAM F. KLOTZ, private, mustered in Aug. 15, 1862; mustered out with company May 24, 1863.

JOHN F. KLOTZ, private, mustered in Aug. 15, 1862; captured Dec. 12, 1862; absent, at camp parole, Annapolis, Md., at muster-out.

BERNARD KELLY, private, mustered in Aug. 15, 1862; mustered out with company May 24, 1863.

WILLOUGHBY KOONS, private, mustered in Aug. 15, 1862; wounded at Antietam, Md., Sept. 17, 1862; absent at muster-out.

JOHN KNAUSS, private, mustered in Aug. 15, 1862; discharged on surgeon's certificate Feb. 16, 1863.

WILLIAM F. KRUM, private, mustered in Aug. 15, 1862; died at Smoketown, Md., of wounds received at Antietam Sept. 17, 1862; buried in National Cemetery, Sec. 26, Lot B, Grave 180.

HENRY LANGE, private, mustered in Aug. 15, 1862; mustered out with company May 24, 1863.

WILLIAM LEED, private, mustered in Aug. 15, 1862; mustered out with company May 24, 1863.

JONAS LOCKE, private, mustered in Aug. 15, 1862; discharged on surgeon's certificate Dec. 24, 1862.

HENRY MANSFIELD, private, mustered in Aug. 15, 1862; mustered out with company May 24, 1863.

JONATHAN L. MILLER, private, mustered in Aug. 15, 1862; mustered out with company May 24, 1863.

MANNES MAYER, private, mustered in Aug. 15, 1862; died at Smoketown, Md., of wounds received at Antietam, Sept. 17, 1862.

EDWARD P. MEELICK, private, mustered in Aug. 15, 1862; killed at Antietam, Md., Sept. 17, 1862.

LUKE MASTERSON, private, mustered in Aug. 15, 1862; deserted Aug. 16, 1862, at Camp Curtin.

Appendix

JOHN McGOVERN, private, mustered in Aug. 15, 1862; discharged April 10, 1863, for wounds received at Antietam, Md., Sept. 17, 1862.

MICHAEL McCULLOUGH, private, mustered in Aug. 15, 1862; killed at Antietam, Md., Sept. 17, 1862.

JAMES PATTERSON, private, mustered in Aug. 15, 1862; mustered out with company May 24, 1863.

ALFRED POH, private, mustered in Aug. 15, 1862; mustered out with company May 24, 1863.

MICHAEL REILY, private, mustered in Aug. 15, 1862; mustered out with company May 24, 1863.

HUGH REILY, private, mustered in Aug. 15, 1862; mustered out with company May 24, 1863.

HUGO RONEMUS, private, mustered in Aug. 15, 1862; mustered out with company May 24, 1863.

JONATHAN C. RUCH, private, mustered in Aug. 15, 1862; died at Smoketown, Md., of wounds received at Antietam, Sept. 17, 1862.

THOMAS RIGBY, private, mustered in Aug. 15, 1862; deserted Sept. 11, 1862, at Boonsborough, Md.

PAUL SOWERWINE, private, mustered in Aug. 15, 1862; mustered out with company May 24, 1863.

DAVID SHAFFER, private, mustered in Aug. 15, 1862; mustered out with company May 24, 1863.

JACOB SHINGLER, private, mustered in Aug. 15, 1862; mustered out with company May 24, 1863.

BERNHARD SMITH, private, mustered in Aug. 15, 1862; mustered out with company May 24, 1863.

THOMAS SMITHAM, private, mustered in Aug. 15, 1862; mustered out with company May 24, 1863.

ROBERT SYNARD, private, mustered in Aug. 15, 1862; mustered out with company May 24, 1863.

JOHN STACY, private, mustered in Aug. 15, 1862; mustered out with company May 24, 1863.

WILLIAM SCHOONOVER, private, mustered in Aug. 15, 1862; mustered out with company May 24, 1863.

H. B. SCHOONOVER, private, mustered in Aug. 15, 1862; mustered out with company May 24, 1863.

JOHN F. SALMON, private, mustered in Aug. 15, 1862; promoted to commissary-sergeant Aug. 15, 1862.

THOMAS SPROLL, wagoner, mustered in Aug. 15, 1862; wounded at Antietam, Md., Sept. 17, 1862; absent at muster-out.

Appendix

JOHN TONER, private, mustered in Aug. 15, 1862; deserted Aug. 16, 1862, Camp Curtin.

JOHN WEISLY, private, mustered in Aug. 15, 1862; mustered out with company May 24, 1863.

WEAVER TILGHMAN, private, mustered in Aug. 15, 1862; mustered out with company May 24, 1863.

HENRY WINTERSTEEN, private, mustered in Aug. 15, 1862; discharged Feb. 28, 1863, for wounds received at Antietam, Md., Sept. 17, 1862.

MICHAEL WELSH, private, mustered in Aug. 15, 1862; discharged on surgeon's certificate March 20, 1863.

RUFUS WALTERS, private, mustered in Aug. 15, 1862; deserted Aug. 16, 1862, Camp Curtin.

EDWARD YEMMONS, private, mustered in Aug. 15, 1862; mustered out with company May 24, 1863.

COMPANY H.

GEORGE W. JOHN, captain, mustered in Aug. 16, 1862; resigned Dec. 9, 1862.

MARTIN M. BROBST, captain, mustered in Aug. 16, 1862; promoted from first lieutenant Dec. 9, 1863; mustered out with company May 24, 1863.

ISAIAH W. WILLITS, first lieutenant, mustered in Aug. 14, 1862; promoted from first sergeant Dec. 9, 1862; mustered out with company May 24, 1863.

HENRY H. HOAGLAND, second lieutenant, mustered in Aug. 16, 1862; died Dec. 14 of wounds received at Fredericksburg, Va., Dec. 13, 1862.

P. R. MARGERUM, second lieutenant, mustered in Aug. 14, 1862; promoted from corporal Dec. 16, 1862; mustered out with company May 24, 1863.

A. H. SHARPLESS, first sergeant, mustered in Aug. 14, 1862; promoted from corporal Dec. 16, 1862; mustered out with company May 24, 1863.

SAMUEL F. SAVORY, sergeant, mustered in Aug. 14, 1862; mustered out with company May 24, 1863.

GEORGE REEDY, sergeant, mustered in Aug. 14, 1862; promoted to corporal Jan. 22, 1863; mustered out with company May 24, 1863.

HIRAM W. BROWN, sergeant, mustered in Aug. 14, 1862; promoted to corporal Jan. 22, 1863; mustered out with company May 24, 1863.

Appendix

WILLIAM McNEAL, sergeant, mustered in Aug. 14, 1862; mustered out with company May 24, 1863.

THEODORE KREIGH, corporal, mustered in Aug. 14, 1862; mustered out with company May 24, 1863.

ROLANDUS HERBINE, corporal, mustered in Aug. 14, 1862; mustered out with company May 24, 1863.

SAMUEL J. FREDERICK, corporal, mustered in Aug. 14, 1862; mustered out with company May 24, 1863.

FRANCIS M. THOMAS, corporal, mustered in Aug. 14, 1862; wounded at Fredericksburg, Va., Dec. 13, 1862; mustered out with company May 24, 1863.

JOHN P. HOAGLAND, corporal, mustered in Aug. 14, 1862; promoted to corporal Nov. 21, 1862; mustered out with company May 24, 1863.

EPHRAIM L. KRAMER, corporal, mustered in Aug. 14, 1862; promoted to corporal Jan. 20, 1863; mustered out with company May 24, 1863.

D. HOLLINGSHEAD, corporal, mustered in Aug. 14, 1862; promoted to corporal Jan. 20, 1863; mustered out with company May 24, 1863.

THEOBALD FIELDS, corporal, mustered in Aug. 14, 1862; promoted to corporal Jan. 20, 1863; wounded at Chancellorsville, Va., May 3, 1863; mustered out with company May 24, 1863.

GEORGE HARBER, musician, mustered in Aug. 14, 1862; mustered out with company May 24, 1863.

BURTON W. FORTNER, musician, mustered in Aug. 14, 1862; mustered out with company May 24, 1863.

MORGAN G. DRUM, wagoner, mustered in Aug. 14, 1862; mustered out with company May 24, 1863.

H. H. BRUMBACH, private, mustered in Aug. 14, 1862; mustered out with company May 24, 1863.

JOHN R. BROBST, private, mustered in Aug. 14, 1862; mustered out with company May 24, 1863.

WILLIAM H. BERGER, private, mustered in Aug. 14, 1862; wounded at Chancellorsville, Va., May 3, 1863; mustered out with company May 24, 1863.

WILLIAM BEAVER, private, mustered in Aug. 14, 1862; mustered out with company May 24, 1863.

JOSEPH BRUMBACH, private, mustered in Aug. 14, 1862; mustered out with company May 24, 1863.

Appendix

JOHN BELL, private, mustered in Aug. 14, 1862; mustered out with company May 24, 1863.

JULIUS A. BARRETT, private, mustered in Aug. 14, 1862; discharged on surgeon's certificate Jan. 31, 1863.

JOHN BATES, private, mustered in Aug. 14, 1862; discharged on surgeon's certificate February, 1863.

WILLIAM J. BRUMBACH, private, mustered in Aug. 14, 1862; discharged Feb. 2, 1863.

CHRISTIAN CLEWELL, private, mustered in Aug. 14, 1862; mustered out with company May 24, 1863.

PHINEAS COOL, private, mustered in Aug. 14, 1862; discharged on surgeon's certificate January, 1863.

HIRAM COOL, private, mustered in Aug. 14, 1862; discharged January, 1863, for wounds received at Antietam, Md., Sept. 17, 1862.

JOHN DILLON, private, mustered in Aug. 14, 1862; mustered out with company May 24, 1863.

WILLIAM H. DYER, private, mustered in Aug. 14, 1862; died at Belle Plain, Va., December, 1862.

JOHN DERR, private, mustered in Aug. 14, 1862; killed at Fredericksburg, Va., Dec. 13, 1862.

ALBERT ERWINE, private, mustered in Aug. 14, 1862; died at Belle Plain, Va., Dec. 15, 1862; buried in Military Asylum Cemetery, D. C.

WILLIAM FETTERMAN, private, mustered in Aug. 14, 1862; mustered out with company May 24, 1863.

DANIEL FETTERMAN, private, mustered in Aug. 14, 1862; mustered out with company May 24, 1863.

CHRISTOPHER M. FEDDER, private, mustered in Aug. 14, 1862; mustered out with company May 24, 1863.

HENRY B. FORTNER, private, mustered in Aug. 14, 1862; mustered out with company May 24, 1863.

SAMUEL A. FIELDS, private, mustered in Aug. 14, 1862; mustered out with company May 24, 1863.

LLOYD W. B. FISHER, private, mustered in Aug. 14, 1862; mustered out with company May 24, 1863.

JACOB G. FISHER, private, mustered in Aug. 14, 1862; mustered out with company May 24, 1863.

JOHN D. FINCHER, private, mustered in Aug. 14, 1862; discharged on surgeon's certificate, date unknown.

SCOTT HITE, private, mustered in Aug. 14, 1862; mustered out with company May 24, 1863.

Appendix

JOHN HAMPTON, private, mustered in Aug. 14, 1862; absent, sick, at muster-out.

ARTHUR HARDER, private, mustered in Aug. 14, 1862; mustered out with company May 24, 1863.

THOMAS E. HARDER, private, mustered in Aug. 14, 1862; mustered out with company May 24, 1863.

ETHAN HAMPTON, private, mustered in Aug. 14, 1862; mustered out with company May 24, 1863.

W. H. H. HARTMAN, private, mustered in Aug. 14, 1862; discharged on surgeon's certificate April 12, 1863.

CLARK HARDER, private, mustered in Aug. 14, 1862; discharged on surgeon's certificate Jan. 21, 1863.

GEORGE H. HANKINS, private, mustered in Aug. 14, 1862; died Oct. 4; bu. rec., Oct. 10; of wounds received at Antietam, Md., Sept. 17, 1862; buried in National Cemetery, Sec. 26, Lot B, Grave 221.

HENRY T. JOHN, private, mustered in Aug. 14, 1862; mustered out with company May 24, 1863.

WILLIAM E. JOHN, private, mustered in Aug. 14, 1862; mustered out with company May 24, 1863.

JEREMIAH S. KREIGH, private, mustered in Aug. 14, 1862; mustered out with company May 24, 1863.

EDWARD KRAMER, private, mustered in Aug. 14, 1862; mustered out with company May 24, 1863.

RALPH M. LASHELL, private, mustered in Aug. 14, 1862; mustered out with company May 24, 1863.

EMANUEL L. LEWIS, private, mustered in Aug. 14, 1862; mustered out with company May 24, 1863.

JOHN LUDWIG, private, mustered in Aug. 14, 1862; mustered out with company May 24, 1863.

JAMES P. MARGERUM, private, mustered in Aug. 14, 1862; mustered out with company May 24, 1863.

WILLIAM MARKS, private, mustered in Aug. 14, 1862; mustered out with company May 24, 1863.

JOSEPH MARTZ, private, mustered in Aug. 14, 1862; mustered out with company May 24, 1863.

ADAM R. MENSCH, private, mustered in Aug. 14, 1862; mustered out with company May 24, 1863.

COMODORE P. MEARS, private, mustered in Aug. 14, 1862; mustered out with company May 24, 1863.

Appendix

CHARLES MALONEY, private, mustered in Aug. 14, 1862; mustered out with company May 24, 1863.

ISAIAH W. MASTELLAR, private, mustered in Aug. 14, 1862; mustered out with company May 24, 1863.

PATRICK McGRAW, private, mustered in Aug. 14, 1862; died at Warrenton, Va., Nov. 6, 1862.

JOHN F. OHL, private, mustered in Aug. 14, 1862; mustered out with company May 24, 1863.

IRVIN C. PAYNE, private, mustered in Aug. 14, 1862; mustered out with company May 24, 1863.

WILLIAM J. D. PARKS, private, mustered in Aug. 14, 1862; died Dec. 28 of wounds received at Fredericksburg, Va., Dec. 13, 1862; buried in Military Asylum Cemetery, D. C.

DAVID PHILLIPS, private, mustered in Aug. 14, 1862; killed at Fredericksburg, Va., Dec. 13, 1862.

TOBIAS RINARD, private, mustered in Aug. 14, 1862; mustered out with company May 24, 1863.

FREDERICK REESE, private, mustered in Aug. 14, 1862; mustered out with company May 24, 1863.

LLOYD T. RIDER, private, mustered in Aug. 14, 1862; mustered out with company May 24, 1863.

ELIAS C. RISHEL, private, mustered in Aug. 15, 1862; wounded at Chancellorsville, Va., May 3, 1863; mustered out with company May 24, 1863.

HENRY J. ROBBINS, private, mustered in Aug. 14, 1862; mustered out with company May 24, 1863.

JEREMIAH RHODES, private, mustered in Aug. 14, 1862; absent, sick, at muster-out.

WESLEY RIDER, private, mustered in Aug. 14, 1862; died at Belle Plain, Va., December, 1862.

JAMES M. RICHARDS, private, mustered in Aug. 14, 1862; killed at Antietam, Md., Sept. 17, 1862.

JOSIAH G. ROUP, private, mustered in Aug. 14, 1862; died of wounds received at Antietam, Md., Sept. 17, 1862.

BENJAMIN B. SCHMICK, private, mustered in Aug. 14, 1862; mustered out with company May 24, 1863.

CHARLES S. SCHMICK, private, mustered in Aug. 14, 1862; mustered out with company May 24, 1863.

JEREMIAH H. SNYDER, private, mustered in Aug. 14, 1862; absent, sick, at muster-out.

Appendix

CLARK B. STEWART, private, mustered in Aug. 14, 1862; mustered out with company May 24, 1863.

JOHN H. STOKES, private, mustered in Aug. 14, 1862; mustered out with company May 24, 1863.

JESSE SHOEMAKER, private, mustered in Aug. 14, 1862; mustered out with company May 24, 1863.

JOHN M. SANKS, private, mustered in Aug. 14, 1862; discharged by special order Oct. 14, 1862.

GEORGE F. STERNE, private, mustered in Aug. 14, 1862; killed at Antietam, Md., Sept. 17, 1862.

CHRISTIAN SMALL, private, mustered in Aug. 14, 1862; killed at Chancellorsville, Va., May 3, 1863.

LEWIS THIELE, private, mustered in Aug. 14, 1862; mustered out with company May 24, 1863.

SAMUEL M. THOMAS, private, mustered in Aug. 14, 1862; died at Falmouth, Va., Jan. 8, 1863.

JOHN TROUP, private, mustered in Aug. 14, 1862; died Oct. 4 of wounds received at Antietam, Md., Sept. 17, 1862.

DENNIS WATERS, private, mustered in Aug. 14, 1862; mustered out with company May 24, 1863.

ROBERT M. WATKINS, private, mustered in Aug. 15, 1862; mustered out with company May 24, 1863.

MONROE C. WARN, private, mustered in Aug. 15, 1862; mustered out with company May 24, 1863.

DANIEL L. YEAGER, private, mustered in Aug. 17, 1862; mustered out with company May 24, 1863.

COMPANY I.

JAMES ARCHBALD, captain, mustered in Aug. 18, 1862; discharged on surgeon's certificate Jan. 7, 1863.

PHILIP S. HALL, captain, mustered in Aug. 18, 1862; promoted from second lieutenant Jan. 14, 1863; wounded at Chancellorsville May 4, 1863; absent in hospital at muster-out.

ROBERT R. MEILLER, first lieutenant, mustered in Aug. 18, 1862; discharged Jan. 7, 1863, for disability.

BENJAMIN GARDNER, first lieutenant, mustered in Aug. 15, 1862; promoted from sergeant Jan. 14, 1863; mustered out with company May 24, 1863.

Appendix

MICHAEL HOUSER, second lieutenant, mustered in Aug. 15, 1862; promoted from private Jan. 14, 1863; mustered out with company May 24, 1863.

GEORGE A. WOLCOTT, first sergeant, mustered in Aug. 15, 1862; promoted from corporal Jan. 14, 1863; mustered out with company May 24, 1863.

GEORGE W. CONKLIN, first sergeant, mustered in Aug. 15, 1862; discharged on surgeon's certificate Jan. 18, 1863.

JOHN M. MILLER, sergeant, mustered in Aug. 15, 1862; mustered out with company May 24, 1863.

JOHN JONES, sergeant, mustered in Aug. 15, 1862; mustered out with company May 24, 1863.

ISAAC CORNELL, sergeant, mustered in Aug. 15, 1862; promoted from corporal Jan. 14, 1863; mustered out with company May 24, 1863.

ABRAM BITTENBENDER, sergeant, mustered in Aug. 15, 1862; promoted from corporal Jan. 14, 1863; prisoner from May 6 to May 22, 1863; mustered out with company May 24, 1863.

ORLANDO TAYLOR, sergeant, mustered in Aug. 15, 1862; discharged on surgeon's certificate Dec. 4, 1862.

ALFRED J. BARNES, corporal, mustered in Aug. 15, 1862; mustered out with company May 24, 1863.

JOSEPH SHARPE, corporal, mustered in Aug. 15, 1862; taken prisoner at Hillsboro, Va., Nov. 8, 1862, exchanged Jan. 1, 1863; mustered out with company May 24, 1863.

OWEN J. BRADFORD, corporal, mustered in Aug. 15, 1862; mustered out with company May 24, 1863.

WILLIAM H. HAGAR, corporal, mustered in Aug. 15, 1862; promoted to corporal Jan. 4, 1863; mustered out with company May 24, 1863.

REED G. LEWIS, corporal, mustered in Aug. 15, 1862; promoted to corporal April 15, 1863; mustered out with company May 24, 1863.

JAMES A. SARGENT, corporal, mustered in Aug. 15, 1862; promoted to corporal Jan. 14, 1863; mustered out with company May 24, 1863.

ROBERT GRAY, corporal, mustered in Aug. 15, 1862; discharged on surgeon's certificate Oct. 6, 1862.

DANIEL S. GARDNER, corporal, mustered in Aug. 15, 1862; killed at Antietam, Md., Sept. 17, 1862.

ORRIN C. HUBBARD, musician, mustered in Aug. 15, 1862; mustered out with company May 24, 1863.

Appendix

THEODORE KEIFER, musician, mustered in Aug. 15, 1862; mustered out with company May 24, 1863.

JOSEPH S. QUINLAIN, wagoner, mustered in Aug. 15, 1862; mustered out with company May 24, 1863.

THOMAS ALLEN, private, mustered in Aug. 15, 1862; mustered out with company May 24, 1863.

MOSES H. AMES, private, mustered in Aug. 15, 1862; killed at Antietam, Md., Sept. 17, 1862.

GEORGE L. BRADFORD, private, mustered in Aug. 15, 1862; mustered out with company May 24, 1863.

WILLIAM BRACY, private, mustered in Aug. 15, 1862; mustered out with company May 24, 1863.

JOHN BURNISH, private, mustered in Aug. 15, 1862; mustered out with company May 24, 1863.

NATHANIEL D. BARNES, private, mustered in Aug. 15, 1862; mustered out with company May 24, 1863.

JAMES BARROWMAN, private, mustered in Aug. 15, 1862; wounded at Chancellorsville, Va., May 3, 1863; mustered out with company May 24, 1863.

THOMAS BARROWMAN, private, mustered in Aug. 15, 1862; mustered out with company May 24, 1863.

BROOKS A. BASS, private, mustered in Aug. 15, 1862; promoted to quartermaster-sergeant Jan. 1, 1863. (See Field and Staff.)

MILTON BROWN, private, mustered in Aug. 16, 1862; mustered out with company May 24, 1863.

LEWIS A. BINGHAM, private, mustered in Aug. 15, 1862; deserted Jan. 1, 1863; returned March 27, 1863; mustered out with company May 24, 1863.

JOHN BERRY, private, mustered in Aug. 15, 1862; discharged at Fort Wood Hospital, N. Y. Harbor, on surgeon's certificate March 13, 1863.

ABIJAH BERSH, JR., private, mustered in Aug. 15, 1862; deserted Sept. 19, 1862.

BURTON J. CAPWELL, private, mustered in Aug. 15, 1862; mustered out with company May 24, 1863.

THOMAS CARHART, private, mustered in Aug. 15, 1862; discharged on surgeon's certificate, date unknown.

GEORGE H. CATOR, private, mustered in Aug. 15, 1862; died Oct. 30 of wounds received at Antietam, Md., Sept. 17, 1862; buried in National Cemetery, Sec. 26, Lot C, Grave 228.

Appendix

HORACE A. DEANS, private, mustered in Aug. 15, 1862; promoted to hospital steward Oct. 1, 1862; returned to company April 6, 1863; mustered out with company May 24, 1863.

FREDERICK M. ELLTING, private, mustered in Aug. 14, 1862; mustered out with company May 24, 1863.

H. L. ELMANDORF, private, mustered in Aug. 15, 1862; deserted at Warrenton, Va., Nov. 15, 1862.

EDWARD FERRIS, private, mustered in Aug. 15, 1862; wounded at Chancellorsville, Va., May 3, 1863; mustered out with company May 24, 1863.

JOHN FERN, private, mustered in Aug. 15, 1862; mustered out with company May 24, 1863.

GEORGE E. FULLER, private, mustered in Aug. 15, 1862; mustered out with company May 24, 1863.

HENRY M. FULLER, private, mustered in Aug. 15, 1862; mustered out with company May 24, 1863.

BENTON V. FINN, private, mustered in Aug. 15, 1862; discharged on surgeon's certificate Jan. 19, 1863.

JOHN FINCH, private, mustered in Aug. 15, 1862; discharged on surgeon's certificate March 28, 1863.

WILLIAM GUNSAULER, private, mustered in Aug. 15, 1862; mustered out with company May 24, 1863.

JOHN GAHN, private, mustered in Aug. 15, 1862; wounded at Fredericksburg, Va., Dec. 13, 1862; mustered out with company May 24, 1863.

ELISHA R. HARRIS, private, mustered in Aug. 15, 1862; mustered out with company May 24, 1863.

SAMUEL HUBBARD, private, mustered in Aug. 15, 1862; mustered out with company May 24, 1863.

J. HIPPENHAMMER, private, mustered in Aug. 16, 1862; mustered out with company May 24, 1863.

CHARLES HAMM, private, mustered in Aug. 15, 1862; mustered out with company May 24, 1863.

RICHARD HALL, private, mustered in Aug. 15, 1862; mustered out with company May 24, 1863.

WILLIAM H. HARRISON, private, mustered in Aug. 15, 1862; mustered out with company May 24, 1863.

HENRY P. HALSTEAD, private, mustered in Aug. 15, 1862; discharged on surgeon's certificate Jan. 5, 1863.

WILLIAM HAZLETT, private, mustered in Aug. 15, 1862; discharged on surgeon's certificate Jan. 2, 1863.

Appendix

JOHN L. HUNT, private, mustered in Aug. 15, 1862; deserted at Acquia Creek, Va., Feb. 15, 1863.

RODERICK JONES, private, mustered in Aug. 15, 1862; wounded at Antietam, Md., Sept. 17, 1862; absent, in hospital, at muster-out.

JOHN J. KILMER, private, mustered in Aug. 15, 1862; mustered out with company May 24, 1863.

H. L. KRIGBAUM, private, mustered in Aug. 15, 1862; wounded at Fredericksburg, Va., Dec. 13, 1862; mustered out with company May 24, 1863.

MICHAEL KELLY, private, mustered in Aug. 15, 1862; mustered out with company May 24, 1863.

GEORGE C. LANNING, private, mustered in Aug. 15, 1862; mustered out with company May 24, 1863.

THOMAS Z. LAKE, private, mustered in Aug. 15, 1862; mustered out with company May 24, 1863.

LYMAN MILROY, private, mustered in Aug. 15, 1862; prisoner from May 6 to May 22, 1863; mustered out with company May 24, 1863.

GEORGE MEUCHLER, private, mustered in Aug. 15, 1862; mustered out with company May 24, 1863.

JAMES J. MAYCOCK, private, mustered in Aug. 15, 1862; wounded at Antietam, Md., Sept. 17, 1862; mustered out with company May 24, 1863.

STEPHEN MOOMEY, private, mustered in Aug. 15, 1862; mustered out with company May 24, 1863.

JAMES H. MILLER, private, mustered in Aug. 15, 1862; mustered out with company May 24, 1863.

ROBERT O. MOSCRIP, private, mustered in Aug. 15, 1862; mustered out with company May 24, 1863.

JAMES S. MORSE, private, mustered in Aug. 15, 1862; discharged on surgeon's certificate Oct. 29, 1862.

JOSEPH NIVER, private, mustered in Aug. 15, 1862; mustered out with company May 24, 1863.

AARON ORREN, private, mustered in Aug. 15, 1862; mustered out with company May 24, 1863.

JOHN OWEN, private, mustered in Aug. 15, 1862; discharged on surgeon's certificate Feb. 11, 1863.

JOHN E. POWELL, private, mustered in Aug. 15, 1862; captured at Chancellorsville, Va.; prisoner from May 6 to May 22, 1863; mustered out with company May 24, 1863.

Appendix

CHARLES PONTUS, private, mustered in Aug. 15, 1862; mustered out with company May 24, 1863.

JAMES A. PARKER, private, mustered in Aug. 15, 1862; deserted at Harper's Ferry, Va., Oct. 29, 1862.

FREEMAN J. ROPER, private, mustered in Aug. 15, 1862; mustered out with company May 24, 1863.

ELEZER RAYMOND, private, mustered in Aug. 15, 1862; wounded at Fredericksburg, Va., Dec. 13, 1862; mustered out with company May 24, 1863.

NELSON RAYMOND, private, mustered in Aug. 15, 1862; wounded at Chancellorsville, Va., May 3, 1863; absent, in hospital, at muster-out.

JAMES S. RANDOLPH, private, mustered in Aug. 15, 1862; dischared on surggeon's certificate Jan. 21, 1863.

GEORGE W. RIDGEWAY, private, mustered in Aug. 15, 1862; discharged on surgeon's certificate, date unknown.

DANIEL REED, private, mustered in Aug. 15, 1862; killed at Antietam, Md., Sept. 17, 1862.

WILLIAM H. SMITH, private, mustered in Aug. 15, 1862; mustered out with company May 24, 1863.

WILLIAM H. SEELEY, private, mustered in Aug. 15, 1862; mustered out with company May 24, 1863.

LATON SLOCUM, private, mustered in Aug. 15, 1862; mustered out with company May 24, 1863.

MICHAEL SISK, private, mustered in Aug. 15, 1862; mustered out with company May 24, 1863.

JOHN SOMMERS, prIvate, mustered in Aug. 15, 1862; mustered out with company May 24, 1863.

RICHARD A. SMITH, private, mustered in Aug. 15, 1862; died Oct. 15 of wounds received at Antietam, Md., Sept. 17, 1862.

ORVICE SHARP, private, mustered in Aug. 15, 1862; died Nov. 16, 1862.

REILY S. TANNER, private, mustered in Aug. 15, 1862; mustered out with company May 24, 1863.

JAMES L. TUTHILL, private, mustered in Aug. 15, 1862; prisoner from May 6 to May 22, 1863; mustered out with company May 24, 1863.

HENRY VUSLER, private, mustered in Aug. 15, 1862; deserted Sept. 18, 1862.

DAVID J. WOODRUFF, private, mustered in Aug. 15, 1862; mustered out with company May 24, 1863.

Appendix

SAMUEL WIGGINS, private, mustered in Aug. 15, 1862; mustered out with company May 24, 1863.

DANIEL WINNICH, private, mustered in Aug. 15, 1862; mustered out with company May 24, 1863.

BURR C. WARNER, private, mustered in Aug. 15, 1862; mustered out with company May 24, 1863.

JOHN B. WEST, private, mustered in Aug. 15, 1862; killed at Antietam, Md., Sept. 17, 1862.

HARRISON YOUNG, private, mustered in Aug. 15, 1862; mustered out with company May 24, 1863.

COMPANY K.

RICHARD STILLWELL, captain, mustered in Aug. 18, 1862; discharged March 31, 1863, for wounds received at Fredericksburg, Va., Dec. 13, 1862.

JACOB B. FLOYD, captain, mustered in Aug. 18, 1862; promoted from first lieutenant March 31, 1863; mustered out with company May 24, 1863.

NOAH H. JAY, first lieutenant, mustered in Aug. 14, 1862; promoted from second lieutenant March 31, 1863; mustered out with company May 24, 1863.

SYLVESTER WARD, second lieutenant, mustered in Aug. 14, 1862: promoted from sergeant to first sergeant Dec. 25, 1862; to second lieutenant March 31, 1863; mustered out with company May 24, 1863.

FRANCIS ORCHARD, first sergeant, mustered in Aug. 14, 1862; promoted from sergeant March 31, 1863; mustered out with company May 24, 1863.

GEORGE M. SNYDER, sergeant, mustered in Aug. 14, 1862; promoted from corporal Sept. 24, 1862; mustered out with company May 24, 1863.

JOHN BOTTSFORD, sergeant, mustered in Aug. 14, 1862; promoted from corporal Sept. 24, 1862; mustered out with company May 24, 1863.

WILLIAM C. KEISER, sergeant, mustered in Aug. 14, 1862; promoted from corporal March 31, 1863; mustered out with company May 24, 1863.

MARTIN L. HOWER, sergeant, mustered in Aug. 14, 1862; died Oct. 17 of wounds received at Antietam, Md., Sept. 17, 1862.

PHILETUS P. COPELAND, corporal, mustered in Aug. 14, 1862; wounded at Chancellorsville, Va., May 3, 1863; mustered out with company May 24, 1863.

Appendix

GEORGE COURSEN, corporal, mustered in Aug. 14, 1862; mustered out with company May 24, 1863.

GEORGE A. KENT, corporal, mustered in Aug. 14, 1862; wounded at Antietam, Md., Sept. 17, 1862; mustered out with company May 24, 1863.

GEORGE W. JOHNSON, corporal, mustered in Aug. 14, 1862; promoted to corporal Sept. 24, 1862; mustered out with company May 24, 1863.

JOHN S. SHORT, corporal, mustered in Aug. 14, 1862; promoted to corporal Sept. 24, 1862; wounded at Fredericksburg, Va., Dec. 13, 1862; absent in hospital at muster-out.

GEORGE H. TAYLOR, corporal, mustered in Aug. 14, 1862; promoted to corporal Sept. 24, 1862; mustered out with company May 24, 1863.

EMIL HAUGG, corporal, mustered in Aug. 14, 1862; promoted to corporal March 31, 1863; mustered out with company May 24, 1863.

AUSTIN F. CLAPP, corporal, mustered in Aug. 14, 1862; promoted to sergeant-major Nov. 1, 1862. (See Field and Staff.)

LORENZO D. KEMMERER, musician, mustered in Aug. 14, 1862; mustered out with company May 24, 1863.

WILLIAM SILSBEE, musician, mustered in Aug. 14, 1862; mustered out with company May 24, 1863.

JOHN M. KAPP, wagoner, mustered in Aug. 14, 1862; mustered out with company May 24, 1863.

AUGUSTUS ASHTON, private, mustered in Aug. 14, 1862; taken prisoner at Fredericksburg, Va., Dec. 13, 1862; mustered out with company May 24, 1863.

DAVID BROOKS, private, mustered in Aug. 14, 1862; mustered out with company May 24, 1863.

CHARLES H. BOON, private, mustered in Aug. 14, 1862; mustered out with company May 24, 1863.

LEWIS H. BOLTON, private, mustered in Aug. 14, 1862; mustered out with company May 24, 1863.

ADOLF BENDON, private, mustered in Aug. 14, 1862; discharged on surgeon's certificate Dec. 6, 1862.

CHARLES A. BULMER, private, mustered in Aug. 14, 1862; discharged on surgeon's certificate Oct. 14, 1862.

WILLIAM H. CARLING, private, mustered in Aug. 14, 1862; promoted to adjutant's clerk January 25, 1863; mustered out with company May 24, 1863.

Appendix

WILLIAM W. COOLBAUGH, private, mustered in Aug. 14, 1862; wounded at Chancellorsville, Va., May 3, 1863; mustered out with company May 24, 1863.

HARRISON COOK, private, mustered in Aug. 14, 1862; mustered out with company May 24, 1863.

JACOB M. CORWIN, private, mustered in Aug. 14, 1862; mustered out with company May 24, 1863.

JOHN COOLBAUGH, private, mustered in Aug. 14, 1862; mustered out with company May 24, 1863.

WILLIAM H. COON, private, mustered in Aug. 14, 1862; discharged on surgeon's certificate Nov. 29, 1862.

MOSES Y. CORWIN, private, mustered in Aug. 14, 1862; promoted to hospital steward April 6, 1863. (See Field and Staff.)

BENJAMIN A. C. DAILY, private, mustered in Aug. 14, 1862; mustered out with company May 24, 1863.

FRANCIS J. DEEMER, private, mustered in Aug. 14, 1862; promoted to sergeant-major Jan. 24, 1863. (See Field and Staff.)

RICHARD DAVIS, private, mustered in Aug. 14, 1862; died Jan. 2, 1863, of wounds received at Fredericksburg, Va., Dec. 13, 1862; buried in Military Asylum Cemetery, Washington, D. C.

THOMAS D. DAVIS, private, mustered in Aug. 14, 1862; died near Washington, D. C., Nov. 25, 1862; buried in Military Asylum Cemetery, Washington, D. C.

JACOB ESCHENBACH, private, mustered in Aug. 14, 1862; killed at Antietam, Md., Sept. 17, 1862.

CHARLES FREDERICK, private, mustered in Aug. 14, 1862; mustered out with company May 24, 1863.

GEORGE GABRIEL, private, mustered in Aug. 14, 1862; wounded at Chancellorsville, Va., May 3, 1863; mustered out with company May 24, 1863.

JOHN C. HIGGINS, private, mustered in Aug. 14, 1862; mustered out with company May 24, 1863.

PETER HARRABAUM, private, mustered in Aug. 14, 1862; mustered out with company May 24, 1863.

JAMES H. HAVENSTRITE, private, mustered in Aug. 14, 1862; mustered out with company May 24, 1863.

GEORGE HINDLE, private, mustered in Aug. 14, 1862; mustered out with company May 24, 1863.

EDWARD F. HENRY, private, mustered in Aug. 14, 1862; dis-

Appendix

charged from Emory Hospital, Washington, D. C., on surgeon's certificate Jan. 8, 1863.

WILSON HESS, private, mustered in Aug. 14, 1862; discharged on surgeon's certificate Feb. 21, 1863.

JOHN P. HEATH, private, mustered in Aug. 14, 1862; deserted on march from Antietam to Harper's Ferry, Sept. 21, 1862.

MICHAEL KIVILIN, private, mustered in Aug. 14, 1862; mustered out with company May 24, 1863.

ROBERT KENNEDY, private, mustered in Aug. 14, 1862; mustered out with company May 24, 1863.

JESSE P. KORTZ, private, mustered in Aug. 14, 1862; died near Falmouth, Va., Dec. 25, 1862.

GEORGE W. LINN, private, mustered in Aug. 14, 1862; mustered out with company May 24, 1863.

ANDREW LANDSICKLE, private, mustered in Aug. 14, 1862; mustered out with company May 24, 1863.

JOHN LINDSEY, private, mustered in Aug. 14, 1862; mustered out with company May 24, 1863.

GEORGE MATZENBACHER, private, mustered in Aug. 14, 1862; mustered out with company May 24, 1863.

SAMUEL W. MEAD, private, mustered in Aug. 14, 1862; mustered out with company May 24, 1863.

WILLIAM L. MARCY, private, mustered in Aug. 14, 1862; mustered out with company May 24, 1863.

GEORGE B. MACK, private, mustered in Aug. 14, 1862; mustered out with company May 24, 1863.

CHARLES A. MEYLERT, private, mustered in Aug. 14, 1862; promoted to second lieutenant Co. A, Feb. 24, 1863.

JEPTHA MILLIGAN, private, mustered in Aug. 14, 1862; killed at Antietam, Md., Sept. 17, 1862; buried in National Cemetery, Sec. 26, Lot A, Grave 13.

RICHARD NAPE, private, mustered in Aug. 14, 1862; mustered out with company May 24, 1863.

DANIEL J. NEWMAN, private, mustered in Aug. 14, 1862; mustered out with company May 24, 1863.

JOHN R. POWELL, private, mustered in Aug. 14, 1862; mustered out with company May 24, 1863.

JOSEPH PELLMAN, private, mustered in Aug. 14, 1862; mustered out with company May 24, 1863.

Appendix

DOWNING PARRY, private, mustered in Aug. 14, 1862; mustered out with company May 24, 1863.

JOHN RYAN, private, mustered in Aug. 14, 1862; mustered out with company May 24, 1863.

SAMUEL RUPLE, private, mustered in Aug. 14, 1862; mustered out with company May 24, 1863.

SIMON P. RINGSDORF, private, mustered in Aug. 14, 1862; discharged on surgeon's certificate Feb. 6, 1863.

GEORGE SMITHING, private, mustered in Aug. 14, 1862; mustered out with company May 24, 1863.

HENRY M. SEAGER, private, mustered in Aug. 14, 1862; wounded at Fredericksburg, Va., Dec. 13, 1862; mustered out with company May 24, 1863.

DANIEL W. SCULL, private, mustered in Aug. 14, 1862; mustered out with company May 24, 1863.

JOSEPH SNYDER, private, mustered in Aug. 14, 1862; mustered out with company May 24, 1863.

SIMON P. SNYDER, private, mustered in Aug. 14, 1862; mustered out with company May 24, 1863.

WILLIAM D. SNYDER, private, mustered in Aug. 14, 1862; mustered out with company May 24, 1863.

CHARLES B. SCOTT, private, mustered in Aug. 14, 1862; mustered out with company May 24, 1863.

PETER SEIGLE, private, mustered in Aug. 14, 1862; mustered out with company May 24, 1863.

JOHN SCOTT, private, mustered in Aug. 14, 1862; mustered out with company May 24, 1863.

WALTER A. SIDNER, private, mustered in Aug. 14, 1862; mustered out with company May 24, 1863.

MARTIN L. SMITH, private, mustered in Aug. 14, 1862; mustered out with company May 24, 1863.

JAMES STEVENS, private, mustered in Aug. 14, 1862; mustered out with company May 24, 1863.

JOHN STITCHER, private, mustered in Aug. 14, 1862; discharged Nov. 28, 1862, on account of wounds received at Antietam Sept. 17, 1862.

ALLEN SPARKS, private, mustered in Aug. 14, 1862; died Sept. 18 of wounds received at Antietam, Md., Sept. 17, 1862.

OBADIAH SHERWOOD, private, mustered in Aug. 14, 1862; died

Appendix

Nov. 20 at Smoketown, Md., of wounds received at Antietam Sept. 17, 1862.

SAMUEL S. SNYDER, private, mustered in Aug. 14, 1862; died at Philadelphia, Pa., Jan. 9, 1863.

JAMES SCULL, private, mustered in Aug. 14, 1862; died near Falmouth, Va., Feb. 11, 1863.

SOLON SEARLE, private, mustered in Aug. 14, 1862; died at Acquia Creek, Va., Jan. 26, 1863.

ALONZO L. SLAWSON, private, mustered in Aug. 14, 1862; discharged, date unknown.

LEANDER J. SMITH, private, mustered in Aug. 14, 1862; deserted from Camp Whipple Sept. 1, 1862.

DAVID VIPON, private, mustered in Aug. 14, 1862; mustered out with company May 24, 1863.

GEORGE C. WILSON, private, mustered in Aug. 14, 1862; wounded at Antietam, Md., Sept. 17, 1862; mustered out with company May 24, 1863.

MARTIN WILMORE, private, mustered in Aug. 14, 1862; mustered out with company May 24, 1863.

ORESTES B. WRIGHT, private, mustered in Aug. 15, 1862; wounded at Fredericksburg, Va., Dec. 13, 1862; mustered out with company May 24, 1863.

JOHN WESTPHALL, private, mustered in Aug. 14, 1862; mustered out with company May 24, 1863.

HENRY C. WHITING, private, mustered in Aug. 14, 1862; discharged on surgeon's certificate Nov. 27, 1862.

JOHN W. WRIGHT, private, mustered in Aug. 14, 1862; died at Harper's Ferry, Va., Oct. 23, 1862.

ALBERT WHEELER, private, mustered in Aug. 14, 1862; deserted from Walnut Street Hospital, Harrisburg, Dec. 19, 1862.

CONRAD YOUNG, private, mustered in Aug. 14, 1862; mustered out with company May 24, 1863.

WILLIAM H. YOUNG, private, mustered in Aug. 14, 1862; mustered out with company May 24, 1863.

W. L. YARRINGTON, private, mustered in Aug. 14, 1862; mustered out with company May 24, 1863.

DANIEL C. YOUNG, private, mustered in Aug. 14, 1862; died Dec. 26 of wounds received at Fredericksburg, Va., Dec. 13, 1862.

Library of Congress Cataloguing in Publication Data

Hitchcock, Frederick L. (Frederick Lyman)
War from the inside.
Reprint. Originally published: Philadelphia:
J.B. Lippincott, 1904.
1. Hitchcock, Frederick L. (Frederick Lyman)
2. United States. Army. Pennsylvania Infantry Regiment, 132nd (1862-1863)—Biography.
3. United States—History—Civil War, 1861-1865—Personal narratives.
4. United States—History—Civil War, 1861-1865—Regimental histories.
5. Pennsylvania—History—Civil War, 1861-1865—Personal narratives.
6. Pennsylvania—History—Civil War, 1861-1865—Regimental histories.
7. Soldiers—Pennsylvania—Biography. I. Title.
E527.5   132nd.H58   1985   973.7′448   84-16142
ISBN 0-8094-4476-3 (library)
ISBN 0-8094-4475-5 (retail)

Printed in the United States of America